Dear Reader:

I am pleased that as a community we will be reading *The Education of a Lifetime* for our 2015 UM Common Reading Experience. This book was selected by a committee of faculty, staff, and students from more than 150 nominations. The selection was based on the issues the book raises, its appeal to a wide University audience, and the potential discussions it will stimulate on our campus. This memoir provides a behind-the-scenes account of some of the most significant moments in University of Mississippi history and will foster compelling exchanges among students, faculty, and staff in the best tradition of collegiate, intellectual exploration.

The Education of a Lifetime is the story of a young Mississippian who steps on the Oxford campus, lost and uncertain of his way, not unlike many of our first-year students. His accomplishments and setbacks as a student and later as chancellor make for a fascinating read. The book is filled with wonderful stories and anecdotes about the people who have contributed so much to the success of our institution, and we are honored to have the author, Chancellor Emeritus Robert C. Khayat, as our keynote speaker at the University's Fall Convocation on August 25, 2015. The selection of this unique memoir provides an opportunity for many of you to better know Chancellor Emeritus Khayat, an iconic Ole Miss leader, as a student, athlete, and administrator.

I hope that you will read this book along with your peers and participate in the campus and class conversations that are so much a part of our Common Reading Experience.

Sincerely,

Daniel W. Jones, M.D.
Chancellor

A *New York Times*
BESTSELLING EDUCATION BOOK
• • •
SILVER IPPY AWARD
FOR BEST NATIONAL MEMOIR
• • •
Author of the Year Award
MISSISSIPPI LIBRARY ASSOCIATION

Praise for
The Education of a Lifetime

"Robert Khayat's extraordinary life has had more rough patches than most observers would believe. In this engaging memoir, he provides an unflinching look at the challenges, the adversity, and the ups and downs of a career that ultimately transformed a great American university."
— John Grisham

"From the playing fields of the NFL to the groves of academe, where he broke the shackles of the Old South at his alma mater, Robert Khayat has led a remarkable life, and his memoir is full of wonderful anecdotes and wisdom. As an ancient scholar said of Aesop and his fables, 'He makes use of humble incidents to teach great truths.'"
— Curtis Wilkie
author of *The Fall of the House of Zeus*

"Robert Khayat needs no introduction as both an educator and an indomitable torchbearer for a better Mississippi. The grand surprise of *The Education of a Lifetime* is Dr. Khayat's storytelling. Having clearly absorbed the state's rich narrative tradition, Dr. Khayat quilts an array of magnificently told stories — about watching a bad movie with Elvis to kicking a 50-yard field goal against the New York Giants to painfully exorcising the malign remnants of Ole Miss's history — into a remarkable, candid, and deeply inspiring memoir."
— Jonathan Miles
author of *Dear American Airlines*

"A highly readable and entertaining story of leadership and vision taking on a stagnant culture. Inspirational and insightful."

— Ace Atkins
New York Times bestselling author

"Maybe once or twice in a thousand years, fate places a person who will do the right thing in the right place at the right time. Robert Khayat left the nest of quiet bayous and coastal rhythms to tackle life, learning, and the law. His toughest adversary along the way: tradition. Armed with a cowboy hero's fortitude and a certain guileless charm, Robert managed to kick one through the uprights for his oft-maligned Mississippi."

— Rheta Grimsley Johnson
author of *Hank Hung the Moon*

"It's not just that *The Education of a Lifetime* should be required reading for all University of Mississippi students and alumni and friends. It's that it should be read for all who feel called to be leaders, and by all who have been led. By all who've dedicated their lives to improving their communities, and by all who've had moments of struggle and doubt while doing so. By all who love the South, and by all who can't conceive of such love. In short, this is a book for everyone. Here we have episodes from a long and challenging career — the charming of an eccentric donor; the attempt to separate Ole Miss from the racially charged symbol of the Confederate flag, which resulted in death threats for Robert Khayat and his family; the hosting of the Presidential debate, in an effort to show the world the university's progress. With candor and humor, Robert Khayat tells the stories behind the stories that have made him a respected leader and an inspiration to so many."

— Tom Franklin & Beth Ann Fennelly
co-authors of *The Tilted World*

"Charismatic, energetic, visionary, Robert Khayat inherited in 1995 an underfunded and dwindling state university haunted by Mississippi's racist history. Over the dozen years under his leadership, the university transformed itself into a thriving public institution committed to academic excellence and proud of being chosen to host the first Presidential debate between John McCain and Barack Obama. In this memoir, *The Education of a Lifetime*, the beloved former chancellor tells us how. I have taught at the University of Mississippi for twenty-five years, and I'm moved to read the history of its extraordinary changes."

— Ann Fisher-Wirth
award-winning poet

"Robert Khayat has written a delightful, insightful account of who he is and why. Joyous reading. A real winner!"

— Perian Conerly
author of *Backseat Quarterback*

"I left Mississippi over fifty years ago to make movies in Hollywood. I made a few. Robert, my dear friend and chancellor, has written a book that has made me wish I had stayed home. If I had, I might've accomplished half as much as he has. A must-read for all."

— Larry Gordon
producer of *Field of Dreams* and *Die Hard*

"It is one thing to fight for academic excellence. It is another to fight for principle. And it is yet another to take on deeply held beliefs and traditions that serve to divide rather than unite. Khayat took them all on, and in *The Education of a Lifetime* we get a front-row seat to marvel at how he did it."

— Ronnie Agnew, executive director
Mississippi Public Broadcasting

"When the College Board asked Robert Khayat to articulate his vision for The University of Mississippi, he said he wanted to make Ole Miss one of America's great public universities. *The Education of a Lifetime* provides ample evidence that he achieved his goal."

— historian David Sansing

". . . a memoir about moving on at Ole Miss."

— *PBS Newshour*

"This book tells of a special place — one that has been through tough times — that emerged from a turblulent past."

— *MSNBC's Morning Joe*

"Meanwhile, thanks to his book, we learn that Robert Khayat's life, like most of ours, has not been all sunshine and roses and not dominated entirely by setbacks and failures. And we learn that achievement is not the product of luck or magic or any other charm. Just the courage to make decisions and the stubbornness to persevere."

— *Columbus Dispatch*

"That searing introspection and its inspiring results are well worth the read.

— *Mississippi Business Journal*

"...one of the most influential administrators of higher education in state history."
— *The Clarion-Ledger*

"Khayat showed courage and ingenuity in his education career."
— Bill Minor
syndicated columnist

"Robert Khayat met the tests as chancellor of the University of Mississippi from 1995 to 2009, and he became a pivotal, transformational leader in the history of both the university and the state. His story is a lesson in leadership, and there's little doubt it will be studied for years to come."
— *The Daily Journal*

"Khayat takes readers on a journey from his childhood on the Mississippi Gulf Coast to his efforts to challenge the image of Ole Miss as an institution still mired in racial hostility and shape it into one of America's premier public universities."
— *The Daily Mississippian*

"This is a story that deserves the broadest circulation. A story of a thoroughly decent, honorable individual who rose from modest circumstances to a position that enabled him to act nobly in the cause of equal opportunity for all through affordable public-supported higher education. All who believe thusly owe Robert Khayat a salute for sharing his story with us."
— Harold Burson
founder Burson-Marsteller

"It inspired me during a time when I needed to be uplifted, and honestly, after reading *The Education of a Lifetime*, I wanted to put on some pants, go out, and be a better person."
— Emily Gatlin, *Bookriot.com*

"The nation now takes Ole Miss seriously, and you can thank Robert Khayat."
— Tad Wilkes, *HottyToddy.com*

Robert Khayat

The Education of a Lifetime

The Nautilus Publishing Company
OXFORD, MISSISSIPPI

For information contact Nautilus Publishing, 426 South Lamar Blvd., Suite 16, Oxford, MS 38655.

In some instances, names of individuals have been changed in the interest of privacy.

ISBN: 978-1-936-946-53-2

The Nautilus Publishing Company
426 South Lamar Blvd., Suite 16
Oxford, Mississippi 38655
Tel: 662-513-0159
www.nautiluspublishing.com
www.RobertKhayat.com

Front cover design by Le'Herman Payton. Front cover photo by Robert Jordan

Back cover design and art by Connor Covert and Carroll Chiles Moore

Library of Congress Cataloging-in-Publication Data has been applied for.
Printed in Canada

10   9   8   7   6   5   4   3   2

Confederate flag → central point
he wanted to change the atmosphere
and academics

To my family and Ole Miss

"Through the lives of our graduates, we can make the greatest contributions to mankind."

Robert C. Khayat

May 5, 1997

1

"Chancellor," the police officer said as he walked through my office door, "we need to talk."

I stood, took off my glasses, and invited him to have a seat.

not a good reputation

During the last four months our campus had become a circus — and all eyes were on us. Not only were we under scrutiny from *The New York Times*, *The Los Angeles Times*, and the major television news networks, but we were also caught in the crosshairs of the Ku Klux Klan, the Heritage Defense Committee, and a band of individuals who still called themselves the Confederate States of America.

On February 28, 1997, media reports broke nationwide that we had hired a consulting firm to help us understand how we were perceived by the outside world. The review was designed to be comprehensive, including a look at school symbols. But there was only one thing people wanted to talk or write or report about — the Confederate flag.

The Lyceum, a stately 149-year-old, Greek Revival style building that housed my office, was swarming with University Police Department officers. They had recently directed our administrative staff to wear surgical masks and latex gloves when opening the mail. The letters, which came from every state in the union and even some foreign countries, accused me of *cultural imperialism* and *ethnic cleansing*. The writers used words like *revile* and *nauseate* and *disgust* to describe their feelings about me. One writer encouraged me to *resign and go someplace where I'd be appreciated . . . like Hell*. Another group had envelopes custom-printed with the phrase *Stop the Lynching of Ole Miss. Stop Robert Khayat from destroying our university*.

The police officers divided the hate mail into different bins marked "KKK," "Heritage Defense Committee," and "CSA."

But it wasn't just letters that arrived on campus. Protesters and radicals from across the nation descended on the Lyceum, the Circle, the Grove and, of course, the Confederate monument. A group from Georgia wore Civil War battle regalia and marched around the loop. Another gentleman stood under the marble statue waving a huge Confederate flag and yelled, "Your Chancellor is killing the heritage of the South!" Then he called on Ole Miss students to join him in seceding from the United States. One of Mississippi's own state senators protested the process by staging a beheading. A man dressed in a black robe and hood (ostensibly portraying me) dramatically chopped off the head of a man dressed as Colonel Rebel.

The officer handed me a one-page fax. "You need to see this," he said.

I put on my glasses and picked up the handwritten note. It opened, *Dear Traitor, It is clear from your last name that you were not born in the United States of America.*

The writer launched into a diatribe of curses and accusations, not unlike hundreds of other letters we had received. But then it took a darker turn.

Try as you may to vilify our heritage and spit on the graves of our ancestors, but I can promise you will never live to see that day. You may think you are safe, but you will never see us coming. Your family will never see us coming.

I handed the letter back to the police officer. "What do we do about this?" I asked.

The officer looked down at the floor. "First, we need to alert the FBI." He paused and looked back up at me. "Then, we need to talk about how to protect you and Margaret. And your children."

People were mad about him taking away the flag.

Summer of 1956

My Moss Point football uniform

2

"Stay off the road to Memphis," my brother Eddie said. Then he drove away.

I stood outside Garland dormitory holding my bag and watched as he disappeared around the corner. We had left Moss Point in the early morning hours and drove straight through so I could be on campus by 3:00 p.m. I wandered around for a few minutes. There wasn't another living soul in sight.

I'd arrived on Saturday — a day before official move-in. For nearly twenty-four hours, I didn't see or speak to anyone except the guy who took my order for a hamburger. I missed my family and friends and felt like going back home.

The next morning I was relieved, and a bit excited, to see students getting out of cars at the dorms. The campus suddenly seemed to come alive.

No one spoke to me. And I was too timid to initiate a conversation, so I just stood back and watched. I had never seen such fine suitcases. And I'd never seen so many shirts, jackets, and shoes. Some of the boys owned cars, and they all seemed sophisticated. envious

I walked across the campus to the green space surrounded by a circular drive. I sat down on the ground at the trunk of one of the large oaks feeling very sorry for myself.

A car stopped and parked on the circle. An attractive woman got out and walked toward me. She stood above me and smiled.

"You must be one of my boys," she said.

I didn't understand.

"Can I help you?" she asked.

I knew she couldn't get me back to Moss Point, and that was what

I wanted. "No thank you, Ma'am," I said.

She didn't walk away. "What's your name?"

"Robert Khayat."

"You *are* one of mine," she said. Then she reached her hand down and said, "Come with me."

As we walked toward the car, she told me her name was Sara Davidson. She and her husband, the freshman football coach Wobble Davidson, lived in the athletics dorm. Mrs. Davidson gestured for me to climb into the backseat of her car.

I settled in back, and Sara introduced me to the woman behind the steering wheel.

"Robert," she said, "this is Midge Kinard." She paused and added, "She's married to Bruiser Kinard."

Mrs. Kinard dropped us off in the parking lot at Garland dormitory, the same spot where my brother had left me the day before. Garland Hall, Mrs. Davidson explained, was the *varsity* football dormitory. She led me to her apartment and introduced me to her two young children, Don and Deb. Then she served me a big bowl of ice cream.

As I sat in the Davidsons' apartment and ate ice cream, Mrs. Davidson assured me that I would make many friends at Ole Miss. She added that I was about to be part of an extraordinary football program.

"Your world will be broadened by the brilliant minds of your professors," she said. Then she smiled, "And there's no school in the world with prettier girls."

I told Mrs. Davidson that I had been feeling a little homesick. But she and her children made me feel welcome.

She put her hand on my shoulder. "There is no better place on earth for an eighteen-year-old boy."

3

[handwritten: what he thought he wanted to be.]

I wanted to be a physician . . . because I wanted to be like Gene Wood. Gene, four years my senior, was handsome and smart and he played quarterback for the Moss Point Tigers. When I was in junior high, people talked about Gene's bright future, his intelligence and drive, and how he was *going to be a wonderful doctor*.

Through my fourteen-year-old eyes, Gene was larger than life. His clothes always looked freshly washed and perfectly pressed, his hair always combed. He was admired by young and old in Moss Point and most of my friends idolized him. I was no exception. If Gene Wood was planning to study medicine, so was I.

During my senior year in high school, I mentioned to Coach Tom Swayze, Ole Miss' recruiting coordinator, that I planned to study medicine.

"Fine," he said without missing a beat, "as long as it doesn't interfere with football practice."

Then Coach Swayze recommended that I attend summer school to get afternoon labs out of the way — to assure no conflicts with fall football practice. As a result, I had enrolled in Chemistry 105.

On the morning of June 5, 1956, I walked into the chemistry building on campus. I surveyed the large auditorium with about 100 wooden seats. Large windows lined both walls, which descended with the slope of the floor from the entrance of the room to the lab table at the bottom of the auditorium. A chalkboard stretched across the wall behind the black marble table. There appeared to be about fifty other students enrolled in the class.

This felt like the beginning of an adventure. I imagined myself years from now seeing patients, making house calls, delivering babies, and curing people of all sorts of ailments.

I took a seat and noticed a chart mounted high on the wall to the left of the chalkboard. It read "Periodic Table of Elements." I had never seen the symbols featured on the chart, and I had no idea what it was or why it was there.

A tall, thin, slightly balding professor wearing horn-rimmed glasses rushed into the auditorium. He placed his book and folders on the lab table and turned toward us.

"I am C.N. Jones," he said. "You should give your hearts to God today because for the next twelve weeks your asses are mine."

Then Professor Jones launched into a lecture. He talked about conversions and polarity. He mentioned something about cohesion. Then he wrote mathematical formulas on the board and kept using words like "entity" and "denotes."

I was slightly paralyzed. It was bad enough that I'd never heard these words, but Professor Jones' nasal twang made it difficult for me to understand exactly *what* he was saying. He rambled on for an hour, laid down some ground rules, and said he would see us at one o'clock for our first lab. The other students stood and walked up the aisles and out of the room. I remained in my seat knowing I was someplace I didn't need to be.

I walked down to the lab table.

"Mr. Jones," I said apprehensively, "after you introduced yourself, I didn't understand another word you said."

He laughed through his nose and snorted.

"Don't worry about it," he said, gathering his books.

Easy for you to say, I thought, *but I'm headed for the U.S. Army if I don't do well in school.*

"I think I need to get out of this class," I told him.

He laughed through his nose again and said, "We'll take it one day at a time." Then he added, "I'll tutor you at night if you're having trouble."

There was nothing left for me to say. I thanked him, told him I'd see him at the afternoon lab. Then I walked up the aisle and out of the building into the damp Mississippi summer air.

4

As a high school sophomore, I was introduced to college recruiting. I received letters from an array of colleges and universities. Sometimes, alumni from those schools would introduce themselves and encourage me to consider their alma maters.

As I progressed athletically, recruiting picked up and during my eleventh grade year, coaches and scouts from universities started to show up for football games and even practices. At times, I received invitations to attend a college game or visit a campus.

By the time I was a senior, I was inundated with letters, notes, phone calls, and personal visits from coaches and recruiters from Alabama, Auburn, Mississippi State, Tulane, LSU, and Ole Miss. I tried to focus on classes, sports, part-time jobs, and my daily routine, but the attention was distracting. At times, my ego got the best of me. I'll never forget receiving a bright purple and yellow envelope with an "LSU Athletics" return address — a purple and yellow ballpoint pen enclosed. It was heady stuff. For a moment, I felt like a big man on campus.

When Barney Poole, the three-time All-American and former NFL player came to Moss Point High, everyone knew he was on campus. He was recruiting for LSU. He was here to see me.

Coach Poole hung his size 52 XXL blazer on the coat hook and asked me to join him in the coach's office. Meeting with him behind closed doors was as thrilling as anything I had encountered in my seventeen years. He told me all the reasons I should choose LSU. He assured me I would be a star. Then he offered me a full scholarship.

I could barely contain my excitement. I wanted to tell him there, on the spot, that I would be an LSU Tiger, but signing day was still weeks away — on December 7.

Mr. Poole wasn't the only coach to come calling that fall. A few days later the coach from Mississippi State appeared.

"You shouldn't go to Ole Miss," he told me. "They make you wear dress pants to class."

The following week the coach from Tulane visited.

"If you come to Tulane," he said, "you'll be the starting fullback by your sophomore year."

"Thank you, sir," I said. "With my speed, if I'm your starting full-back, our record will be 0-10."

As signing day approached, Coach Swayze came to visit.

In 1951 and 1953, Ole Miss had prepared for the Sugar Bowl at the Biloxi High School stadium. My friends and I drove over to watch them practice. The uniforms were beautiful, and the players were so fast. Also, in 1953, Dixie Howell, a great Ole Miss player, was hired at Moss Point. He had been my head coach for the past three years. I knew I would go to Ole Miss if given the opportunity.

Coach Swayze sat down in the coaches office and said, "Robert, you're a lucky young man."

"Yes, sir?"

"I'm here to offer you a scholarship to Ole Miss."

"Thank you!" I said, a bit surprised.

"Accept it now," he said, "or I'll withdraw the offer."

I committed on the spot.

Although I knew I was not the top recruit at Ole Miss, I felt good about my chances of making the team. In high school, I was named All-Big 8, had been selected to play in the Mississippi All Star Game, and had garnered a number of awards during my time on the field.

Naturally, I assumed football practice would go a bit better than my first chemistry class.

At 5:00 p.m., after attending chemistry lab, my roommate, Ken Kirk, and I walked across campus to the field house. We were the only two freshman football players attending summer school.

We arrived to find the varsity players casually jogging and engaged in calisthenics. A few were tossing the football around. Ken and I, dressed in shorts and t-shirts, joined in.

The varsity players appeared to be in extraordinary physical condition. They were big, fast, and perfectly coordinated. They ran pass routes with perfection. Their throwing, running, and catching techniques were textbook.

Then, I saw a man — the likes of whom I'd never seen — jogging toward the field. He was six feet three inches tall and 240 pounds. But there wasn't an ounce of fat on his body.

Ken leaned over and said, "That's Gene Hickerson . . . the All-American."

I could see the muscles bulging under Gene's shirt. A dark five-o'clock shadow grew on his solid jaw.

I didn't yet need to shave regularly.

One of the varsity players called for fifty-yard sprints. I lined up with four other players.

One of the varsity yelled, "Go!"

Within seconds I saw the other players sprint ahead. I ran as hard as I possibly could. When I crossed the line, I was dead last.

The practice went downhill from there. It was apparent I was out of my league. My size was average, but I was woefully slow. I had hoped to play end for Ole Miss, to follow in the footsteps of legendary Barney Poole.

By the end of practice, I knew I'd never play end for this team. My glory days at Moss Point were over. And I doubted I'd ever see any playing time.

I took off my clothes, wrapped a towel around my waist, and headed for the shower. I was beginning to feel a bit self-conscious, a boy among men, the only one in the locker room without chest hair, when I heard someone yell.

"Freshmen! Get over here."

It was Hickerson. He told us to sit down on a bench. Then he smiled.

One of the other varsity players pulled out an electric razor. I felt the vibration at the base of my neck. Then the razor moved forward across the back of my head and over the top of my scalp. I saw my blond hair fall to the floor.

That evening, as I walked back to Mayes dormitory with Ken Kirk, I ran my hand over my newly cropped hair. My pale scalp was totally exposed.

As was my future.

5

Chemistry proved to be terribly difficult for me. I quickly memorized the chart of elements. I knew it well, but that is all I knew. I had no idea *why* the chart mattered or *how* the elements interacted with each other.

On a Monday during the second week of class, I visited Mr. Jones. I was nervous. Ken had told me his nickname: C.N. "Cyanide" Jones. In Mr. Jones' office, I explained my state of ignorance and my lack of understanding that grew each day. I tried to explain the condition that plagued me in his beloved field of science.

"Meet me at my home in the evenings," he said. "I'll tutor you."

Several nights every week, I went to Mr. Jones' home for tutoring, but I still didn't grasp the subject matter. Then, in early August I was absent from chemistry class for a week. I had committed to play in the Mississippi High School All Star Football Game.

Unlike the C_{12}s and H_{22}s and O_{11}s of chemistry that even Mr. Jones' tutoring couldn't help me understand, the Xs and Os of football made perfect sense.

But being away from class for a week, just ten days shy of the final exam, did not help me prepare for the test.

Exam day came. My classmates and I sat for the test and responded to a couple of dozen questions that included working problems.

Sheepishly, I handed my exam paper to Mr. Jones.

"Meet me in my office in an hour," he said.

When I stepped into his office, Cyanide looked at me, glasses on the end of his prominent nose, and said, "You stupid son of a bitch. I spent the entire summer trying to teach you a little about the fundamentals of basic chemistry." He took his glasses off and tossed them onto his desk. "Do you want to know how many points out of a possible 100 you earned?"

I didn't want to know, but I said, "Yes, sir."

"Eight," he said.

"Eight?" I asked.

"Eight!" he repeated.

I reminded Mr. Jones that I had tried to explain to him that I didn't understand. All summer I'd tried, but it was futile.

"I can recite the chart of elements," I offered.

"Bullshit!" Cyanide barked.

He stared at me, and I stood in front of his desk for what seemed like a lifetime. I remembered the story of my first day of school at Moss Point. My mother said I sat down on the kitchen floor and cried. I was inconsolable. I pleaded with my mother, begging her not to send me to first grade. When my mother finally calmed me down, she asked why I was so afraid to go to school.

"Cause I don't know nothin,'" I said.

I'd heard my mother repeat that story a thousand times but never remembered how I had felt until this moment.

Then Mr. Jones broke the silence. "I am going to give you a passing grade on the condition you *never* come inside this building again."

Those were the sweetest words I'd heard since my tenth grade girlfriend said she loved me.

I thanked Mr. Jones and left his office.

Later that day, I slipped into the chemistry building to see if Cyanide had posted our grades. As I scanned the alphabetical sheet posted on the wall, I found my name.

Khayat, it read, *D-minus, Complimentary*.

My academic career at Ole Miss was underway.

The Interview
March 5, 1995

6

"Dr. Khayat," Nan Baker asked, "what is your vision for the University of Mississippi?"

Ms. Baker, president of the Board of Trustees of Mississippi's Institutions of Higher Learning, was seated behind a U-shaped conference table. To her left and right sat a dozen fellow IHL board members.

In the center of the U, facing the board, was a straight-backed wooden chair. My seat.

The windowless room was well-lit. Large black and white photos — aerial views of the eight public universities in Mississippi and the University of Mississippi Medical Center — adorned the off-white walls. The boardroom, with its beige wall-to-wall carpet, was designed to project an air of neutrality. It was also designed for an audience of one hundred, but on this day there were only fourteen of us.

When I was in college, I was spellbound by the Ole Miss campus — beautiful, green, and lush — and by the stately Georgian buildings that housed our classrooms. The faculty was outstanding and the students were, for the most part, bright. By the time I enrolled as a freshman, the University of Mississippi had already produced thirteen Rhodes Scholars.

After graduation, Oxford remained my home base. I served on the faculty at the law school and, later, as a vice chancellor. It was from this vantage point that I watched as time took its toll on Ole Miss.

The integration of the campus in 1962 was a pivotal event in the history of the university. The evening news broadcast footage of riots to the entire nation. In the eyes of the public, Ole Miss became a place of military troops and tear gas. The effects of the integration riot were felt for years. Enrollment declined. Brilliant young professors rejected offers to teach at the university. They had seen the news footage.

Some of Mississippi's most promising students chose to attend out-of-state universities. From 1991-1994, enrollment at the university dropped from 11,000 to 10,181. The loss of tuition dollars resulted in lower salaries and fewer funds for building maintenance and new construction projects. The once-stately academic buildings began to look worn and tired. The grounds were neglected. The campus had lost its luster. *no one was coming*

Even the once-mighty football team fell. The Ole Miss Rebels, a football team that had ruled the Southeastern Conference for nearly two decades, were placed on probation twice in seven years. Ole Miss didn't play in a bowl game for ten full seasons.

It appeared that Ole Miss, weighed down by negative press and a tarnished public perception, had simply given up. We were viewed by many as a third-tier university, and we had acted like one for far too long.

Over the years, it was painful for me to watch.

I looked around the room as the IHL board awaited my reply. I saw my old friends Will Hickman and Frank Crosthwait. I nodded at my new friend, IHL Commissioner Tom Layzell. Then I looked at Ms. Baker and told her my vision for the University of Mississippi.

"To be — and to be perceived as — one of America's great public universities."

Deliberation
Spring 1995

My M Club sweater

7

After the interview in Jackson, I drove back to Oxford and waited to hear from the Board of Trustees.

During those weeks, I vacillated between believing that I might be the best person to fill the position of chancellor to thinking I had made a terrible mistake by putting my name up for consideration. I spent my days in March of 1995 going back and forth between the two extremes.

I also thought about my own experience as an undergraduate at our university. *didn't seen to have a good experience*

My summer school experience was disastrous. The fall semester couldn't have been more different.

In my history class, a tall, thin, dignified woman with short gray hair entered the classroom.

She turned and wrote her name at the top of the chalkboard: *Margaret Moore*. Then, under her name, she wrote an outline of the first day's lecture. I recognized every single word, and I understood why one event led to the next. She was speaking English, not chemistry.

Mrs. Moore delivered the most extraordinary lecture I'd ever heard. She was engaging and told colorful stories and brought the history lesson to life. I didn't want the class to end.

A few weeks later, Dr. Doris Raymond, the Latin teacher, asked me if I would like to accompany the university scholars on a trip to Memphis to see an opera. I had never seen an opera — or heard one for that matter — and my only trip to Memphis had been a wild weekend with Ken Kirk and Carl Comer to see Elvis Presley.

I accepted Dr. Raymond's invitation. Good fortune was with me that night. The opera was *La Bohéme*. I was immediately transfixed — and transported to the Latin Quarter of Paris where Rodolfo, the poet, and Marcello, the painter, were burning pages from Rodolfo's latest drama to keep warm. As each character entered the story, they came alive. The philosopher, the musician, the landlord, the toy vendor and, of course, Mimi the seamstress. When the wind blew out Mimi's and Rodolfo's candles and they fell in love talking under the moonlight, I sat in wonder. I'd never seen anything like it. The music, the color, the excitement, the energy.

For the first time, I saw the majesty of the world outside of the United States. Dr. Raymond's gift was generous. She understood the importance of *cultural enrichment*; I'd never heard the term. But that night in Memphis was one I would always remember.

As the semesters passed, I thrived in the classroom. Liberal arts was where I needed to be. But I also had a bit of success in the sciences.

The biology lecture was held in Fulton Chapel, and enrollment was roughly four hundred. The professor, the legendary Dr. Irwin Kitchin, taught the class as if only twenty of us were in the room. Not only was Dr. Kitchin a riveting speaker, he was also an accomplished artist. As he talked about microorganisms or amoebas, he sketched elaborate illustrations on the chalkboard to help us understand the complex science.

Dr. Kitchin and Cyanide Jones were equally talented teachers, I'm sure, but I thanked God every day for biology. It made sense to me.

Though the fall of 1956 brought great relief in the classroom, my football future was still in question. We reported for preseason practice two weeks before fall classes began. The first few days we went through physical examinations and light workouts. Then real practice started.

We practiced once in the morning and once in the afternoon — at the hottest, most humid time of the day. Team meetings were held at night.

Freshmen did not practice on the same field as varsity, but we were often called down to "Vaught's Valley" to serve as fodder in scrimmages. *it was hard to be a football player*

All of the freshmen suffered from culture shock. Most of us had been team captains or All-Stars or All-District, or had earned some other distinction. We were accustomed to being the best on the field. Not only were the size and speed of the varsity team sobering, but the players also treated us as if we were subhuman. We were subjected to punishment on and off the field.

The coaches were unreasonably rough. Wind sprints until players were physically sick. Disinterest or disdain for injuries. Limited water regardless of the heat. We weren't sure if they were trying to make us the best players possible or if they were trying to send us back home.

The on-field winnowing continued after practice in the form of hazing. During our first dinner together, one of the varsity players stood and called for everyone's attention.

"We will be having a mandatory freshman meeting," he announced, "immediately following supper."

At that meeting, the freshmen were told to form a line.

"Step forward one at a time," the varsity player yelled. "Tell us your name, hometown, and any honors you received in high school."

That first meeting most of us proudly announced our athletics and academic and extracurricular awards. And the varsity players kept count.

Using a baseball bat, shaven flat on one side, the varsity players gave us a lick on our behinds for every honor announced. It didn't take us long to learn. The second freshman meeting revealed that none of us had received any high school recognition or honors and, in fact, none of us could imagine how we were able to receive scholarships from Ole Miss. With shaved heads and blistered tails, any of us who needed humbling got it. Those who were already humble realized that true humility has no limits.

That part of the hazing ritual was dangerous and cruel. The balance came in the form of personal servitude. We performed menial tasks for the varsity players. We shined shoes, dropped off laundry, made up beds, served as chauffeurs, and delivered food from the grill.

The tasks, for the most part, weren't difficult, but we were asked to perform them when we needed to be resting. We practiced morning and afternoon. We were tired and dehydrated. While varsity players took naps or sipped on Cokes, we performed our assigned tasks. Freshmen were always tired.

Survival became our primary objective and many of us didn't make it. The day fall practice started, sixty freshmen were on the field. By the end of the second week, our numbers had dwindled to 35. We all wondered who would be the next one to pack his belongings and leave the team.

I survived the practices and the hazing, but only because I was blessed to have two seniors — Eddie Crawford and Lee Paslay — who adopted me as *their* freshman.

Under their mentorship, I did all the usual domestic chores, errands, and driving for Eddie and Lee, but my primary task was to read aloud. Following lunch each day, I reported to their room, made sure the space was in order and then, as they rested on their beds, I read. Their favorite selections were *Field and Stream* magazine and the *Police Gazette*.

As I read, as weary from practice as they were, I tried to pace the delivery so that my voice gently, slowly rocked them to sleep. When it worked, I could slip away and go to my room and lie down. At other times, they would close their eyes and pretend to be asleep. I would keep reading in a soft voice and tiptoe toward the door.

About the time my hand touched the doorknob, Eddie or Lee would shout, "Freshman, sit your ass down and read."

And I did. I learned more about crappie and bass, fishing lures and waders than I ever wanted to know. But I was glad to be their friend and thankful they protected me from some of the more violent varsity team members.

persivered

My freshman year of football was difficult, but I stuck with it. By my sophomore season, wonderful things started to happen on the football field. I was lucky enough to be a member of some of the greatest teams in college football history. I was a backup lineman and a starting kicker, but the young men who surrounded me were extraordinary.

My sophomore year, ~~got better~~ our record was 9-1-1, and we whipped Texas in the Sugar Bowl by a score of 39-7. My junior year, the Rebels were 9-2 and beat Florida in the Gator Bowl. And my senior year, on the famed 1959 team, our record was 10-1. It was topped off by a 21-0 Sugar Bowl victory over LSU. We were ranked No. 1 in the nation.

Our teams were so dominant in the three-year stretch between 1957 and 1959 that we outscored our opponents 776 to 139.

The Ole Miss football team continued to dominate the SEC and once held the record for the most consecutive bowl appearances in college football history. Every year from 1957-1971, Ole Miss made an appearance in a postseason bowl, at a time when there were only a handful of bowl games.

But times had changed. As I sat in Oxford awaiting a decision from the IHL board, football at Ole Miss was in shambles. We'd not seen bowl action in several years. And we were coming off two separate NCAA sanctions. In recent years, the students at Ole Miss had not experienced anything like the championship football squads that took the field when I was a student at the university.

I planned to do something about that as well.

8

My first brush with the heartache of public failure came on the evening of November 15, 1958, in Knoxville, Tennessee. We entered the game with a 7-1 record. Our only loss came to a mighty LSU team that would go on to win the 1958 national title.

The game against Tennessee was close. In the waning moments of the fourth quarter, we were trailing the Volunteers by two points. I was called in to attempt a twenty-nine-yard field goal. If I made it, Ole Miss would win by a point. If I missed, there wasn't enough time for another scoring drive.

As I stood in the backfield, I went through my regular pre-kick ritual — *focus on the spot where the ball will be placed, don't look up, keep your eye on the ball, and remember to kick straight through the ball and finish high.* I also included a short prayer asking for God's help in making the kick. Apparently, God had more pressing matters. The center snapped the ball, Billy Brewer placed it perfectly on the tee, and I kicked through and high just like I practiced every day. I watched as the ball soared into the air and drifted about a foot outside of the left upright.

We lost the game by two points.

My twenty-year-old heart was broken. The next morning's headline in the *Clarion-Ledger* read: "Golden Toe Turns to Brass." For the next few days, I thought I might die. That kick, that moment, was seared in my mind. It was not only a personal failure, but it also showed an inability to deliver when my teammates and coaches were counting on me most.

But even this failure paled when compared to the disappointment I felt on Halloween night of 1959.

At midnight on October 31, 1959, I leaned over the rail of the Baton Rouge ferry and stared into the darkness of the Mississippi

River. The lonely sound of the foghorn intensified my pain. I rode back and forth across the river, alone and silent, trying to understand a dejection I'd never experienced before.

During my twenty-one years, I had suffered personal failure, embarrassment, and pain. But nothing compared to how I felt when I looked at the scoreboard earlier that evening in Tiger Stadium: LSU 7, Ole Miss 3. It had only been about two hours, but it already felt like a nightmare.

The anticipation of this game actually began twelve months earlier, in 1958. LSU, the `58 national champions, had beaten us 14-0. They had a better football team than ours, and though the loss was tough to accept, in fairness, the better team won.

In the locker room after the 1958 game, those of us who would return the next season vowed that it wouldn't happen again. And from that day forward, we worked as a team to be ready to win the 1959 game.

Spring football practice in 1959 was a time of heavy lifting. We pounded one another. There were separated shoulders, sprained ankles, and torn knee ligaments. The twenty days of practice, including the spring game, determined which players would be on the traveling squad in the fall of 1959.

Since we played one-platoon football (all of us played offense and defense, and there were no specialists who focused solely on kicking or punting), the traveling team comprised thirty-six players, and the competition for each of those slots was furious.

At the beginning of practice, the coaches had created a depth chart: the first team (red), the second team (blue), and the third team (green). Everyone knew where he stood on the team. The practice jersey matched the color of a player's status, as well as his self-perception. I was on the blue squad.

If a blue or green team player thought he should be in red, all he had to do was tell the position coach that he *challenged*. Then, a one-on-one dogfight ensued. The battle between the two men — blocking and resisting — went on until one man overpowered the other. One of the most humiliating moments for an Ole Miss player in those days was to remove his red jersey on the spot and hand it to his challenger.

And any time the loser felt he could regain the first-team status, he could issue a similar challenge.

There were additional players on the squad. Some wore orange jerseys; the remainder wore white. The orange and white teams assumed the roles of our weekly opponents. They executed the opponent's offense and defense and helped the red, blue, and green teams prepare for games. The color-coded jerseys provided a well-established class system. But in the end, we were all treated like dogs.

The months between the brutal spring practice and the fall football season flew by. A day didn't pass without thoughts of LSU. We had beaten Mississippi State for so many consecutive years — with a rare tie or two along the way — that we no longer viewed them as a true rival. But when we thought about football, which was every day, we thought about LSU.

August 29, 1959, finally arrived and we returned to campus. Classes didn't begin until the third week in September, so we were the only students at Ole Miss for those first two-and-a-half weeks. Our team was of one mind: have an undefeated season.

September 1st brought two-a-day workouts. Practice in the morning and the afternoons, followed by evening team meetings. That fall we lived in the new athletics dorm for football players only. Our meals were served in the athletics cafeteria, a private dining room for football players. Other sports athletes had a separate dining hall during football season, but we all shared a cafeteria in the spring. We joked that football players enjoyed steak in the fall and Spam in the spring.

We had not merely bonded; we were joined at the hip. We did everything together. We ate, practiced, met, studied, and traveled as a group. We shared our clothes, our belongings, and our joys and sorrows. We knew all about each other's personal habits, grades, girlfriends, and families. We probably understood more about our teammates than we knew about our siblings and parents. The friendships of teammates are for life. And in those preseason days of 1959, we were a tightly knit, focused group.

We breezed through the first six games of the 1959 season. We scored 189 points and gave up only seven.

We attended our regular Sunday afternoon, post-game meetings at the coach's office riding a crest of lopsided victories. We were ranked third in the nation, and we anxiously anticipated our Friday flight to Baton Rouge. Practices during the week before the game were *in shells*. No pads or helmets and no physical contact. Practicing in shells is fun. You feel light and fast, and you know that you aren't going to be hit or have to hit another player. Our coaches knew that we were in top physical condition. No need to beat on each other all week. We wanted to be rested and healthy for the game, so we spent the week refining our offensive and defensive plans. We also worked on punts, kickoffs, and field goals/extra points.

On Friday at noon, we boarded the twin-engine Martin 404. We were all excited to be bound for Baton Rouge and ready to exact revenge on the Tigers.

Every player wore a jacket and tie. So did the coaches and managers. There were no wealthy alums on the team plane. We were serious about our business, and we believed that more was at stake than a football game. We represented the university, but we genuinely felt that we were Mississippi's finest — the one group that could overcome all the negative perceptions about our state. And we achieved this by winning football games.

The team buses were waiting at the Baton Rouge airport to take us to the stadium for our Friday afternoon practice. The city and the LSU campus were electric. Signs and banners covered buildings. Horns and cheers and boos were directed at us as the buses slowly drove toward the stadium. In the heart of the LSU campus, Tiger stadium seemed larger than the Roman Colosseum. And in the previous year, we had experienced a fate similar to the Christians. We didn't intend to repeat it.

The visitors' dressing room was under Tiger Stadium, near the access portal to the field. We gathered in a circle. Some players took a knee; others stood. Coach Vaught made a few pre-game comments. Then, it was time for Doc Knight's prayer.

Wesley Isador Knight, known to all as "Doc," was our trainer, supporter, and healer. Doc, a devout Episcopalian, father of five children, and devoted husband, asked us to join him in prayer.

He knelt.

"God, our Father," Doc began, "watch after our team as we take the field today. Know that we are your servants and that all we do is in honor and glory of your name. Look down, Lord, from your heavenly throne and protect these young men from injury, and help us remember that all victories are gifts from above. Glory to the Father, and to the Son, and to the Holy Spirit; as it was in the beginning, is now, and will be forever. Amen."

"Amen," we said in unison.

Doc stood and shouted, "Now get out there and whip their damn asses! Knock those sons-of-bitches' heads off!"

We joined Doc, yelling and cheering as we ran out onto the field. We were met with a deafening blast of noise. The atmosphere was surreal, unlike anything we had experienced — and the roar never let up.

The two best teams in the nation took the field in front of 67,327 fans. Both teams had allowed only one touchdown from their opponents that season. LSU had a Heisman contender in Billy Cannon. Charlie Flowers was the Ole Miss favorite to receive the Heisman. All eyes and ears in the sports world were on Tiger Stadium.

Tickets were so scarce that one of my friends paid $100 for a Coca-Cola vendor's apron, hat, and tray. Then he walked right into the stadium. Another gentleman had purchased white knickers, a black and white striped shirt, stockings, football shoes, and an official's cap. He entered the stadium right behind the legitimate officials. Scalpers were asking $2,500 per ticket.

As expected, the game was a knock-down, drag-out defensive battle. In the first quarter, Billy Brewer recovered a Billy Cannon fumble. The recovery set up my twenty-two-yard field goal. We led 3-0.

Neither team scored again until the fourth quarter. With 10:59 remaining in the game, Jake Gibbs punted. He'd planned to kick the ball so that it rolled out of bounds, but the ball hit on the LSU ten-yard line and bounced right into the arms of Billy Cannon. Cannon was caught by surprise. He had been instructed by LSU Coach Paul Dietzel to not try to catch the wet ball. But when the ball landed in his arms, his instincts took over and he ran. Along his eighty-nine-yard route to the goal line, eight of our eleven players tried unsuccessfully to tackle him. One of our players had the chance to hit him twice. Those of us on the sidelines watched helplessly as Billy Cannon ran by our bench. But he wasn't alone. The man fraudulently dressed as an official ran along the sidelines, step-for-step with Billy Cannon from the time the punt was received until he crossed the goal line.

Our silk-suited Coach Vaught sank to both knees on the muddy field. When he stood, round, dark spots stained the knees of his trousers.

LSU made the extra point. Both teams sent in their second units. We returned LSU's kickoff to the thirty-nine-yard line. Ten minutes remained in the game. With our blue team, led by sophomore quarterback Doug Elmore, we proceeded to march down the field. When we reached the LSU forty-yard line, Coach Dietzel sent his first team back into the game. We drove down to the LSU seven-yard line. It was first and goal with two-and-a-half minutes left.

Our blue team had been on the field for nearly nine minutes. Our red team — the first string players — were on the bench, rested and ready to come back into the game. But Coach Vaught left us in the game. Three plays later, we were on the one-yard line. With just over a minute left in the game, we were one yard away from victory, one yard away from a national championship, one yard away from securing the Heisman Trophy for Charlie Flowers. We were just one yard away from redemption. But it was fourth down. We had only one shot.

Doug Elmore called our most successful, dependable play. After the snap, a single mental error, a blocking error, was committed by one of our most intelligent, reliable players. Doug Elmore was stopped on the half-yard line by Billy Cannon and Warren Rabb.

The ball was turned over to LSU. The game was over.

I changed into street clothes and caught a ride to the river ferry dock. Alone, I rode back and forth across the river. I didn't know what to do, and I had no idea what to say to my teammates. So I stayed on the ferry until the captain told me it was stopping for the night. It was 2:00 a.m.

Then I walked back toward the hotel through the dark, abandoned streets of Baton Rouge.

9

For most of my life, I have been a member of a team. It began with my family in Moss Point. With a modest income and six of us living in a 1,500-square-foot home, our family depended on teamwork in order to function and maintain domestic tranquility. As a team, our family cooked and cleaned and entertained. We learned the principles of sharing, waiting your turn, and helping each other, as well as learning patience and tolerance for the shortcomings of others and ourselves.

When we worked together — when each of us did his or her part — our family team functioned reasonably well. If, however, one of us stayed in the shower too long, the others suffered through cold baths. If my sister took the comb to school, our dad went to work with disheveled hair. If my brother read *Life* magazine from cover to cover, the stories were stale by the time he shared the magazine.

Soon I joined football, basketball, and baseball teams. Later in life, I joined teams in business, education, development, and law.

There is no more fulfilling experience for a team member than the joy of performing your job well to help your team succeed. Conversely, nothing is more disheartening than failing your teammates.

But one trait exists in all healthy, successful teams: *You win together and you lose together.*

When I missed the field goal and cost Ole Miss the victory over Tennessee, my coaches, teammates, and friends all offered consolation. The coaches allowed me to continue as the placekicker for the team. And my teammates told me they had confidence that I would never cost Ole Miss a game again. It was this dedication and loyalty that triggered an unwavering commitment in me to work harder, to sacrifice, to take any action necessary to avoid failing the people who mattered the most.

Immediately upon returning to Oxford, I spent hours on the field before and after regular practice. I placed the ball at the twenty-nine-yard line on the right hash mark, in the exact spot the ball was placed on Shields-Watkins Field in Knoxville. Then I kicked again and again and again. I kicked until I couldn't lift my leg.

I wasn't alone. Billy Keyes, one of the team managers, was right there with me. For three entire seasons, Billy stayed late to shag footballs for me. We were usually the only people on the field. Even when darkness was near and I wanted to practice a few more kicks, Billy was happy to stay.

Some people might not think about Billy being on the football team. But, for me, he was one of the most important members. Shields-Watkins Field would be my only game-losing kick. Billy Keyes helped me see to that.

I understood the sacred nature of a team. Respect, loyalty, and sacrifice were all vital. I have been privileged to be a member of many fine teams. And I felt blessed.

The 1959 Ole Miss Rebels had some unfinished business with LSU.

On Sunday morning, November 1, 1959, after the defeat at the hands of the LSU team, we gathered at the Baton Rouge airport to fly back to Oxford. Coach Kinard had packed his suitcase in a fit of anger. Before boarding the plane, while he was cleaning his fingernails with a pocketknife, he noticed that about six inches of a necktie were protruding from the seam of his luggage. He bent over, put the knife blade to the necktie, and severed it.

We all knew that practice in the coming week would be hell.

But the coaches didn't even have to push us. We understood what we needed to do. We focused and practiced as if nothing else in the world mattered. We had three regular-season games remaining, and we would make the most of them.

The following week we beat Chattanooga 58-0. Then, we

pounded Tennessee 37-7. We ended with Mississippi State. The score was 42-0.

In a strange turn of events, LSU agreed to play us on New Year's Day in the Sugar Bowl in New Orleans. Exactly two months after the Halloween night debacle, we were set to take the field again against the Tigers.

With the exception of Billy Cannon's punt return, our season had been nearly perfect. Not one of our ten opponents actually drove the football for a touchdown or a field goal. Tulane scored the first touchdown of the year against us. It was set up by a recovered fumble inside our five-yard line. We won that game 56-7. Against Tennessee, they blocked a quick kick inside our ten-yard line. We won that game 37-7. And, of course, Billy Cannon made his eighty-nine-yard return for the historic touchdown and our only loss of the year: 7-3 to LSU.

The 1960 Sugar Bowl was the first bowl game to be telecast in color from coast to coast. And in front of that national audience, we were intent on rectifying the Halloween nightmare.

Coach Vaught had learned a lesson about overly conservative play in the loss to LSU. During the regular-season game, we punted three times on first down. But in New Orleans, he let us loose. We came out running and gunning on offense and rushing through the gaps on defense.

LSU's defense held firm until the very end of the second quarter. Jake Gibbs, who led the SEC in total offense, rolled out and pulled up behind our tackle. He delayed for an instant and let the ball go. Larry Grantham raced down the field. Cowboy Woodruff ran behind him. Then Cowboy cut toward the center of the field, and Jake's pass arched down into Cowboy's hands. No one was within fifteen yards of him. We went into the locker room with a seven-point halftime lead.

The touchdown at the end of the half broke LSU. In the third quarter, Larry Grantham caught an eighteen-yard touchdown pass from Bobby Franklin. And in the fourth quarter, Bobby threw a nine-yard touchdown to George Blair.

The LSU defense had not allowed a passing touchdown all season. We scored three in one afternoon. But that was just the beginning. We dominated the Sugar Bowl. We gained 363 yards in the game; LSU had a minus fifteen yards rushing. Our nemesis, the recently crowned Heisman Trophy winner Billy Cannon, carried the ball six times for a grand total of eight yards. The Sugar Bowl ended Ole Miss 21, LSU 0.

I have thought many times about the two games we played in that season. In 120 minutes of playing time, LSU crossed the fifty-yard line once — when Cannon returned the punt.

We were the better team.

The following week, the final polls were released. Ole Miss was ranked No. 1 in the country by Berryman, Billingsley, Dunkel, and Sagarin. Syracuse was ranked No. 1 by AP and UPI.

The Sugar Bowl victory was sweet, but it didn't come close to erasing the loss on Halloween night — a loss that cost Ole Miss a Heisman Trophy and an undisputed national title.

10

We all have defining moments. One of mine came on the evening of August 12, 1960. I remember that muggy Chicago night as vividly as if it happened yesterday.

I had signed a contract to play football for the Washington Redskins of the National Football League. Professional football, at times, was overshadowed by college football. All but three professional teams were located east of the Mississippi River. Television coverage was rare, and player salaries were modest, at best. The Super Bowl, indoor stadiums, and artificial turf did not yet exist.

Professional football was no threat to the national pastime — baseball. However, a few games each year attracted big crowds and national television audiences: the NFL Championship game, the Pro Bowl, and the Chicago Charities College All-Star Game. The latter was a preseason game that pitted the reigning NFL champions against the College All-Stars. It was a nationally televised game played before a crowd of 75,000 at Soldier Field in Chicago.

In 1960, I was among the thirty-six College All-Stars chosen to challenge the NFL champion, the Baltimore Colts. Our All-Stars included Don Meredith, Mike Magee, Prentice Gault, and a few other All-American players. The Colts' roster included Johnny Unitas, Lenny Moore, Gino Marchetti, and Raymond Berry, among other big-name, proven professional stars. It was a mismatch. Men against boys.

My teammates and I arrived at Northwestern University in Evanston. We had three weeks to train and prepare for the game. Our head coach was the great Cleveland Browns quarterback Otto Graham. He was assisted by perennial all-pros Dick Stanfel and Pete Pihos. Most of the players had been selected for some All-American team, and we held some degree of national notoriety, but we were still intimidated by the coaches — and, in a way, by each other. All of us except Don Meredith. Don Meredith wasn't intimidated by anybody.

After two weeks of workouts, we travelled to Rensselaer, Indiana, to scrimmage the Chicago Bears — to get a taste of what was to come. The Bears' players were bigger, faster, better, older, and tougher than any of us, and they hadn't come close to being a championship team. Late in the fourth quarter, the score was Bears 35, All-Stars 0.

With little time left, we approached the line of scrimmage, and the ball was snapped. All of the Bears' defensive players fell to the ground. Don Meredith had taken the snap and turned his back to the line as he dropped back to pass. When he turned, he saw every receiver open. There was no pass rush. It was insult on top of injury. Don turned toward the bleachers, planted his feet, and threw the ball over the press box and out of the stadium. We walked off the field, crawled on to our buses, and headed back to Evanston.

I don't know what the other All-Stars were thinking during the bus ride, but I was visualizing the massacre that would take place on Soldier Field against the Colts in six days.

As the days passed, our coaches developed a game plan, and we practiced hard. The coaches knew that survival was as much an issue as winning. Wisely, they listed two of us at each position. We would alternate play by quarters. I was a guard and a placekicker, and my alternate was a young man from the Big Ten. He and I were to split time on the field. He would play the first and third quarters; I would play the second and fourth. And, if we should score, I would kick the extra point, as well as kick off.

During pre-game drills, I noticed that the men in the white and blue uniforms didn't move like us. They seemed to glide effortlessly. They caught passes with one hand. And they laughed a lot.

Our uniforms were pretty and new — grey pants and blue jerseys with stars on our shoulders. But we were not laughing, nor were we gliding. In fact we were stiff — like stick men — so tense our knees wouldn't bend.

As the game began, the Colts kicked off to us. I watched my capable alternate attempt to block one of the large Colts. After the collision, the Colts player continued to run down the field in pursuit of our receiver. My alternate lay on the ground. He slowly moved to a hands-and-knees position. Then, much like an animal, he began to crawl. Not toward our bench but toward the darkness beyond the end zone. Soldier Field had been built to host the Olympic games, so it was configured to accommodate a track and, therefore, was a horse-shoe-shaped arena. In the open end of the stadium, darkness prevailed. And that is exactly where my alternate was headed. I watched him crawl into the darkness and disappear. He never returned.

I had been well-trained in replacing injured teammates. I snapped on my chinstrap, adjusted my helmet, and rushed onto the field and into the huddle. Don called the play. We broke the huddle and hustled to the line of scrimmage. I was the left guard. I assumed my position with my hands on my knees, and I looked ahead, expecting to see the face of my opponent. To my surprise, and with great chagrin, I stared straight at my opponent's sternum. The number on his jersey read "76." That number belonged to a man named Eugene "Big Daddy" Lipscomb.

I knew an encounter with Big Daddy was a possibility during the course of this game, but it came too quickly. Big Daddy was six feet eight inches tall. He weighed around 300 pounds. I was six feet two inches and weighed 220 pounds. I was a twenty-two-year-old white kid from Mississippi. He was a thirty-four-year-old black man who grew up in Detroit. Big Daddy's dark, thick beard was tucked behind a gray face mask, and his eyes appeared as dark, shiny agates. Suddenly, the crowd noise disappeared. Time slowed down. I nearly forgot where I was, but then I looked up at him.

Big Daddy said, "Boy, does your mama know you're out here tonight?"

"Yes, sir," I said.

Then the ball was snapped. I was dealt a crushing blow from a huge right arm. Big Daddy brushed me aside as if I were an irritating fly and tackled our ball carrier for a loss.

Since my alternate had disappeared, it was my fate to spend the entire game in front of Big Daddy. I tried to hold and trip him. Other

hoped to simply get in his way. Each time he would cast me
or down.

C'mon, Sweet Pea," he said. Then, offering a hand, he'd add,
"Get up, Sweet Pea."

I knew I'd never beat Big Daddy. But I was determined not to
quit. When our defense was on the field, I sat on the bench and wondered if this was how pro football would be for me. I thought of
home and my mother. And the days when I played at Ole Miss, when
we won just about every game. Then the Colts would score and kick
the ball back to us. Out onto the field I would run, hoping Big Daddy
had decided to take a break. But it was not to be. He played every
play. So did I.

When the game ended, Big Daddy gave me a hug. Then he smiled
and walked off the field.

Eugene "Big Daddy" Lipscomb bruised my body — and my ego.
He showed me my place in the world of football. And I knew I never
wanted to face him on the football field again.

That night, I started to dream of law school.

getting knocked down and
getting back up again →physically
and metaphorically

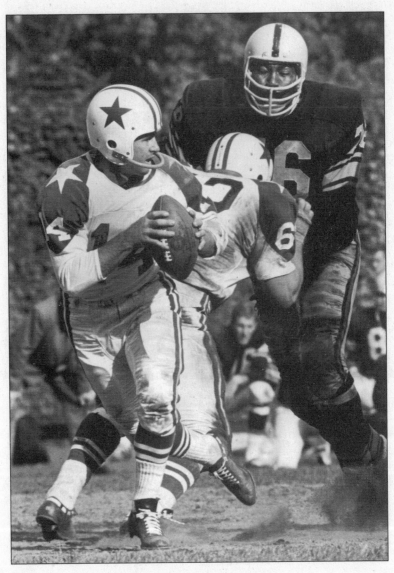

Eugene "Big Daddy" Lipscomb

The Cleveland 🏈 BROWNS

CLEVELAND 14, OHIO

PAUL E. BROWN
Coach and General Manager

January 21, 1960

Cleveland Stadium
TOwer 1-3400

Mr. Robert Khayat
510 Beardslee Stret
Moss Point, Mississippi

Dear Bob:

This is your copy of the contract which was signed with the Cleveland Browns. There is one on file with the League Office and we have the other one.

We have taken special precautions so that there will be no announcement of your signing until such time as you feel it is to your best interest.

I would like to suggest that you put your contract away carefully to protect yourself. When the time comes for announcing your signing, by all means allow us to do it from our offices. In this way the maximum publicity will be gained nationwide. Also, I would suggest that you keep your contract confidential - it is the sign of a big timer.

In the meantime, if you are bothered by other teams I would suggest that you simply tell them that you are not interested in being with them and plan to play with the Cleveland Browns. In this way you will save yourself a lot of trouble and still not specifically tell them that you have signed.

We are looking forward to having you with us. We have need for your services and we have plans for you. Sometime around May or early June you will receive a reporting notice from our offices. It will include all the details.

In the meantime stay in shape and set your heart on making good - it is the next step.

Sincerely,

THE CLEVELAND BROWNS

Paul E. Brown

11

In 1960, I signed a contract with the Cleveland Browns. Cleveland's Jim Brown had led the league in rushing for three straight years behind the extraordinary blocking of Ole Miss great Gene Hickerson. And, of course, Paul Brown was a legend in the National Football League.

After receiving my signed contract, Coach Brown wrote me a letter encouraging me "to stay in shape and set my heart on making good." He added, "We have need for your services and we have plans for you."

But five months later, before I ever set foot in Cleveland, I was traded to the Washington Redskins. During my first year with the team, our record was 1-9-2. We were last place in the Eastern Conference. My second season with the Redskins ended slightly better at 5-7-2. We weren't last in the league, but we didn't come close to making the playoffs.

In April 1963, I received my contract for the upcoming season from the Redskins. They offered me a $250 increase in my annual salary. I had just married Margaret Denton, and we were planning to start a family. I needed to think about my future. The paltry increase was insulting, so I returned the contract to Washington unsigned.

My longtime friend Joe Colingo, who was enrolled in the Ole Miss law school, encouraged me to join him in the June class. I wrote the Redskins and told them I wouldn't be returning because I planned to enter law school.

I started classes and immediately fell in love with the law. It made sense to me, and I quickly understood that law had almost universal application. It is, literally, the foundation upon which our society is built.

Then, in mid-June, I received a new contract from the Redskins proposing a salary increase of $1,500. At $12,500, I would be the highest paid lineman on the Washington roster. I simply couldn't turn down the money. I accepted the offer, signed and returned the contract, and assumed I would have to drop out of law school, or at least delay my legal career. However, in an act of generosity that I will never be able to repay, the law faculty agreed to work with me. I would stay in Oxford to attend class until July 10th, at which time I would report to Carlisle, Pennsylvania, at Dickinson College for training camp. While preparing for the 1963 NFL season, I completed my two summer school courses by correspondence.

I entered my third season as a Redskin with high hopes. We won two of our first three games, but after those wins we fell back into our old mode of play.

I wasn't accustomed to losing, but I wasn't accustomed to quitting, either. I wanted to play as many seasons in the NFL as possible, but I found myself wondering whether that was a better decision than moving on to law school full time. Those two summer courses, the quality of the faculty, and the acumen of my fellow students created an intellectually vigorous environment that struck a nerve.

Going back to the Xs and Os of football was becoming tedious. I suppose if we had been a better team, I may have felt differently, but we were awful. The environment in the locker room was depressing, and our record reflected it. As the season ground on, losing week after week, the thought of a stimulating law school class became more and more appealing. We ended the 1963 season 3-11.

I returned to law school for the spring semester and flourished. I found the classes exhilarating, and I felt like I was in the right place.

In the summer of 1964, I received my new contract from the Redskins. I signed it and reported to training camp, but it was clear that nothing had changed in the Redskins' culture. There were no leadership improvements. The team also had no center and no holder for field goals.

I stayed at training camp for one month. Then I took my notebook to the head coach and told him I was leaving to go to law school full time. He tried to persuade me to stay, promised better days ahead, as well as higher pay, but it was too late. My heart was in the law school — and at Ole Miss.

I drove away from Carlisle, and I thought about my time in the NFL. I'd met some wonderful men, played in the great football and baseball stadiums in cities across the nation, and experienced some degree of celebrity. But as I made my way south, I had no sense of regret. I felt rather liberated. I was headed to enroll full time in law school, and I had saved enough money from playing in the NFL to pay my way through.

Margaret Denton entered Ole Miss in 1960. She was a product of a quiet, low-profile family in Memphis, and a graduate of Miss Hutchison's School for Young Ladies. The school's spirit song was "You Are My Sunshine." Margaret was lovely in every way, smart, and a lot of fun. It is no surprise that she knew nothing about intercollegiate athletics. The Ole Miss cheer — "Who in the Hell Are We?" — was quite a contrast to Miss Hutchison's adopted song.

What Margaret didn't know is that the members of the Ole Miss football team were closer to each other than our own blood relatives. And three of my very best friends, Warner Alford, Bo Ball, and Jimmy Hall, were carefully reviewing the freshman girls, trying to find a girlfriend for me. Early in the fall of 1960, I had a call from Bo.

"We have found the girl for you, Ox," he said.

Then they told Margaret that they'd found the boy for her. And they were right. We began dating in January and fell for each other. We were together constantly in February and March, then I moved to Vicksburg to earn my teacher's certificate. When I had an attack of pancreatitis and was hospitalized for three months at Mercy Hospital in Vicksburg, Margaret stood by me.

Margaret and I were married on March 24, 1962. She was nineteen. I was twenty-three. The wedding was a traditional formal Memphis wedding at the First Evangelical Church at 8:00 p.m. with many bridesmaids and groomsmen and an overflow crowd. Most of the groomsmen were my football teammates. Their bodies, and particularly their necks, stretched the tuxedos with tails to their limits.

Between 1962 and 1964, we moved to and from Washington and had a truly extraordinary extended honeymoon. My salary was generous compared to those of my classmates who worked in banks or taught school. We had no children, apartment living was simple, and Redskins were celebrities in Washington. We were young and free and we enjoyed all that the life of a professional football player had to offer. But Margaret — who I'm sure had never even heard of the NFL before she met me — had quite a surprise when she watched me play football. This nineteen-year-old girl from Memphis sat in the Redskins' stadium when I missed a field goal, and suddenly found herself surrounded by 56,000 people who booed and sneered at the young man she had just married. Still, Margaret made the adjustment from Memphis society to the world of professional football and then back to life in Mississippi with grace and apparent ease.

Law school began in earnest in 1964, and we loved living in Oxford. Our apartment at Avent Acres was small and inexpensive. Other law couples occupied most of the other twenty-three units. On the weekends, we shared barbecue grills and played guitars. It was a great relief from the weekdays and nights of intensive study.

The courses at the law school inspired me like nothing had before. I found that I loved reading, writing, and thinking. To the surprise of many, I turned out to be intellectually curious. I suppose that was the first time I felt sure my career would be in higher education. As a full-time student, I started to think like a lawyer. The law plays into everything we do, say, touch, hear, see, or smell. It often becomes relevant in things we don't do. For me, learning to think like a lawyer meant being sensitive to the potential legal implications of all our actions, as well as everything we encounter.

Margaret used those three years to work as an interior design assistant, take courses in art history, and nurture friendships. She was a superior homemaker and a gourmet cook. She knew about etiquette, crystal, china, linens, and silver. She introduced me to social skills I had never before had occasion to learn or use. At the time, I had no idea how useful that knowledge would someday be for me.

My last year in law school, I was privileged to serve as a member of the *Law Journal*. I graduated in 1966 and joined a law firm on the Mississippi Gulf Coast. But I soon discovered that my love of the law didn't translate into a love for the *practice* of law.

12

Our daughter, Margaret, arrived on March 19, 1967, and life was never the same. It was better. Her mother delivered the baby girl, nursed her, nurtured her, and taught her everything a child needs to learn. Margaret seemed to adapt to motherhood as easily as she had to becoming a spouse. Both of us gave our daughter all the love we could give, but Margaret prepared her for life beyond the nursery.

After three years away from Ole Miss, I received a call from Dean Bill Bunkley. He reached me in Pascagoula on a warm Monday morning in June.

"Bob," he said, "would you be interested in teaching at the law school?"

I didn't even have to think about it. I accepted on the spot. By August 1, the two Margarets and I had moved to Oxford, and I was preparing to teach my first class.

There is no practice teaching for a law professor; there is no orientation program, and nobody tells you how to approach the challenge. One friend who joined our faculty after I had taught for several years asked me what he would need to get started.

"A three-hole punch," I said, "to use as you build your class notebook."

"What else?" he asked.

"Courage."

I soon discovered I loved nothing more than teaching — particularly the law. In one of my torts classes in the late 1970s, I drafted a final exam that included four discussion questions. The issues raised required the students to analyze and identify the legal issues, discuss the scope of negligence, and examine the elements of duty, breach, and cause. One student in the class who was bright, hardworking, and generally prepared was puzzled by the last question. His answers on the first three discussion questions were clear and concise, lucid, and well-thought-out. He had a complete grasp of the material. However, he had absolutely no knowledge of the subject of the fourth question. Instead of leaving the question unanswered, he constructed a well-written, humorous, creative, and clever story. Although the answer had nothing to do with the subject or the law, I admired his tactic and, in fact, was a bit taken with the beauty of the piece.

After grading his exam, I wrote a note in red pencil on the cover of his blue book. "You missed all the legal issues, but you write great fiction."

The young man received a B+ on the exam. His name was John Grisham.

Our son, Robert, arrived in 1973 — a healthy, happy, bouncing baby boy. Robert's infancy and early childhood, just as Little Margaret's had, brought us great joy.

The first years of our marriage (with the exception of the time in Washington) were as typical as any young family in Oxford could expect. Our children were healthy, they attended Oxford public schools, and we were regulars at Sunday school and church.

Among the challenges we faced were the frequent, often serious, illnesses I suffered. Some required major surgery. Margaret didn't talk about it or complain, but she must have felt vulnerable. During my recovery, she was at home with small children, and we had virtually no reserve resources. At times, I'm sure it crossed her mind that she had married a man destined for an abbreviated life. But she stood strong and never hinted that she felt any insecurity.

When Parham Williams was appointed dean of the law school, I took on the role of associate dean. The position put me into even closer contact with faculty, students, and administration. During this time, I also continued to teach law school courses.

Both of my degrees, undergraduate and law, were from the University of Mississippi. In the constantly changing world of academia, that simply wasn't acceptable. Faculty typically opposed applicants with degrees from the same institution. They used the term *intellectual incest.*

I knew that my prospects of moving up in the world of higher education — whether in the law school or in the administration at Ole Miss — were limited.

Our family, 1978

13

Margaret and I agreed it was important that I strengthen my academic credentials. So, in 1979, I sent in an application to the graduate law program at Yale University.

At the time, I was forty-two. Yale's commitment to diversity proved to be an asset. A good ole boy from Mississippi — who actually *was* old — rang just the note Yale wanted to hear. My academic credentials were competitive, but demographics worked in my favor, too. Perhaps equally serendipitous was that the associate dean for graduate studies at Yale was my friend Jim Zirkle. Jim had taught at Ole Miss for a number of years before accepting the position at Yale. He was my advocate for admission. But, more importantly, he was my friend. He was helpful to me, Margaret, and our children as he guided us through life in New England.

Yale granted me a Sterling Fellowship, and Ole Miss gave me a one-year sabbatical at one-half pay. Between the two, I could enroll full time at Yale and we could afford to live in New England.

In the fall of 1980, we moved north. Our daughter, Margaret, was in eighth grade, and our son, Robert, was in second. We hoped this adventure would not only expand my professional options but also expand the horizons of our family.

We leased a saltbox, winterized home overlooking the Long Island Sound in the charming New England town of Madison, Connecticut.

During our first family trip to the grocery store, I suggested we buy a box of grits. I thought it might remind us of home while living 1,200 miles away.

"They don't have grits in New England," Margaret said.

I didn't believe her, so I went in search of the manager.

When I found him, I asked, "Where do you keep your grits?"

Without blinking, he said, "Try international foods."

I found the international aisle, and Martha White was waiting there, smiling at me from the shelf.

The public schools in Connecticut were exceptional, and Margaret and Robert both had remarkable experiences. As did I. My classes were rich and stimulating. We discussed ideas and perspectives and processes that I'd never before considered.

I drove from Madison to New Haven most days. On other occasions, I rode the train. While the children and I were at school, Margaret explored our town. She found it appealing and enjoyed the shops, library, and galleries, but she devoted most of her energy during the week to helping her three students.

During the weekends, we traveled throughout New England. We saw for the first time America's earliest settlements, the sturdy architecture of the buildings, beautiful maple trees, stone mountains and retaining walls, and traditional holiday parades and celebrations foreign to us. The first covered bridge we crossed left us all breathless.

We rode the train into New York and walked the streets of the world's busiest and most diverse city. We saw indescribable wealth and abject poverty. In the afternoons we'd watch a baseball game in Yankee Stadium, and in the evenings we would find a Broadway play. During the Christmas season, we went to Rockefeller Plaza. These images are permanently etched in our minds.

I earned a Master of Laws degree from Yale, and we returned to Oxford in 1981. I came back with an increased appreciation of the strengths of our state and the warmth of our citizens. But I also saw more clearly the challenges facing our people and our culture . . . particularly in education.

14

In early 1993, Dean David Shipley announced that he had accepted a position as dean of the law school at the University of Kentucky. Several friends and alumni encouraged me to apply for the open position.

I had no great desire to be dean of the law school. What I loved most was teaching, spending time in the classroom with students. But I told my colleagues and friends that I would consider it.

During my deliberations about whether to submit my name for the deanship, I received a call from my older sister, Edna. I was needed in Moss Point.

On July 2, 1993, my father died. He was eighty-two.

When I was a child, my father was the centerpiece of my life, as well as the lives of my sisters, my brother, and my mother. He was the vortex around which our family agenda was set. My mother was the stabilizing, substantive presence in our lives, but she took a backseat to the force and energy my father created. Life was relatively simple in our hometown of Moss Point. But our father's energy and activity created a fast-paced, emotionally charged environment at our house.

There was something frantic about the way he lived, as if each day would certainly be his last. It appeared that every second of every day had to be pushed to its limits. Most of my early memories of him are filled with rapid movement — rushing off to work, speeding back home for meals, running off to meetings or speeches, and dashing to bed as if he were compelled to get the cycle underway again by hurriedly sleeping.

He loved his family, but he loved his work — promoting Mississippi and Jackson County — almost as much. And he was consumed by it.

As family and friends gathered for the funeral se[r]
bered one of the rare moments when my father was[...]
meeting. When I was ten years old, he showed me ho[w ...]
ball.

In our side yard, my father pressed two nails into the ground. He bent over and balanced the football against the nails. It stood upright — a perfect substitute for a real kicking tee or the holder for a field goal.

He told me to face the goalpost with my shoulders squared. We didn't have a real goalpost, so I squared my shoulders to the shrubbery at the back of the yard. Then he told me to focus on the ground where the ball would be placed. *Don't look up*, he said. *Stay focused.* Then he told me, *Keep your eye on the ball.* He added, *Kick straight through the ball and follow through high.* He finished the lesson with one final piece of advice. *Practice, Practice, Practice.*

And I did. For hours. Every day.

his father was kicked out of office for fraud

The funeral service was overflowing with friends and family and supporters. My father lived a life dedicated to service and kindness. He had helped literally thousands of residents in Jackson County. But the last years of his life ended in a manner none of us could have imagined.

his dad is his hero

Our father, the man who spent his every waking hour promoting our state and our county, had been indicted and convicted in the 1980s in an investigation known as Operation Pretense. Along with dozens of other supervisors, he was evicted from office by a young, newly elected generation of law enforcement officers in Mississippi.

My father was convicted for doing the very things that won him election after election for thirty-seven years.

Edward A. Khayat, the man around whom our lives had revolved, the gentle man who taught us about respect and responsibility and kindness, the father who taught me how to kick a football, spent the last few years of his life quietly going through the motions of living — continuing to assist and support anyone who asked for or needed

p. But my father had lost his enthusiasm. The spark and energy that had driven him were gone.

With his public life finally behind him, his focus was on his family. He and my mother spent many hours together each day.

She once said, "He *finally* needs me."

I stood next to my mother, my two sisters, and my brother, Eddie, as our father was lowered into the ground at Griffin Cemetery in Moss Point.

Explains why he loved the
state of Mississippi and
UM.

15

I acquired one significant trait from my father: a deep, unwavering affection for the state of Mississippi.

As a product of the public education system of Mississippi, I long believed we had not been good stewards of our public resources. We were poor, granted, but the potential to build a stronger state could be found in the extraordinary talents and gifts of native Mississippians.

For decades, Mississippi had produced and exported national leaders in business, science, education, music, art, entertainment, literature, and athletics.

If we could export leaders throughout the world, I regularly asked myself, *why couldn't we capitalize on those strengths within the state?*

And, since my days as a freshman at Ole Miss, I understood that the University of Mississippi was the state institution to provide that leadership. Throughout its history, Ole Miss had attracted strong faculty and gifted students. As a public university, we provided opportunities for students across the spectrum — bright, average, and struggling.

But recent financial inadequacies made faculty recruitment difficult. We often lost our best professors to more financially sound schools. Despite our financial weakness, a strong nucleus was always in place, and by any objective measure we were nationally competitive in several arenas.

The elephant in the room, of course, was Mississippi's tragic race relations history. The challenge was to move from segregation, separation, and discrimination to an open society and culture with full access for all. The old school Mississippi culture was deeply rooted. Any transition to an open society would be painful. To a great extent, that cultural battle had been fought on and around the campus of the University of Mississippi. The apex of the struggle was staged on the Ole Miss campus in September 1962.

I was also acutely aware that for too long Ole Miss had suffered from an institutional inferiority complex. Too many years of struggling with inadequate funding, the burden of our racial history, faculty and staff morale, and public perception had created a culture that, too often, accepted mediocrity.

Perception was a critical component of any forward movement for the university. And that perception included not only how we were perceived by others, but also how we perceived ourselves.

I am painfully aware of my own weaknesses and character defects, but I also know my strengths. One of them is helping others believe in themselves. Though I often doubt myself, I have never doubted the talents of the people from this state.

Given the chance, and with a great team, I believed we could change this culture. I could identify our institutional strengths and weaknesses, develop a realistic view of the political landscape, determine the extent of our financial challenges, and assemble a management team whose members would fully commit to overcoming the obstacles we faced. Together, I was certain, we could become a great university again.

It was at these moments that I believed I might be the right person for the chancellorship.

16

Back in Oxford, still overwhelmed by the loss of my father and suffering through another bout of pancreatitis, I had to decide whether to submit my name for dean of the Ole Miss law school.

"Robert," my dear friend Bob Weems said, "the law school needs you."

If I were appointed dean, Bob said, my leadership, energy, and outreach abilities would benefit lawyers, law students, and faculty for decades to come.

Guff Abbott, Bill Champion, Carolyn Ellis Staton, Tom Mason, and others on the law faculty encouraged me. Lawyers from the bar association, including my friend Jack Dunbar, called to tell me they not only *wanted* me to be the next dean, they *expected* it. I even heard from Chancellor Turner. He encouraged me to submit my name for the deanship.

Chancellor Turner would ultimately appoint the new dean, but first he instructed the law school faculty to submit a list of candidates they deemed acceptable for the position.

I weighed the pros and cons, talked to members of the faculty, discussed the prospects with Margaret and our children, and, ultimately, decided to submit my name. I knew I might not be selected if a better qualified candidate applied for the position. But surely, I thought, the faculty would find me an acceptable candidate and send my name along to the chancellor.

I interviewed with the faculty and talked to them about my vision for the law school.

Then, in October 1993, the faculty met to determine which candidates to pass along to Chancellor Turner. That same afternoon, as I sat in my living room reading, I saw Bob Weems pull into my driveway.

As he walked to my front door, I noticed an expression on his face I'd not often seen. He was frowning. He looked as if he were in pain.

I opened the door.

"Bob," I said, "are you all right?"

He stepped into the house.

"No," he said. "This is one of the most difficult things I've ever had to say."

"What is it?"

Bob pressed his lips together. "The faculty," he said, "voted you not acceptable."

17

My friends tried to make me feel better about the faculty vote, but I was hurt. In all the losses I'd endured before, my teammates and colleagues had been there, behind me, loyal.

This time was different.

I would have been fine with a better qualified candidate getting the position, but the faculty vote was 7-14. Two-thirds of my colleagues had voted me not acceptable. It was hard to stomach.

The faculty submitted *one* name to Chancellor Turner for consideration. It was a minority candidate. Those who voted against me, I was told, wanted an African-American dean. My friends on the faculty told me that the general consensus among the fourteen individuals who voted against me was that Chancellor Turner would have selected me over the minority candidate. They didn't want to give him that opportunity.

Despite the rationale, I promised I would never again subject myself, or my family, to this kind of public rejection. My years at Ole Miss and the law school had been rich and fulfilling, but it was time to move on.

Sometimes fate intervenes at just the right moment. I received a telephone call from my friend Roy Williams, a lawyer in Pascagoula. Roy represented one of the largest hospital systems on the Mississippi Coast. He told me the Singing River Hospital Foundation was looking for a new director.

"This job may be perfect for you, Robert," he said.

I thanked him, placed the phone in its cradle, and walked into the kitchen where my wife was preparing dinner.

"Margaret," I said, "how would you like to look at new houses on the Coast?"

During 1993 and 1994, Margaret and I made a couple of trips to

Jackson County to look at homes, and I began researching the position at the Singing River Foundation.

In the meantime, I'd accepted a temporary position to plan and organize a yearlong celebration for the 150th anniversary of the founding of the University of Mississippi — the sesquicentennial. I enjoyed the position, especially mining the rich history of Ole Miss, but I was still intrigued by the notion of moving back to the Coast.

The opportunity with Singing River was serendipitous for two reasons. First, I was ready to move on from the law school. Second, my father wasn't a presence in Jackson County anymore. I once tried living and working there when he was alive, but it became apparent rather quickly that his shadow was too large for me to establish any sense, or appearance, of independence.

Margaret and I deliberated whether to make the move, whether to put our house up for sale, and if we were really ready to start a new life in a new place.

Then, in the fall of 1994, we discovered that Chancellor Gerald Turner was interviewing for presidencies at other schools. Shortly thereafter, Southern Methodist University announced that Gerald Turner had been selected as its next president.

That's when my phone started to ring.

18

As soon as it was announced that Gerald Turner was leaving, not a day passed when I didn't receive a phone call or a personal visit or a note from an Ole Miss alum encouraging me to put my name in the search pool for chancellor.

In spite of their kind words and encouragement, I was reluctant to put myself in a vulnerable position again. I told everyone "thanks" and added that I was going to pass on the opportunity.

Frank Crosthwait, a member of the IHL board, called me in the spring of 1995.

"Robert, I hope you're planning to apply for the position."

"No," I said, "I'm not. If you want me to be chancellor, just appoint me."

"Look," Frank said, "it doesn't work that way. There's a formal process." He told me that I needed to complete an application, attach supporting materials, and submit everything to the IHL board before April 1.

The last thing I wanted to do was put myself out there to be rejected again. I thanked Frank and told him I would consider it.

The calls didn't stop. In fact, their frequency, and the urgency in the voices of my friends, increased. They came from former law students, members of the bar, old teammates, colleagues, former bosses, and even former clients.

On a Saturday, one week before the deadline for nominations for the chancellor's position, I called my old friend Jack Dunbar. Jack had been a mentor to me, and we briefly practiced law together in Oxford.

Jack lived in a house originally built by Coach Wobble Davidson and his wife, Sara. The house was spectacular. Situated just west of Coliseum Drive, the entrance to the home was a single-lane drive that meandered through the trees.

Jack invited me into his home and showed me to a chair next to the fireplace.

"Robert," he said, before I could say anything, "You are the right man at the right time for this job."

I didn't say anything, but I thought, *fool me once . . .*

Jack sensed, I think, that I didn't plan to budge from my position. "You really don't have a choice in the matter," he said.

I still didn't say anything, but I thought, *the hell I don't.*

"Look, Robert," he said, leaning forward in his chair, "you are going to regret this decision for the rest of your life." Jack paused for a moment and leaned back in his chair. Then he continued, "Many people will be disappointed if you don't do this."

I was beginning to have déjà vu. Didn't I recently have this conversation with Bob Weems about the law deanship?

"Jack," I said, "I just don't think I can."

"I won't be proud of you if you pass up this chance," he said. Then he paused and added, "And your Daddy would not be proud of you either."

I left Jack's and drove toward my house. I thought of my brother, Eddie, and my sisters, Edna and Kathy.

Eddie had a long football career — ten years as an NFL player and twenty-five as a coach, including two years as the head coach of the Philadelphia Eagles.

But Eddie's playing days weren't easy. He had inherited the Khayat slow gene. Eddie was a Redskin his rookie year, but he was cut from the team after one season. Then he moved to the Eagles for four seasons, including the 1960 championship team. The Eagles traded him back to Washington in 1962. He played on my Redskins squad in 1962 and 1963. Then it was back to the Eagles in 1964 and 1965. Eddie played a final year in 1966 with the Boston Patriots.

Eddie and I played together for the first time on the 1962 Redskins team. At the time, I was the placekicker for Washington. I think my teammates thought of me as nonconfrontational. On the first play from scrimmage at Eddie's first practice, he hit our star guard, Vince Promuto, on the helmet and *rattled his brain*. Vince was as tough as Eddie. As soon as his head cleared, he went after Eddie, and a brutal fight ensued. While the fight was underway, the rest of us watched, being sure to stay out of the fray.

Riley Matson, a six feet seven inch, 270-pound tackle whispered in my ear, "Bobby, is that your brother?" He had difficulty believing Eddie and I were related.

Later, I asked Eddie why he started a fight on his first day.

"I wanted the sons-of-bitches to know I was here," Eddie said.

During his football career, Eddie had to fight for a chance to play college football. He was rejected by both Ole Miss and Mississippi State before signing with Tulane. He was cut by the Redskins once and the Eagles once, but Eddie never gave up. He was focused, driven, and relentless. He simply would not quit.

My sister Edna spent much of her adult life in the nation's capital and in developing countries, primarily in South America. Formerly a teacher in Jackson, she and her husband, Tom, gave up the comforts of the United States to address international poverty through the Lay Overseas Services.

But it was my younger sister, Kathy, who endured the most. Her first husband, almost without warning, required emergency heart surgery. He did not survive.

A thirty-three-year-old widow with two adopted children, burdened with significant debt and virtually no financial resources, deeply saddened by the loss of the man she loved, Kathy moved back to Moss Point where, with support and assistance from our mother and father, she put her life back together.

Four years later, Kathy met a handsome, smart single man and they were married. Within two years of the marriage, she gave birth to a healthy, beautiful son — "a gift from God" to a forty-year-old woman.

They bought a beautiful home on Beardslee Lake and had several happy years together. Then, disaster struck again. Her adopted son was found dead in a rural house, shot between the eyes and lying near a young woman, also shot to death. Lost in unspeakable grief, my sister mourned the loss of her twenty-four-year-old son.

But Kathy's suffering was not over. Her husband, the father of her biological son, was diagnosed with cancer. He was gone within two years.

Never once did I hear her say, "Why me, Lord?"

She cried, she mourned her losses, and then moved forward. Kathy had an innate understanding that we are measured not by our victories and losses but how we react to both. She never doubted God's love for her and her family. Though she had been the victim of life's greatest challenges, she emerged with a smile on her face and joy in her heart.

As I arrived at my house on Gleneagles Road, I knew what I needed to do. I had spent enough time being hurt. I'd wasted too much energy thinking about moving away from a place I called home. And I'd let the votes of a small group of faculty members derail my confidence. It was time to be more like my brother and my sisters.

I walked inside to find Margaret. I had something to tell her.

June 20, 1995

19

On a Tuesday in June, the Board of Trustees met at Ole Miss. They were on campus for their regular monthly board meeting, but they were also in Oxford to further evaluate me.

My day started at 7:00 a.m. with a breakfast in the chancellor's dining room where I met with the university's vice chancellors and deans. At 8:00 a.m., I reported to the lecture room at Barnard Hall. My first meeting was with the Faculty Senate. They asked pointed questions about my qualifications, my thoughts on raising funds earmarked for faculty salaries, my vision for academic excellence, and my plans to restructure the organization of the university. I answered each question as honestly and completely as possible. The meeting ended, and the senate members left the room. They would gather elsewhere to discuss whether they would recommend me to the IHL board. They would then immediately report to board president Nan Baker.

As soon as the senate had vacated Barnard, the seats filled with members of the Black Faculty and Staff Organization and the Commission on the Status of Women. Again a lively question-and-answer period ensued. They, too, were to report to the IHL on my acceptability.

As the morning and early afternoon progressed, I met with the Staff Council and alumni leadership and the foundation directors. Each group would send an evaluation to the board members who were meeting at the alumni office boardroom.

It was a grueling day.

At 3:30 in the afternoon, I addressed the Board of Trustees. Though I was exhausted, I thanked them for the opportunity and privilege of participating in the process. I acknowledged that there had been an unusual amount of interest in the selection of the new chancellor.

"It indicates a level of concern about Ole Miss," I said. "I believe it comes from people who care about this university and who see an urgent need for healing, for unity, for commitment."

I told them I didn't have all the answers to Ole Miss' problems, but that I possessed an abiding affection for the school, the state, and our people.

"My entire life seems to have prepared me for this job, at this time, in this place."

After listing the positions I'd held at Ole Miss — student, athlete, professor, registrar, vice chancellor and interim athletics director — I assured them I had the highest respect for the office of chancellor.

"I would not offer my services if I did not believe I could do the job."

I outlined the greatest challenges I thought we faced and the goals I hoped to meet in tackling those issues. Then I ended the presentation with a final thought.

"The people of this state have invested in the University of Mississippi for 150 years." I paused and made eye contact with the board members. "We must place the interests of the university above our personal interests. When our work is done, we want to deliver the keys to a better university for future generations."

I thanked them again, took my notes, and left the building. Then I went home to wait, just as I had done two years earlier when the law school faculty voted on my acceptability.

20

In a closed meeting, the IHL board reviewed the evaluations of the Faculty Senate, alumni groups, and department heads, as well as the students' comments.

Around the heavy table sat board members Nan McGahey Baker, Frank Crosthwait, Ricki Garrett, Will Hickman, J. Marlin Ivey, James Luvene, Diane Martin Miller, J.P. "Jake" Mills, Sidney Rushing, William Sterling Crawford, and Carl Nicholson Jr.

Frank Crosthwait presented a motion. "RESOLVED, That the Board hereby appoints Dr. Robert Khayat as Chancellor of the University of Mississippi, beginning July 1, 1995, to a four-year contract."

Will Hickman seconded the motion.

Then, President Nan Baker called for a vote.

Each of the eleven members of the IHL board in attendance cast a vote in favor of the motion.

President Baker announced, "Let the minutes reflect that Dr. Robert Khayat has been unanimously selected as the fifteenth chancellor of the University of Mississippi."

The official chancellor's portrait

Getting Started

The Lyceum

talks about being chancellor; had large goals for the school not just one goal

21

Saturday, July 1, 1995, was my first official day as chancellor. I couldn't wait to get started, so I arrived at the Lyceum at 6:30 a.m. Two custodians were the only other people in the building.

I placed a few photographs on a credenza. Then I turned my chair around and looked at the top of my desk. There was nothing on it.

John F. Kennedy recounted his first day in the Oval Office. After fighting so hard to win the election, he arrived in the late afternoon after his inauguration and parade, sat down at the president's desk, rang his secretary, and asked, "So what do I do now?"

I felt the same way, but there was no one to call.

On the first page of a brand new legal pad, I wrote a list of the major issues facing our university.

1. *Enrollment*
2. *Increased Private Support*
3. *Efficient Management*   *many goals*
4. *Morale*

The *issues* list continued with accessibility, accountability, cost containment, diversity, healthcare reform and systems, balancing teaching with research, public perception, economic development, distance learning, preparing leaders for the twenty-first century, and service to the State of Mississippi.

When I was co-chair of the Sesquicentennial Committee in 1993, I asked the chair of the Faculty Senate, Tom Horton, to organize an effort to provide ideas to improve the future of the university. Tom asked Brian Reithel to organize the planning effort.

When the complete list was presented, it contained more than 4,000 ideas. Eventually, the group whittled that list down to 967. Then I distilled those into eleven major goals.

I flipped the page, and at the top I wrote *Goals*. The list read:

- *Unite our faculty, staff, students, and alumni. Work toward common goals.*
- *Increase enrollment on Oxford campus to 12,000 by the year 2000.*
- *Continue development of the Medical Center and the expansion of healthcare services in the state.*
- *Increase our endowment to $100 million by the year 2000.*
- *Become one of the top 100 Research Universities in America.*
- *Increase the number of Ph.D.s awarded annually to 100+.*
- *Increase library holdings to 1,000,000+ volumes by the year 2000.*
- *Increase faculty and staff salaries to regional averages.*
- *Establish a leadership position for our technology initiative.*
- *Develop a teacher evaluation plan for the IHL system.*
- *Collaborate with other public educational institutions.*

I looked over the list and knew that it was a tall order. It would take focus and attention and luck. It would require an extraordinary effort on behalf of the administration, faculty, staff, students, and alumni. It would depend on a shift in the culture of the university from a bureaucratic, state-run institution to a model based on business in which everyone is accountable for his or her performance.

It would also require faith, hope, and money. But most of all, we had to have a great team.

22

My criteria for selecting the team members to lead the university were simple. I wanted men and women who would be better, more talented, and more capable in their areas of responsibility than I would be. I wanted individuals who would inspire and challenge me and each other.

My highest priority was our academic mission — faculty-student ratios, faculty and staff salaries, buildings and equipment, the library, and making the transition to an electronic information technology system.

In 1986, when I was vice chancellor, we had submitted an application to Phi Beta Kappa, but we were told we were lacking.

One of their concerns was library collections. We needed one million volumes to compare to other top schools. Our collection stood at 800,000. The library also needed to implement new, state-of-the-art technology.

The average Ole Miss freshman ACT scores were below standard. But I knew that some of Mississippi's brightest students might choose Ole Miss if we could offer competitive scholarships and nationally competitive academic programs.

We also needed faculty salary enhancements, including endowed chairs, professorships, and lectureships, as well as technology enrichment grants to give our teachers the best tools. To accomplish this, we would have to be focused and disciplined. And I would need an exceptional leader in the academic field. My first call went to Gerald Walton.

Gentle, wise, and dedicated, Gerald Walton had already left a remarkable legacy at Ole Miss. He came to the university in 1959 as a graduate student and teaching assistant in the English department. Gerald courageously stood up in support of opening the doors of our university to all, when the 1962 integration crisis nearly destroyed our school. He went on to earn his master's and doctoral degrees while teaching and serving in a number of administrative positions. Gerald directed the university writing program, and served as dean of the College of Liberal Arts and associate vice chancellor of academic affairs. He led efforts to strengthen programs such as Southern Studies, as well as our museum, and his students loved him (one of those admiring former students was my wife, Margaret).

"Gerald," I said, "I'm asking you to stay three more years. We need you."

Gerald looked a bit surprised and said, "I was planning to spend a bit more time with my family."

I knew Gerald was ready to rid himself of the burdens of administration and pursue other interests. I also understood that I was asking him to place the interests of the university ahead of his personal interests.

"Stability in a time of change is critical," I said, "and almost impossible to attain. But you could provide that for us. And nothing is more important to this university than this position."

Gerald was one of a small number of incumbents who could soften the impact of a new chancellor's presence. We both knew it. And we both knew that he would be the best person to lead us to new heights in academic quality.

Before I left his office, and perhaps against his better judgment, Gerald agreed to place his experienced, well-respected hand on my shoulder and guide me through the early years of my chancellorship.

He had only one caveat — he would stay no longer than three years.

23

As I sat behind the chancellor's desk on my first day in the Lyceum, I wished my father could have seen me. When I was young, he would say, "Robert, you're going to be a senator some day." At other times, he'd tell me that I'd make a great governor. And when I joined the faculty, he set his sights on the chancellorship. He set the bar high for all of his children. Despite the pressure we felt to perform well, his drive helped us all succeed.

However, on this day, my thoughts went mainly to my mother. She made tremendous personal sacrifices for our family. She had always been a homemaker with the exception of several years as a licensed practical nurse. Watching her manage a complicated family with limited financial resources and a busy husband was equivalent to witnessing a perfect ballet. She elevated the mundane of simple home life to a work of art, and she gave dignity to otherwise simple, basic tasks.

She was anything but a socialite. She didn't belong to a bridge club. She was not a leader in the PTA, and she was not a member of the garden club. Her home was her base, and we knew she would be there when we needed her. My mother insisted on maintaining a spotless house. Clothes were washed every day, and it seemed there was a constant rotation of sheets, shirts, and towels blowing in the breeze on the clothesline. Every item was starched and ironed. I can still remember the fragrance of freshly washed and ironed cotton clothing. Standing over her ironing board in a hot house with no air conditioning, she whistled and sang as she ironed.

As I relived those days, I saw that she was grooming her four children to learn to take care of themselves, to accentuate the positive, to value cleanliness, and to embrace respect. For my mother, respect was all inclusive — it meant respect for others, for yourself, for prop-

My mother, Eva Pates Khayat

erty, for God.

Retrieving a letter she had written to me in 1973, upon the arrival of our son, Robert, I read —

The days are so golden and beautiful lately. I'm always happy when morning comes (7 a.m.) because there are so many things to do. Seemingly trivial things that one doesn't notice unless they are not done. Like cleaning house, hanging clothes out and watching the wind blow them on the line and knowing how fresh they are going to smell when you press them...cooking a pot of stew...working in the yard...and thanking God every minute for all of this energy and good health.

The real reward comes late in the evening when I sit on the patio and watch the moon flowers open before my eyes as they unfold their petals and this heavenly fragrance fills all of the air around...and then the Hummingbirds come from nowhere and feast on the nectar of the blossoms. Oh, I'm a simple, simple fool but these are the things that make me happy.

I folded the letter and placed it in the top drawer of my desk. I would keep it close by for the duration of my tenure.

My mother rarely preached to us, and she was never heavy-handed in delivering a lesson. But her stewardship of, and respect for, God's gifts were passed along to all four of her children.

For me, these lessons resulted in a love of yard work. I loved nothing more than spending the early morning hours on Saturdays mowing and raking and trimming our yard. It gave me a great sense of spiritual peace.

My neighbors and friends thought my meticulous maintenance was borderline obsessive, but I saw it as an act of respect, an appreciation for the things we were blessed to own.

At 11:30 a.m., Margaret met me at the Lyceum. We were joined by the talented, young photographer Robert Jordan, who spent an hour with us taking photographs at the chancellor's home, the Lyceum, Ventress Hall, and the library. Afterward, Margaret returned home, and I decided to take a walk through campus. Stepping outside the large double doors of the Lyceum, I stopped to survey the Circle.

Those who selected the land to be developed for this university in the early 1840s followed the time-tested rule that buildings should be placed on sites so that it appears the buildings have grown from seeds planted in the soil. The compatibility of nature and our facilities created a stunning landscape.

For the most part, the red brick, Georgian-style buildings complemented each other. The architecture suggested that the university placed a high value on beauty and function. And, thankfully, those responsible for the campus for the past 150 years had consistently protected the green spaces and trees.

I walked the same sidewalks I'd navigated nearly forty years earlier as a freshman.

My heart sank. Despite the natural beauty of Ole Miss, the campus looked tired. Roofing had been allowed to darken with mold, stonework on the buildings had not been cleaned in years, lawns were neglected, and virtually no flower beds were being maintained.

Trees were not trimmed. Fertilizer was sparsely utilized. Sprinkler systems were practically nonexistent.

As I walked, I noticed that litter was everywhere. I gathered a few cans and shreds of paper and looked for a trash receptacle. I couldn't find one.

Across campus there were huge patches of red clay with little or no grass. Landscape maintenance was nearly nonexistent. It had not been a priority. Joe Symons, who was director of grounds for many years, did the best he could with limited resources. Joe had a very small staff, obsolete equipment, and a miniscule budget. I often thought of how frustrated he must have been.

Of course, crews from the physical plant did mow patches of grass, pick up fallen limbs, and remove trees that died, but that was the extent of it. No one, apparently, had given much thought to shrubbery, flower beds, outdoor art, sidewalks, outdoor seating, inviting green spaces, and lakes.

That was going to change.

24

At 6:30 p.m. on Sunday, July 2, the community gathered for a worship service at Oxford-University United Methodist Church. The sanctuary was packed with friends and well-wishers. We prayed and sang together, and the minister asked God to bless this transition.

At the end of the day, in our new home — the chancellor's home — Margaret and I sat at the dining room table. I told her about my first day in the office. I recounted who had called and left cards. I rattled off my top priorities, and challenges, for the coming years. Then I told her about my disappointing walk across our neglected university grounds.

"Robert," she said, "this is a big campus." Then she paused and gently added, "Try to remember you can't maintain it like you did our front yard. It's too big."

Margaret's advice was reasonable, so I nodded, pretending that her cautionary words resonated with me.

But secretly, her comment struck a nerve. First, I wanted the word "can't" removed from the vocabulary at Ole Miss. And, second, treating the campus like my front yard was exactly what I planned to do.

talks about goals, his wife tells him it might not be possible. it puts him down.

↓

he continues to do it anyways.

25

On Monday morning at 8:30 a.m., I met with Andy Mullins. Andy was most widely known as one of Governor William Winter's "Boys of Spring" (a group of young men who served as assistants to the governor), but Andy had accomplished much more than that. He was involved in every aspect of the Education Reform Act of 1982 — a legislative act that changed the face of public education in Mississippi, including the implementation of public kindergartens. He later served as a special assistant to the state superintendent of education. In 1989, Andy, along with Amy Gutman, created the Mississippi Teacher Corps — an innovative program that brought top, recent college graduates from all over the country to Mississippi to teach in critical-needs schools in an attempt to end educational inequity in the state.

Andy was young, talented, and energetic, and he knew just about everyone in the education field in Mississippi. But his greatest strength may have been his relationships in our state government and an insider's understanding of how it operated.

In our first meeting, Andy came ready to work. Bright-eyed and smiling, he reviewed the agenda for the week. We discussed the goals for a transition team; set an aggressive schedule of speeches, development, and recruiting trips around the state; and developed a plan to visit each major department at the university.

As we would do almost every morning during my tenure, we talked about what was the most urgent issue facing the university. On our first Monday together, our highest priority — our most pressing issue — was obvious to both of us.

I said, "I guess we need to start with . . ." Andy joined in to finish my sentence.

In unison, we said — "Enrollment."

I had so many dreams for Ole Miss, but before I could pursue most of them, I needed to listen.

My first week in office, I worked with Donna Patton and Gloria Kellum to set appointments for weekly visits with each of the major departments of the university. In honor of my summer with Cyanide Jones, I started with the Department of Chemistry. Then I visited the School of Pharmacy and the departments of English, History, Social Work, and Modern Languages. At each meeting, I made a brief introduction, told the faculty and staff a bit about my hopes for the university, and then I asked for their thoughts, grievances, opinions, and ideas.

Our institutional self-perception was terrible. Within each department, individuals were aware of their own strengths and advancements, but their perception of other departments was dismal. We weren't doing a good job telling our own story.

After a visit with the Ole Miss mathematics department, I walked back toward the Lyceum and thought about my eighth grade math teacher, Mr. Mallette.

One of Mr. Mallette's math assignments focused on angles. To illustrate the practical application of somewhat abstract material, he required each of us to build a birdhouse. He gave us six weeks to complete the project.

Many of my classmates had fathers who were accomplished carpenters or, at the very least, owned saws, hammers, planes, and paint. In our home, we didn't own any tools. None of us would have known how to use them anyway. Adhesive tape was all we needed at the Khayat home. It worked to repair a broken lamp, chair, or bone.

I worked hard to construct the birdhouse. Using thin veneer from vegetable crates, I taped and glued together the roof, floor, and four sides of the small box. With a kitchen knife, I cut a jagged hole into one of the panels. Then, I glued a popsicle stick just below the hole as a perch.

We didn't own any paint, so I used food coloring. It turned the raw, thin wood a sickly blue tint.

I hid the birdhouse under my bed so no one else would see it. When the day arrived to turn in the project, I wrapped it in a towel to prevent anyone from seeing it on my way to school.

I watched as the other boys stepped off the bus. They proudly displayed their Hyde Park-quality birdhouses under their arms. Some had small shingle roofing with painted brick siding; others were neatly painted and included window boxes complete with small flowers; one was a multilevel, three-story affair with interior and exterior stairways extending from the floor to the roof.

My heart sank.

In the classroom, we were required to stand, hold our creation up for the world to see, and affirm that we had built the houses by ourselves, without assistance from adults.

When my turn came to stand, I removed the towel and held up my birdhouse. Laughter erupted. Compared to the artistic creations of the others, my pitiful box stood out. For all the wrong reasons. Even Mr. Mallette laughed. He couldn't help himself.

When the hooting finally subsided and Mr. Mallette had regained his composure, he said, "Robert will receive an A on this project."

My classmates were shocked.

"His box," Mallette added, "is the only one I'm certain was built with no help from others."

After class, I threw my box on the roof of one of the school porches. By the following Monday, two small birds had taken residence in the ugliest of blue birdhouses.

When I arrived back at my office, T.J. Ray was waiting for me. T.J. was an outstanding professor in the English department with an impressive record of public service on campus and off. He was also president of the Faculty Senate.

I understood the importance of building trust with this group. The relationship between the Faculty Senate and former chancellors had been less than ideal. I didn't want that to be a part of my chancellorship.

T.J. and I discussed a number of issues and opportunities. We agreed to meet monthly, at the very least. I also committed to speak to the Faculty Senate at least once each semester . . . and more often if necessary. I asked T.J. to spread the word among faculty members that my door would always be open. Then, I told him about my plan to elevate the position of vice chancellor of academic affairs to provost.

I understood that the majority of the faculty at Ole Miss viewed me as a non-scholar. I also sensed concern among the group about my ability to evaluate teaching, research, and scholarship.

In addition, as chancellor, my duties would frequently take me off campus. And in my absence, someone had to be in charge. That position, I told T.J., would be the provost. The provost would be the chief operating officer at the university, handling the day-to-day responsibilities for the university and communicating with faculty; elevating the position would send a clear message to the faculty — and the Faculty Senate — that a scholar was in the front-line leadership position.

T.J. listened and rubbed his thick salt-and-pepper beard. Then he stood to leave and said, "You probably ought to read this letter."

I took the letter, scanned the page for a signature, and asked, "Who wrote this?"

"Oh," he replied, "it's anonymous."

With my thumb and forefinger pressed against the top corner of the paper, I held the letter at arm's length, away from me as if the letter might have been a snake.

"T.J.," I said, "please watch this and spread the word."

I walked over to the corner of the room and dropped the letter in my trash can.

"I am wide open to meetings, telephone calls, and communication with all faculty members," I said. "But I will never read an anonymous letter."

T.J. looked a bit shocked.

"I can't respond to an unknown writer," I said. "I want open lines of communication." Then I added, "If you have the opportunity to let others know, please do."

T.J. smiled and nodded. We shook hands, and he left my office. As I sat down behind my desk, I knew I had an honest critic in T.J. Ray.

I also had a feeling we were going to be friends.

26

As the weeks of summer passed and Mississippi schools opened, Andy Mullins and I spent a great deal of time visiting towns in and around Mississippi, including Senatobia, McComb, Meridian, Jackson, Hattiesburg, Tupelo, Pascagoula, and Iuka.

We treated these trips much like a political campaign. After morning meetings at school, I would spend the lunch hour speaking to civic groups such as Rotary, Lions, or Kiwanis clubs to tell about our exciting plans and programs at Ole Miss. After lunch, I would meet with the editor, or editorial board, of the local newspaper. Whenever possible, I scheduled meetings with alumni and/or potential donors.

I had many years' experience in seeking financial gifts. I had asked for gifts for Ole Miss, the United Way, my church, and other worthy organizations since I was in my mid-twenties. Though I enjoyed meeting like-minded people — those who loved Ole Miss and wanted to give back — I understood that it was never easy to get a financial commitment.

As vice chancellor, I had visited personally with hundreds of prospective donors. Many asked what contribution would make the greatest difference for the university. Most seemed truly interested in our work, as well as our needs. Some had great affection for a specific aspect of university life. Others cared about the school because of friends or family. But with few exceptions, when I met with an individual about giving, Ole Miss held a special place in his or her heart.

A June 12, 1985, visit was one of those exceptions. My appointment was scheduled for 2:00 p.m. As I drove through Jackson's exclusive Eastover neighborhood, I passed enormous houses with beautifully landscaped grounds. I had admired the homes on previous trips, often to visit friends who lived in Eastover. But on this day, I was headed to the home of a woman who had no connection to Ole

Miss: Gertrude Castellow Ford.

The meeting had been arranged through Charles Ray Davis, Mrs. Ford's attorney and a law school colleague of mine. I knew little about Mrs. Ford except that she was from a well-to-do family in Georgia. Her father, a Georgia congressman, had introduced his daughter to Aaron Lane Ford, a four-term congressman from Mississippi. The two married but had no children. Mr. Ford had passed away in 1983.

I parked my car in front of Mrs. Ford's one-story home. The buff brick, ranch-style house had been built on a lot some twelve feet below street level. As I walked down her sidewalk, I noticed, in the carport, the largest Cadillac I'd ever seen. Attached to the corner of the garage was a fenced dog run. It extended the entire length of the west wall of the house. Inside the fence, close to a dozen white Chihuahuas were yelping and yapping.

The temperature was bumping up against 100 degrees and the humidity was working hard to match it. I wore a blue suit, white shirt, and red tie. And I was starting to sweat.

I tapped on the door and waited.

The door opened. A woman, about five feet three inches tall, stood in the entrance. She could not have weighed more than ninety pounds. In one hand, she held a highball; in the other, a cigarette. She was dressed in a sleeveless, sheer nightgown, turned inside out. She looked over the reading glasses perched on the end of her nose and said in a heavy smoker's voice, "You must be Mr. Canoe."

I wasn't sure how to respond, but Mrs. Ford followed with "Your damn name is so hard to pronounce, I'm going to call you *Canoe*."

"That's great," I said.

I stood outside her door perspiring; the dogs yapped incessantly. I wondered if I would be invited in.

"I wouldn't let the little SOB from that other school inside," she said, looking me over as if she still was not sure what to do with me. "But," she said, "Mr. Davis said you were OK." She took a deep pull on her cigarette, coughed out a bit of smoke, and took a sip from her drink. "Come on in, Canoe. I have some things to teach you."

We walked down the hallway through her house. There were

eleven bedrooms — one for her and ten others for her beloved Chihuahuas. She had built a four-bedroom apartment onto the back of her house for her husband and his attendant. The house had a safe room for her jewelry. In the kitchen, a stove had been removed. A small organ occupied the space.

We ended up in a sunroom with lots of windows . . . and no air conditioning. Mrs. Ford sat in a recliner and told me to have a seat on the ottoman.

"You probably didn't know that Shakespeare is a complete fraud," she said. "Didn't write a word attributed to him."

I thought it best to simply listen.

Mrs. Ford explained that the seventeenth Earl of Oxford had written all of the works claimed by Shakespeare.

"The little SOB plagiarized. Stole all the work of the earl, and I can prove it."

As Mrs. Ford explained her theories and documentation, she quoted from the sonnets and plays. She used no notes or books. This was clearly a brilliant woman but an angry one, too. Not just at the Bard but at those "damn faculty who perpetuate the lie."

Mrs. Ford would occasionally stop to smoke her cigarette and sip from her drink.

I did learn a great deal that day. In addition to the lessons on the Earl of Oxford, I learned that Mrs. Ford's safe room was full of diamonds and rubies and emeralds. Next to her dogs, jewelry was her delight.

I also discovered that Mrs. Ford didn't like being asked for money. Especially from institutions. As an alumna of George Washington University, Mrs. Ford was regularly contacted about donating to her alma mater. After receiving a solicitation from the university, she returned the package to the school with a handwritten "deceased" written on the envelope. The next issue of the university's alumni magazine featured a four-page tribute to memorialize her. She kept a copy of the magazine by her bed. Right next to her loaded handgun.

In the course of our conversation, Mrs. Ford made it clear that she had $100 million in liquid assets. She said she planned to leave every dime to the American Society for the Prevention of Cruelty to Animals.

It was apparent to me that Mrs. Ford's love of animals was matched only by her disdain for most humans. I sensed she only deemed a handful acceptable: Leon Lewis, her financial manager; Tom Papa, her accountant; a friend, Cheryl Sims; and Charles Ray Davis, her attorney.

By the time Mrs. Ford finished talking, my blue suit was soaked in perspiration. As I stood to make my exit, she invited me to come visit her again. I accepted.

As Mrs. Ford opened the door to show me out, she said, "But let's get one thing straight, Canoe."

"Yes, ma'am?" I said.

She looked me straight in the eye and said, "I'm not giving one red cent to Ole Piss."

27

As a new chancellor, I worried about maintaining balance. At once, I wanted to aggressively recruit and raise funds and increase morale and beautify our campus, while I also knew I needed to be patient, to listen, and to learn from those who walked before me. It was difficult terrain to navigate. I knew of one thing that had the potential to knock me off course if I didn't pay careful attention. Football — and all that goes along with it — could consume my time, energy, and resources to the exclusion of other programs.

The spectacle of college football is beautiful. The games bring friends and former classmates to the campus. The university gains widespread national and international exposure. Game-day picnics create communities of people who view those moments as sacred. The bands, cheerleaders, and athletes create magical moments for the fans. Coffee shops across the nation are filled with men and women who gather on Monday morning to recap the weekend events. Great rivalries and competitions develop and continue for generations. Quarterback, gridiron, and touchdown clubs meet weekly to share meals, speeches, films, and a good bit of teasing among the members. And when a team is winning, its fan base is more likely to support non-athletics' endeavors at the college or university.

Our football program was in disarray. We were on probation with the NCAA for rules violations . . . for the second time in ten years.

It was a sad day for me, personally, when our popular head coach Billy Brewer was terminated. Billy was not just a teammate. He was a friend. He held the ball for just about every field goal attempt I made my senior year at Ole Miss. Billy and I also played together for the Washington Redskins.

Billy had produced good teams at Ole Miss. The Rebels played in four postseason bowls under his leadership. He made significant contributions to the university and, even more significantly, to the lives of his players. But he could not remain as our coach.

An additional casualty of that time was my close, longtime friend Warner Alford. He and I met in high school and roomed together in the athletics dorm for four years at Ole Miss. During Warner's seventeen-year tenure as director of athletics, we made vast strides in the Ole Miss sports program. He expanded the football stadium and added luxury boxes. Under his leadership, we expanded, enlarged, and improved our athletics field house and built the finest tennis facility in the conference. Warner hired the SEC's first black head coach. In a partnership with the city of Oxford, we built the finest baseball stadium in the South. And, at the time of his resignation, he had been selected to serve as president of the National Athletics Directors Association.

In view of the two probations under his watch, Warner felt honorbound to resign from his post. Chancellor Turner, in his last year at Ole Miss, accepted Warner's resignation and asked me to replace him as interim director of athletics.

I didn't want to take Warner's place. I knew nothing about directing athletics, but at Warner's urging, I accepted the job. Thank goodness it was short-lived, and I returned to my position as sesquicentennial director and law professor.

Gerald Turner hired Pete Boone as director of athletics. Pete started work on January 2, 1995, and his first order of business was to find a head football coach. He asked me to assist in his efforts and to come along for the interviews.

Our top two candidates were Tennessee's offensive coordinator David Cutcliffe and Texas A&M's defensive coordinator Tommy Tuberville.

First, Pete and I flew to Knoxville to meet Coach Cutcliffe. I had known about David through Archie Manning. Archie's son, Peyton, had just finished his freshman season with the Volunteers.

Pete, David, and I met at the Knoxville airport. I was impressed. David not only demonstrated an extraordinary knowledge of football, but his experience and success were beyond reproach. What I liked about him most were his honesty and candor. He was clearly an honorable man.

Then we went to College Station, Texas, to see Tommy Tuberville. Tommy had charisma. The man sparkled when he talked, and the conversation couldn't have gone any better. He was also prepared. He rattled off who would be on his staff, and he explained how he would deal with the NCAA sanctions. He seemed ready to come on board right away.

Pete and I discussed both candidates, and we tried to decide who would be best for Ole Miss. It was Pete's responsibility as athletics director to make the call, and he offered the job to Tommy Tuberville.

A few days later, I was at the alumni house for the press announcement and spent some time with Tommy before he stepped in front of the media for the first time as head football coach. While we waited for Tommy's wife, Suzanne, to arrive, he asked, "Do you have any advice for me?"

"Do you *really* want my advice?" I asked.

"Please," he said.

The advice I had for Tommy wasn't about football. It was a given that attracting good players and coaches was critcal, second only to hard work and dedication. The advice I had for him was about something else.

In theory, head football coaches answer to the director of athletics, but in this age of celebrity coaches and astronomical salaries, that simply was no longer true. The coach of a major football program has all the power. And a winning coach is deified.

Almost without exception, the head football coach will be the highest paid person on campus. Directors of athletics — and sometimes university presidents — have to be adept at working closely with head coaches. If the coach and the director of athletics are at odds, the AD will lose. Even when the coach loses, his contract — often negotiated by an agent — usually includes a long-term payout.

Warner Alford tells a story about head coaches of major football programs. To begin, Warner generally steps just outside a doorway.

"You take a perfectly rational, decent man who has coached football his entire life," he announces. "Then," Warner says, "he accepts a position as head football coach . . . "

At this moment, Warner steps over the door's threshold, spreads his arms in amazement, and says, "And he goes insane!"

Backstage, Tommy Tuberville waited for my answer. I figured it might be the last time he *really* listened to me.

"There are three traps I hope you will avoid," I told him.

Tommy sat, listening intently.

"First," I said, "don't be greedy." I assured him he was going to make plenty of money as the head coach of an SEC team. "The money will come."

"Second," I gently suggested, "maintain control of your ego." I explained that if he wins, he will be exalted and idolized. "But don't forget you are just a human being — a normal, mortal, imperfect one."

"Finally," I said, "if extramarital relationships interest you, be very careful." I paused. "People will watch *everything* you do. And if you should find yourself discovered in a compromising situation, your success as a coach will pale by comparison to the attention that behavior will receive."

"That's it?" he asked.

I nodded.

"That's easy," Tommy said. He stood up and walked to the other side of the room. "I'll never fall victim to any of that."

28

I hoped Tommy Tuberville would turn our football program around. If he produced winning teams, my job would be much easier. Ole Miss alums wanted the school to be academically competitive, but they really liked to be winners on the football field.

As the fall semester began, Andy Mullins and I held our breath. Enrollment at Ole Miss had fallen by nearly a thousand students during the past four years. We were making efforts every day to recruit, but that wouldn't pay off until the next academic year.

When the dust settled and all students had registered, the 1995 fall semester enrollment stood at 10,181. That number wasn't nearly what we wanted or needed.

Tommy Tuberville's first game as head coach at Ole Miss was played in Auburn. We lost the game 46-13. The following week, we played Indiana State University in the home opener. Attendance was just over 33,000, the lowest in years, but the Rebels won the game 56-10. Then we defeated the Georgia Bulldogs 18-10. Considering the state of our program, it was a great start.

Football games gave me the opportunity to host new and old friends who came to campus for fall games. One of those friends was Jim Barksdale.

Jim, a native of Jackson, was one of the Ole Miss business school's most successful graduates. He had served FedEx as vice president and chief operating officer. From there, Jim was appointed CEO of McCaw Cellular/AT&T Wireless. And in January 1995, he was hired to head one of the most innovative software companies in the world — Netscape.

Under Jim's leadership, Netscape introduced the very first Web browser that allowed all computer users to surf the Internet regardless of computer hardware. In each quarter of 1995, company revenues doubled. Netscape went public on August 9, 1995, with the stock valued at $14.00 Before the day ended, the stock soared to $28.00. By the time Jim and his wife, Sally, arrived on the Ole Miss campus for a fall visit, Netscape was valued at $2.9 billion. It was the darling of Silicon Valley.

Jim and I took a drive around campus and talked about his new venture, as well as mine. We drove around the loop, by the Lyceum, past Vaught-Hemingway Stadium and past the Turner Center. As we turned right at Bishop Hall and approached Bondurant, Jim shouted, "Stop!"

I pulled the car into the Bondurant parking lot.

Jim pointed to the northwest corner of the building and smiled, "That's where I met Sally."

A few weeks later, in mid-October, Jim and Sally returned to campus. This time all three of us took a drive. On several occasions, Jim noted that the campus looked *old and dingy*. At one point, he used the word *neglected*.

"I promise," I said, "if you come back here in twelve months, you'll see a different campus."

We took the same route we'd taken in September and, again, I pulled into the Bondurant parking lot. I drove to the northwest corner of the building. I saw Jim and Sally exchange a glance. Then they saw it. I had asked staff members to paint and erect a sign on the very spot the Barksdales had first laid eyes on each other.

In bold blue letters, the sign read: "Where Jim Met Sally."

They both laughed and Sally said, "You will do *anything* for a gift!"

"Yes, I will," I admitted. Then I told them both I hoped they would consider helping Ole Miss.

That's when they invited me to visit them in Palo Alto.

29

In 1955, the year before I enrolled at Ole Miss, the University of Mississippi Medical School moved from the Oxford campus to Jackson. Since that time, it had been generally viewed as separate — independent from Ole Miss. I planned to bring us back together.

Andy Mullins and I flew to Jackson to meet with Dr. Wally Conerly, the top executive at the medical center. Dr. Conerly was a much beloved and respected M.D. His official title was vice chancellor for health affairs. In the printed organizational chart of university authority, the position of chancellor was placed above his position. But that piece of paper was only a chart and did not reflect the actual relationship. In the past, turf had always been an issue. The leaders of the medical center protected their autonomy. In fact, over the years they had even dropped the official UMMC (University of Mississippi Medical Center) name and had started using the label UMC (University Medical Center).

Everyone understood that chancellors on the Oxford campus had enough to do and, in truth, weren't competent to serve as CEOs of the medical center. Of course, that included me. But I knew that we could be stronger together.

In our first visit together, I told Dr. Conerly that I planned to be at the medical center for a full day each week. I explained that I did not and could not *run* the center. My role would be to counsel him and offer support where I could be helpful. I made it clear, however, that UMC was going to become UMMC again. I planned to participate in faculty and staff meetings, assist with private gift solicitation, and participate in the annual commencement exercises. When we appeared before the Legislative Budget Committee, I said, we would appear together, though Dr. Conerly would take the lead role.

Dr. Conerly didn't say a word. He sat quietly as I told him my reasons.

First, I explained, our separateness hurt funding for both campuses. With students on the Jackson campus being counted outside the Ole Miss population, our enrollment appeared to be 2,000 fewer. One of the major factors in state appropriations and allocation of funds is student population and credit hours produced. Of course, other universities in Mississippi encouraged the separateness. The split allowed them to claim higher enrollment. Additionally, without being allowed to count UMMC funds, Ole Miss was being penalized by accrediting agencies, since total budgets were a measure of success.

Second, Ole Miss was denied the authority to operate a nursing program (other Mississippi universities and community colleges had them) since one already existed in Jackson. I wanted nursing students to enjoy a traditional college experience on the Ole Miss campus and then spend their last two years on the medical center campus in a clinical environment.

Finally, almost every health sciences campus in America was an integral part of the home campus, even when physically separated.

Dr. Conerly remained quiet and deferential. I suspected he was reluctant about my proactive involvement. We both understood that my presence at the medical center ran counter to forty years of convention, but I felt certain it was the right thing to do.

I planned to be proactive in another area, too — faculty relations. During my years at Ole Miss as a member of the staff, faculty, administration, and the Faculty Senate, I had firsthand experience with the fractures that can develop between faculty and the chancellor. I planned to do everything in my power to keep that from happening. The first order of business was the university airplane.

Faculty, staff, and media tracked the use of the airplane — known as *UM 1* — with a watchful eye. My predecessor, Gerald Turner, was severely criticized for using *his plane*. I'm not sure the fuss was really about use of the airplane, but it was an easy target. Some faculty members started calling it *Turner Air*. I thought the criticism was unfair, but I wanted to address the issue before it addressed me.

In a memo to university employees, I wrote:

The university owns an airplane that is for use in conducting university business. The airplane is not the Chancellor's plane, though I will undoubtedly be the individual who flies on the plane most often. Please know that any member of the faculty or staff who has business in the same city or town to which we are flying is invited to ride with us on the plane at no charge. If the plane isn't scheduled, you are free to reserve the plane and pay for its use out of your departmental funds. The plane is to be used for official university business only.

I knew it would take much more than memos to make headway in building sound relationships with faculty members. I also planned to make some friends.

Among the brightest and best of our faculty members was a young historian named Charles Eagles. Professor Eagles was admired and loved by his students and was gaining national acclaim for his writing and scholarship. I had not met Dr. Eagles, but I saw him almost every day. His home was about one mile from his office in Bishop Hall. Weather permitting, Dr. Eagles walked to and from work each day, and his route took him directly past my office window.

During my years at the law school, I had followed some of Dr. Eagles' public comments in the student newspaper, and it seemed to me that just about everything he said was critical. I wondered if he was happy at Ole Miss.

Dr. Eagles had joined the faculty in 1983, and later held one of our few endowed chairs. Due to his growing reputation, I was sure other universities would attempt to lure him away from Ole Miss. I wanted to keep him here.

On several consecutive mornings in September, I caught a glimpse of Professor Eagles walking briskly past the Lyceum. One morning, when I saw him coming, I jumped from my chair and rushed out to greet him.

"Dr. Eagles," I said, extending my hand, "you don't know me, but

I have followed your work at Ole Miss. I wanted us to meet."

We exchanged pleasantries for a moment. Then it was clear he was ready to get on with his day.

"I follow your comments in the press," I said.

He looked a bit surprised.

"You seem," I said, "consistently critical."

Dr. Eagles raised an eyebrow.

"I want you to know something," I said. "The success of my chancellorship will be determined by your happiness."

He paused for a moment to think. Then he flashed a smile. "Don't put that burden on me." Then he went on his way.

30

I continued to take daily, early-morning walks across campus. And as the weather began to cool, I invited students and staff to join me.

My favorite walks were with students. A dozen or so of us would meet at the Lyceum, introduce ourselves, and then take a brisk stroll through the Circle, around the Grove, and across campus.

It gave me a chance to get to know students outside the Lyceum. And it let students get to know me as a person, not as an administrator in a navy-blue suit.

As I walked, whether with students or colleagues, I took note of what we could do to improve the appearance of our property.

On a Saturday morning walk with Andy Mullins, I noticed the large entrance doors to the "Y" Building. The 1853 structure sat on our central circle just east of the Lyceum. The enormous doors were filthy and had not been painted in years.

"Andy," I said, "we have to paint those doors."

"I'll take care of it," he told me.

A few weeks later, on the same route, we noticed that nothing had been done to improve the eyesore.

Andy called the director of the physical plant to inquire about the job.

"That's seventy-eighth on our 'to-paint' list," the director told him.

Andy waited one week, then called back to see where the job stood.

"It's up to thirty-fourth now," he was told.

Andy and I had talked ad nauseum about shifting the culture of Ole Miss from a bureaucracy to a business model. We saw an opportunity to start those changes in the physical plant.

"If those doors aren't painted by Friday," Andy told him, "the

An early-morning walk with students

chancellor and I are going to buy two gallons of white paint and spend all Saturday morning painting those damned doors."

They were painted the next day.

Though the campus needed work, the natural beauty of the trees at Ole Miss always brought me great joy. Passing these magnificent creations every day, I would stop to admire the giant catalpa tree near the student union. In the spring, no tree was more stunning than the flowering dogwood north of the law school. In the fall, the brilliant, champion Osage orange that stood next to the university museum looked like God had plugged its leaves into an electrical socket. And, of course, the ancient magnolia trees in the Grove and loop were green throughout the year.

The one tree I missed most — a coastal species that wouldn't grow in North Mississippi — was the live oak.

The first time I remember being aware of a live oak, I was three years old. I vividly recall watching my mother standing in front of the kitchen sink, washing dishes, and gazing outside at a tree we all referred to as "Mama's oak."

The tree sat on a vacant lot adjacent to our yard. Its trunk was eight feet in diameter. Huge limbs reached toward the sky while others arched close to the ground. The oak shaded more than 5,000 square feet of soil.

Mama's oak was a playground for the neighborhood children and me. I would walk on the lower limbs like a tightrope or tell stories in the cradle created ten feet off the ground where the trunk parted and formed huge limbs. The more daring kids explored the upper reaches of the tree by saddling one of the vertical limbs and slowly inching upward. The tree was all the amusement a young boy could want.

But the tree was much more than that to my mother. For sixty years on Beardslee Street, the oak was my mother's companion. She basked in the shadows, created by moonlight filtered through the canopy of limbs, as she stood in the humid darkness. She understood that the tree's shade and relief on a hot July day were a blessing. She was grateful even when the falling leaves permeated the air with an aroma of death because she understood they would ultimately bring forth the joy of birth.

The oak had a soul, and it brought my mother comfort and stability and joy.

I don't get to spend much time with the oak tree anymore, but I can still smell its pungent bark. Thankfully, my mother always talked about her tree whenever we were together.

She reminded me of the victory garden our family planted near the tree during World War II. She basked in the memory of the backdrop the tree provided for family wedding receptions. She and I shared the memory of panic, during hurricanes, huddled inside the safety of our home, knowing the tree was outside to face the high wind and rain.

To hear my mother tell stories of the oak tree was to know true love. Most relations are flawed, but the one between my mother and her oak tree was perfect.

In late October, another mother and son were having a conversation. It took place in Atlanta between Larry Martindale and his mother, Charlotte.

Larry Martindale attended Ole Miss from 1966 to 1969. Born into a family of modest means, Larry came to the university on a basketball scholarship. He lettered in varsity basketball in 1967, 1968, and 1969. Then he went into the army.

After his discharge, a former teammate of Larry's gave him a job as a cook. He took full advantage of the opportunity and quickly moved up the company ladder. Soon he became a partner in an Atlanta-based company that signed on as the first franchisee of Waffle House restaurants. It grew to be the largest franchise in the United States. Then, in a move at the other end of the social spectrum, Larry and his partners developed the Ritz-Carlton Hotel into a brand that is now one of the hospitality industry's greatest success stories. Larry's Ritz-Carltons were consistently ranked among the top five hotel properties in the world.

While Larry was building his business empire, his wife, Susan, devoted her time to improving life for children in her community. She raised funds for a home for troubled children in Atlanta, sponsored Christmas parties for underprivileged children, and supported the Cobb Street Ministry, an organization that provides assistance and training to homeless mothers.

Over dinner at Larry and Susan's, the conversation led to Ole Miss.

"Larry?" his mother asked, "have you ever paid back the scholarship Ole Miss gave you?"

It was a question Larry had never considered. "What do you mean?"

"Your scholarship to Ole Miss paid all your expenses for college," she reminded him.

"I earned it," he said. "I played basketball for four years."

"Well," she said, not buying Larry's rationale, "I think you should pay it back."

Shortly thereafter, I was sitting in the den of the Atlanta home of Larry and Susan Martindale. They expressed an interest in helping the university, but they weren't sure what gift might be most helpful. The list of needs at the university was staggering. As tempted as I was to make a suggestion for a gift, I had a better plan.

"Let's talk details later," I said. "Why don't the two of you come visit us in Oxford?"

Jim Barksdale in a 1995 publicity shot from Netscape

31

On November 3, 1995, I boarded a plane with Jim Barksdale's brothers Tommy and Bryan. We flew to Palo Alto to spend the weekend with Jim and Sally Barksdale.

We all stayed in their beautiful home, and the Barksdales could not have been more gracious. They took us to watch Stanford play Southern California (the game was a thriller, ending in a 31-30 victory for USC), and we dined at some of the best restaurants in the Bay Area.

We also spent a great deal of time talking about gifts the Barksdales could make that would help Ole Miss get back on its feet.

I went through a litany of ideas, including a new business school and an information technology center. I assumed they would be interested in some kind of technology since Jim was leading the world's best-known Internet company, but I was mistaken. None of my thoughts seemed to excite them. But I pressed on.

After suggesting a performing arts center and a general fund for scholarships, Jim and Sally asked me to join them at the dining room table.

"What can we do that will have the greatest impact on Ole Miss?" Sally asked.

Without blinking, I said, "Create an honors college."

They seemed intrigued. Then Jim asked, "Why an honors college?"

I told them about my trip to Memphis with the University Scholars to see *La Bohéme* when I was a freshman and how that moment changed my life forever. I added that I thought an honors college would attract exceptional students who might otherwise choose another school.

"Ole Miss owes the brightest students in Mississippi the oppor-

tunity to stay in state for undergraduate education," I said. "They should understand that no private or public university in the nation can offer them a better college experience."

Then I added that it was imperative we have a top honors college if Ole Miss had a prayer of sheltering a Phi Beta Kappa chapter.

They exchanged glances, then looked at me. "Let us think about it," Jim said, "and let us know how much money you will need."

When I returned to Oxford, I set up a meeting with Carolyn Ellis Staton. She and I served together on the law school faculty. Her record was more than distinguished. She earned degrees from Tulane and Yale Law School. While at Yale, her best friends were a bright young couple named Bill and Hillary Clinton.

Carolyn had a strong record of scholarship. She was the recipient of a Fulbright, and she was a favorite among her students and faculty colleagues. As an interim dean at the Ole Miss law school, she provided enlightened, courageous, and visionary leadership.

As fate would have it, Gerald Walton had lured her away from the law school to serve as his partner in the Office of Vice Chancellor for Academic Affairs. I assumed Gerald was grooming Carolyn to take his place when his three-year commitment ended.

Carolyn was as smart as they come. She was full of great ideas and energy, and she had already begun to suggest exciting new academic programs. Carolyn also had a gift for motivating and inspiring others, as well as an extraordinary skill for selecting the right people to lead specific programs and initiatives.

I met with Carolyn in my office and asked her to organize a small group of our brightest faculty to develop a plan for an honors college at Ole Miss. I asked her to find a building, create a comprehensive plan, propose programming, and estimate class size.

At the end of our meeting, I said, "Carolyn, when you and the committee finish the plan, I'll need one more concrete detail."

"Yes?" she said.

"A price tag."

32

I was stunned by how quickly the fall semester passed. As the students began to prepare for final exams, I took a bit of time to reflect on, and assess, my first few months as chancellor.

I felt good about the team we were building. Of course, I needed more talented people to fill voids, but Andy Mullins, Gerald Walton, Carolyn Ellis Staton, Pete Boone, and the very capable administrative assistant to the chancellor, Leone King, were already starting to make a difference in moving the university forward.

In five months, Andy and I had made stops in more than thirty-five communities. While we were on the road with our recruiting and public relations trips, Gerald and Carolyn managed the day-to-day business on campus.

Many of the leaders from Gerald Turner's administration were still with us, but some of those who were uncomfortable with me — or my management style — began to take jobs elsewhere. Others retired or asked to go back to full-time teaching. We made changes without much acrimony, and I was able to search for the best, most energetic people to fill vacancies with "no blood on the rug."

Some outside factors were working in our favor, too: primarily, the economy. It was booming. In February of 1995, the Dow Jones index had surpassed the 4,000 point mark. In November, it topped 5,000. It was the first time in history that the Dow surpassed two millennium marks in a single year. And the technology boom seemed to be here to stay. In October, *Forbes* magazine announced that Bill Gates had just eclipsed Warren Buffett as the world's richest man.

A good economy was working in our favor, but Ole Miss was also blessed by extraordinary relationships with our leaders in government. Mississippi's two U.S. Senators, Thad Cochran and Trent Lott, were classmates of mine — in both undergraduate and law school. They were also personal friends. They had both worked hard to secure federal funds for buildings and programs. Senator Cochran had directed generous support to our National Center for Natural Products Research. We actually owned and operated the only legal marijuana field in America, leading the way to remarkable research on medicinal uses of the illegal substance that attracted international acclaim and millions of dollars in research funding.

We lost a great friend in Congress when Jamie Whitten retired. His fifty-three years of service were the longest in the history of the U.S. House of Representatives. He passed away shortly thereafter, but not before securing federal funding for the university's National Center for Physical Acoustics.

Our relationship with state officials looked promising, too. In the November elections, Kirk Fordice had won the governorship. Ronnie Musgrove was elected lieutenant governor.

Governor Fordice was not an Ole Miss graduate, but he was a businessman. I knew he would be behind our move from a bureaucracy to a business model. Lieutenant Governor Musgrove was an Ole Miss graduate — and my former student — who would lead the state legislature. He would certainly be a friend to the university.

There was good news from our football team, too. Our university attorney, Mary Ann Connell, was leading the effort to complete our NCAA probationary period. Her integrity and credibility would go a long way toward getting our team back in good standing. And despite our limitations under probation, Tommy Tuberville led the team to six victories, including an upset over Georgia and a season finale victory over Mississippi State.

Despite all the good things, there were problem areas. The most visible was game day in the Grove. It was a nightmare for all of us responsible for the campus. We simply weren't prepared to host a picnic for 15,000 people in a relatively small space.

The postgame clean up was a two-to-three day affair. On Monday mornings, our office was deluged with complaints — primarily from faculty and staff. And they were justified. The grounds were littered and trampled, but an even more distasteful, unexpected problem was discovered. Our academic buildings were being used as restrooms. Academic buildings and inebriated football fans turned out to be a bad mix. When a bathroom was available, it was sometimes utilized in a less-than-appropriate manner. Worse, if no restroom could be found, some unthoughtful individuals would simply use the hallway as a bathroom.

Not all the game-day problems were due to abusive fans. We faced a severe lack of parking. Traffic didn't flow, it stood still. Fans were bringing golf carts and four wheelers to drive through the Grove. So many people were selling merchandise that some sections of the Grove could have been mistaken for a flea market. Other unexpected issues included unloading in the Grove, fights over tent locations, fake handicapped stickers for better access, electricity problems, gas-operated generators, and, of course, trash clean up.

After our last home game, against Vanderbilt, on top of all the other issues we mishandled, we discovered a window had been knocked out of a science lab at Shoemaker Hall.

I walked into Andy Mullins' office.

"Andy," I said, "we need a governing system for game day."

Andy listened. We knew it was going to be a difficult task. We also knew regulating the Grove, changing late-night, postgame behavior, wouldn't be popular with some of our alumni.

Andy agreed to take on the monumental task. I promised him that I'd find someone else to head game-day operations if he would take the lead in setting the boundaries and guidelines. No one was better equipped to return order to game day.

Two other problem areas were less visible, publicly, but vital to our long-term success: finances and public perception.

I couldn't get a good grip on the budget for the university. The bureaucratic financial reports simply didn't make sense to me. When I inquired about why we did things a certain way, the answer seemed to be "we've always done it this way."

The second problem was public perception. We weren't doing a very good job of telling the positive story of Ole Miss.

I needed the Christmas break to regroup and recharge, and I needed to spend time with my family. However, I also planned to work during the holidays, drafting objectives for the new year, planning to build on the work we'd done that fall, and finding committed individuals to lead us in the realms of finance and university relations.

On my last day in the office before Christmas break, I opened my 1996 calendar. On the January 3, 1996, schedule, I wrote down two names: Rex Deloach and Gloria Kellum.

Investiture
1996

33

During the Christmas holidays, I read an editorial in *The Clarion-Ledger* attacking the administrations of the University of Southern Mississippi and Jackson State University for the apparent loss of more than $500,000 worth of school-owned equipment. According to the editorial, officials at USM and JSU blamed mistakes in accounting for the alleged losses.

That afternoon, I went to my office and made copies of the editorial for every department head, as well as individuals responsible for keeping records of university property. I underlined the "mistakes in accounting" phrase and added a handwritten note — *Each of us is responsible for the property and funds assigned to us. We need to be prudent, responsible, and accountable.* Then I called for an audit of university property — all four million items.

The audit was a first step in my attempt to understand, and become thoroughly familiar with, the university budget and finances. Since all my questions about the budget had been answered with "that's how we've always done it," I knew we needed a fresh look at our financial practices.

About that time, perhaps providentially, I met Rex Deloach. Rex had recently retired as managing partner of the Memphis office of Arthur Anderson. I learned from Memphis friends that the business community held him in the highest regard. In fact, some major international firms in Memphis had seen remarkable successes built around Rex's reviews, recommendations, and consultations.

Rex's story is a great example of the possibilities for upward mobility in America. Raised on a farm in the Mississippi Delta about five miles east of Alligator, Rex, his father, mother, and two brothers lived in a home without electricity or running water. The five of them scratched out a living on the farm. They had no expectations of opportunities for a higher standard of living. On a hot Delta summer day, they were chopping cotton when an automobile stopped on the highway and a young man walked across the field to talk to Rex's father. He said one of Rex's teachers had told him that Rex needed — and had what it would take — to go to college. Of course, Mr. Deloach replied, *that would be nice, but we can't afford college.* The recruiter from Delta State was relentless. He asked the family to drive to Cleveland. Rex and his mother walked on the Delta State campus the next day, and, within hours, Rex had a job in the cafeteria and a room in a dormitory. He was enrolled in college.

Rex studied at Delta State and Birmingham Southern. At the same time, he also worked odd jobs, including pumping gas at a service station. When he was twenty years old, he joined the Navy.

Four years as a sailor eventually led Rex to Memphis State, where he earned an accounting degree. He passed the Certified Public Accountant Exam and was immediately hired by a national accounting firm. That's when he set about the business of building a remarkable career.

Rex accepted my invitation for a lunch meeting at the Downtown Grill on the Square in Oxford.

"Rex," I asked, "would you teach me the university budget?"

At first, he seemed a bit reluctant, but I eventually convinced him to give it a shot. The following afternoon, I arranged to have the 500-page university budget delivered to his home.

As I waited for Rex's analysis of the university budget, I realized I had no idea how the various divisions, schools, or departments managed resources. For years, as a faculty member and administrator, I had heard the pleas for more funding. I just assumed the requests and complaints were genuine and well-founded. I do not recall ever hearing a chancellor or other administrative leader use the words *efficient*, *prudent*, *performance-based* or *best practices*.

On January 31, Rex Deloach walked into my office. He wore a dark suit. His angular features, silver hair, and bright eyes, combined with his quiet demeanor and clear intellect, created an aura of stability and integrity.

"I have good news and bad news," Rex said, as he handed me a thirty-six-page report — his analysis of the budget. "Which would you like to hear first?"

"The bad news, I guess."

"You are broke," he said.

I took a deep breath. "And the good news?"

"You can fix it," Rex answered, "if you have the courage."

Rex presented me with a number of strategies to make the university more efficient, to eliminate waste, and to generate revenue.

The courage I was supposed to muster had yet to be tested. None of us know how we will perform under pressure until the moment arrives. But I was so intent on getting the university moving that I was willing to try anything that made sense — and was legal.

First, Rex and I identified the five sources of revenue for a public university:

(1) State Appropriations
(2) Tuition and Fees
(3) Research Grants
(4) Self-generated income from the bookstore, residence halls, food service, etc.
(5) Private gifts

In recent years, funding from the state had been reduced, so we agreed that we needed to look at increasing revenue through tuition, self-generated funds, grants, and private support through the University of Mississippi Foundation.

Enrollment increases would be the greatest source of revenue growth — and that would also increase self-generated income.

"I know the business of a university is education," Rex said, "but Ole Miss has not been using best business practices."

I sensed this was a problem. Every time I had asked a question about university finances, the answers I got were indirect and deflected.

Rex explained that the university operated on a "use it or lose it" policy. All unspent funds at the end of the fiscal year were swept back into the central university budget.

"Obviously," Rex said, "budget officers try to spend every dime budgeted."

He showed me a graph of university spending. It spiked from June 1 to July 1 — the last month of the fiscal year.

"They're spending money on supplies they might need in the future," Rex said.

Because so many departments spent money on future needs, the university had to rent space to store the supplies.

"The university rents a building on College Hill Road," he said. "It's not climate controlled, and it has a leaky roof."

"So, the supplies are water damaged?"

"Or mildewed," he said.

I was shocked at the waste and inefficiency, but it perfectly illustrated the need to abandon our old bureaucratic ways and adopt business models.

"There's more," Rex said.

"What?"

"We're paying $30,000 per year to rent the building."

34

In 1989, I took a three-year leave of absence from the university to organize an educational foundation in Kansas City for the NCAA. Those three years with the foundation expanded my experience and introduced me to national leaders. When I returned to the university as professor of law, I was overjoyed to be back home and in the classroom.

Chancellor Gerald Turner, with whom I had worked as vice chancellor from 1984 until 1989, asked me to chair the university's sesquicentennial celebration (and also to organize a major gifts campaign). I accepted, but I suggested to Chancellor Turner that he appoint a co-chair. I knew the perfect candidate: Gloria Kellum.

I had known Gloria long before I was chancellor. She was one of those bright lights on the campus. She was an outstanding teacher, highly respected for her research and scholarship in speech and hearing, and well-known and liked on campus. My wife, Margaret, had been an adult student in one of Gloria's classes and raved about the experience.

In the spring of 1994, I was walking down the hallway of the Lyceum when I bumped into Dr. Kellum.

"Gloria," I said, "I was just talking about you."

"You were?" she said.

"How would you like to co-chair the Sesquicentennial Celebration Committee with me?"

"The what?" she said.

"The 150th anniversary of the university," I explained.

I gave Gloria a quick overview of what I had in mind, including solicitation of private gifts for academic support . . . a major development initiative.

Before we parted, Gloria agreed to co-chair the committee.

Then she added, "As long as I don't have to spell *sesquicentennial*."

Gloria and I invited active faculty and staff to serve as members of the committee. Donna Patton, a staff support person, joined us as a volunteer "keeper of the records." Donna and many others, who quietly worked in departments across campus, made incredible contributions to the life of our university.

Our committee held several strategic planning committee meetings to develop our "wish list" for the university. There was a consensus internally and externally that we could use the sesquicentennial to revitalize the university. There had been too many years of disappointing state support. Too many years of deferred maintenance. Too many years of low morale. And, of course, our football program was still on probation.

On the bright side, the national economy was beginning to improve, and Silicon Valley was becoming a household term. But Ole Miss was in the dark ages when it came to the world of electronic information.

During one of the committee meetings, we were discussing that we had fallen behind so many other universities in the realm of technology.

"How much would it cost to catch up?" I asked.

"A lot," Gloria said.

Then, a gentleman from the finance department said in a low voice, "Nobody knows this yet, but the university is about to receive one million dollars that no one expected. It's not earmarked for anything specific."

"Where is it coming from?" Gloria asked.

"Casino revenues," he said.

I immediately walked over to Chancellor Turner's office and asked him if the sesquicentennial committee could use the one million dollars for a technology initiative.

"What do you plan to do?" Chancellor Turner asked me.

"Put a computer on every desk," I said.

With Chancellor Turner's blessing, Gloria and I ordered 900 new desktop computers, one for every faculty member and staff.

As fate would have it, the computers arrived in the seventh month of my chancellorship. I received a great deal of credit for something that was born under Gerald Turner's tenure.

The faculty responded positively to the surprise. Suddenly, they believed the administration really *was* interested in academic programs.

I received lots of pats on the back from faculty, but the honeymoon was short-lived. It didn't take us long to realize that very few of us — faculty included — understood how to use these electronic miracles.

Several Ole Miss faculty members, from different schools on campus, came to the rescue. They volunteered to design and create a Faculty Technology Development Center. The nucleus of the leaders included T.J. Ray, Lee Bolen, Phil Malone, Mark Tew, and Brian Reithel. They came from engineering, English, physics, and business, but they worked together beautifully.

Another benefit of my co-chairing the Sesquicentennial Celebration Committee was preparation for the chancellorship. In 1994 and 1995, Gloria and I had held a number of strategic planning meetings and developed a big dream list of objectives.

Gloria and I were partners of sorts, not only in planning the 150th celebration but also in our deep love for Ole Miss — and an obsessive concern for the future of the university.

Gloria was tireless, creative, and always positive and committed to the goals we agreed upon. But she was also always honest with me. She told me if she thought I was wrong. Gloria was exactly the kind of person I wanted on the university leadership team.

In January of 1996, I asked Gloria to serve as the sole chair of the Sesquicentennial Celebration Committee. The celebration would culminate in 1998. It would be an opportunity to showcase our history and bring the Ole Miss community together to celebrate. Gloria accepted the position, and I knew she would do a terrific job.

But I had much bigger plans for Gloria Kellum.

I felt like our core leadership team was now in place — Andy Mullins, Gerald Walton, Carolyn Ellis Staton, Pete Boone, Gloria Kellum, and Mary Ann Connell. The only missing pieces were a chief financial officer, a leader of our research program, and a leader of student life. And I wanted Rex Deloach. The CFO's role was critical, as were the vice chancellors' for research and student life.

As chancellor, I knew I would be the leader of the leaders. My approach would be fairly simple. Relationships would be based on respect, common sense, and an unwavering awareness that our success depended on every person on the team being invested in our mission.

The leadership rules I wanted to follow included:

1. Select leaders at every level who are better at their jobs than I would be.

2. Delegate full responsibility to each leader.

3. Give each leader not only responsibility but also *authority* to make decisions in the management of his or her area.

4. Be sure that successful leaders received *public credit* for their work. If an initiative failed, it would be my responsibility; if it was successful, the victory belonged to the leader and his or her department members.

5. Give leaders full responsibility and authority to manage their departmental budgets, thereby dropping the "use it or lose it" rule and creating incentives for sound, prudent management of resources.

I had other guidelines depending on the circumstances, but for the most part these were our guiding principles.

As for leading by example, I planned to work hard and always be visible and accessible to faculty, staff, and students. As chancellor, I knew I would have to travel, but I was determined to be on campus more often than not. I would not be an absentee chancellor.

Visibility and accessibility were going to be essential in the years to come.

35

In February of 1996, the university lost two great friends — George Street and Charlie Conerly.

George Street was a university icon. He dedicated his life to Ole Miss. George came to the university as an undergraduate after serving in the Army during World War II. After graduation, he enrolled in the Ole Miss law school and earned a Juris Doctor in 1949. He moved steadily through the ranks of Ole Miss during his thirty-nine-year tenure. He not only moved up the ladder quickly but also created new positions at the university, including the university's first placement bureau and office of financial aid. He helped build the Carrier Scholarship program and eventually served as the Ole Miss director of university relations.

George had a huge impact on so many students' lives. The Episcopal priest Lowell Grisham said, "George Street turned frogs into princes. And there are a lot of us little tadpoles running around with crowns on our heads."

I was no exception. As an undergraduate, I met with George to discuss my future.

"What would you like to do?" he asked.

"I might like to work for the university," I told him. "Sort of what you do."

"Then get an advanced degree," George said. "You might think about law school."

It was the very first time I had considered the idea.

Shortly after George passed away, football great Charlie Conerly died.

On February 15, I sat in Clarksdale's First United Methodist Church. The pews were packed with friends and former football teammates. I saw Frank Gifford, as well as members of the Mara family, who owned the Giants. Dozens of former Ole Miss players attended, including Archie Manning, who sat next to Coach Johnny Vaught.

When Coach Vaught was offered the job as head football coach in 1947, he had one question: *Will Charlie Conerly stay and play football for Ole Miss?* He knew that our only chance for success was to have Charlie Conerly as the Ole Miss quarterback-tailback.

Charlie's college football career had been interrupted by service in World War II and he was eligible to move on to the NFL by the time Coach Vaught arrived. The Redskins wanted him, but he accepted Coach Vaught's invitation. The Rebels won the SEC championship that year, as well as the Delta Bowl. Coach Vaught was so unsure of the 1947 team that he committed to the Delta Bowl (a new bowl game to be played in Memphis) before the season even started. The 1947 team led by Charlie was so good that Ole Miss would have played in the Sugar Bowl but for that prior commitment.

Charlie went on to a remarkable career in the NFL. As a quarterback, he set a rookie record for touchdown passes. He led the New York Giants to many successful seasons, including the 1958 NFL Championship game — the first ever professional overtime game. At the time, professional football and the NFL were gaining traction and popularity. Charlie played for the Giants until he was in his early forties.

As the advertising business on Madison Avenue boomed, he was selected as the first Marlboro Man. He was generally known as Mr. New York. His wife, Perian, wrote a bestselling book titled *Backseat Quarterback*.

After his football career ended, Charlie declined offers to become a lead commentator for CBS TV, and, instead, he recommended that the network consider Pat Summerall, who went on to have a long and successful career in television.

Charlie was shy and consistently declined speaking opportunities. He continued his role as the Marlboro Man and later owned a chain of shoe stores. He maintained warm relationships with Frank Gifford and other Giant stars, as well as the Mara family.

On one rare occasion, Charlie was forced into agreeing to give a speech. In front of a large audience and after being elaborately introduced by the master of ceremonies, Charlie rose slowly, approached the microphone, looked out on the audience of 500 attendees, and said, "Any questions?"

Charlie's funeral was short and to the point, just as Charlie would have liked it. During the recessional, in perhaps the most fitting music ever played at a funeral, the organist broke out into the Yankee Stadium version of *New York, New York*.

Charlie's funeral was a reunion of sorts for former players and Coach Vaught. I remember the first time I heard Coach Vaught speak. I was a nineteen-year-old sophomore competing for a position on a very good 1957 Ole Miss football squad. I sat in the wooden bleachers inside the football locker room. My teammates and I talked while we waited.

Then Coach Vaught walked into the room. He didn't have to say a word. The moment he entered, the locker room went silent.

He walked in front of the bleachers and stood perfectly still. With shoulders back and perfect posture, Coach Vaught wore a baseball cap, white t-shirt, and khaki pants. A whistle rested against his strong chest.

He looked us over for a moment and said, "You represent all that is good about Mississippi. And the best way you can represent this state is to play championship football."

He paused for a moment to let it sink in.

"If you are champions," Vaught continued, "the state will be a champion. We owe it to ourselves and to the people of Mississippi to be the best we can possibly be.

"This team is the bright spot of our state — a state that is often maligned."

Then Coach Vaught clapped his hands together and said, "All right, let's go!"

Coach Vaught's words, and the success of our teams, [ ]affected the way I viewed my personal responsibilities to[ ]Mississippi. In 1957, when my attitudes and feelings we[ ]shaped by my coaches and teammates, I could never have imagined that I would lead the most influential and significant institution in Mississippi. But when I was selected chancellor, I knew it was an opportunity — no, a responsibility — to use my position as a springboard for progressive ideas and forward movement.

I would have many allies in this endeavor. So many citizens of the state wanted the best for Mississippi and all its people. These are the individuals William Alexander Percy described as "the bright lights."

But I also knew I would be fighting against decades of complacency, and, of course, racism. Race relations were, obviously, a major impediment to progress, but beyond race stood the twin blockades of ignorance and poverty.

Many Mississippians, it seemed, were satisfied with mediocrity. Some wanted nothing more than the status quo. I knew others would intentionally try to impede any change. *collectively as a group*

At times, collectively, we refused to look at ourselves objectively. We were reluctant to accept our destructive reality and do what was necessary to break the cycle that had been in place for generations. We allowed our public schools to be segregated and underfunded, and that assured continued mediocrity at best for the larger population. In many cases, our reluctance to change guaranteed inferiority.

Mississippi is a rich state in many ways. We have produced world leaders in business, music, sports, television, film, and literature. But, financially, Mississippi is among the poorest.

I had parents who instilled in me an understanding that our meager resources were precious. I grew up knowing that any asset should be used efficiently.

Mississippi's leaders, in the past, had generally been poor stewards of our limited resources. We provided duplicate government services on the basis of race. For political reasons, in a state so hungry for education, we established eight universities, a medical center, multiple campuses, fifteen community colleges and facilities in eighty-one communities — each with its own administrative salaries, building costs, and operational expenses. None of the schools was adequately funded — which guaranteed substandard performance.

I wanted to change this cycle. We simply had to use our limited funds wisely. I was determined to get Ole Miss on sound financial footing. Only then could we attract the best faculty, staff, and students. I longed for the day Ole Miss realized its potential.

Throughout my life, I remember being embarrassed by the frequent disparaging comments made about my state. But that was nothing compared to the embarrassment I felt by the egregious behavior of some of the people of our state.

Coach Vaught introduced me to a higher standard. He made me believe that a football team could change the way the world viewed our state. His lessons stayed with me. If an exceptional sports team could do that, then imagine what an outstanding flagship university could accomplish.

With the town of Oxford as our partner, I believed Ole Miss could be a bright and shining light.

This was my dream.

36

In the fall of 1996, I created an inauguration planning committee. I asked the members to think about, plan, and implement an investiture ceremony that would put Ole Miss in the national spotlight. I saw the event as an opportunity to announce to the academic world, our alumni, faculty, staff, and students that we were serious about achieving "great university" status.

The committee was chaired by Gerald Walton and included faculty, staff, and students. The group accepted my challenge, and the inauguration planning took on a life of its own.

The committee scheduled a series of wide-ranging programs for the week prior to the inauguration. Mississippi's leading writers, musicians, and historians made presentations that energized the campus and attracted large crowds. One of the most memorable was a lively program that featured Mississippi authors Larry Brown, Ellen Douglas, Willie Morris, Barry Hannah, and John Grisham.

The investiture of a chancellor is certainly a time to celebrate, but it is also a time to reflect on the history and traditions of the university. For my investiture, Dr. Ron Bartlett, a language faculty member who also happens to be a talented sculptor, created a university mace. In the Middle Ages, ceremonial maces were carried by bodyguards of French and English monarchs. It later became an important symbol of office in both civil and academic processions. Many universities have designed symbolic relics to reflect the character and traits of the institution. Ole Miss had not had one. Ron created a beautiful mace for the university, symbolizing the defense of truth.

After the ceremony, the mace would become a part of the collection of treasures of the university that also includes the university medallion.

More than 4,000 people gathered in Tad Smith Coliseum for the inauguration. Representatives from ninety-one colleges and universities from across the nation — all dressed in academic regalia — attended. They added great color and spectacle to the event.

As I stood in the portal leading into the Coliseum at the very front of the processional line, and the university symphony began to play, I felt as if I were watching a movie. It was as surreal a moment for me as any I'd ever experienced.

One of the organizers gave me a cue to move forward. On my first step down the stairs, my shoe caught the hem of my gown and I nearly tumbled down the stairs. It jarred me back to reality.

Once we were in our places, the program began. I sat next to Gloria Kellum. She was on the inauguration committee, but she had only offered one piece of advice during the planning process: *Please don't promise anything we can't deliver.*

After the other speakers had their turns at the microphone, I walked to the front of the stage. I put my speech on the podium and looked out over the audience at Tad Smith Coliseum. I was overwhelmed that so many had gathered for the event. Then, I looked over the podium at the front row and I saw my family. At the center, I saw the glowing face of my mother.

I smiled and nodded in appreciation to my family and opened the notebook that held my speech. That week, we had celebrated our past and present.

It was time to talk about our future.

in his speech, it shows how passionate and how much he cares about this school

37

Then I read . . .

When the Board of Trustees granted me the privilege of serving as chancellor, we, as a community, decided this inauguration would be a celebration of the university and a tribute to the people of Mississippi. We are glad you could be here.

One hundred and forty-eight years ago, George Frederick Holmes, our university's first president, stood where I stand today. He began his inaugural address with these words: "I come as a stranger among you — and feel the usual difficulties of a stranger."

I come not as a stranger. I am one of you — I am a product of this university, and I welcome you to the inauguration of the university's fifteenth chancellor. In my remarks, I will refer to the university as "we" and "us." I do so because there is and always has been a special bond between the university and its people. We exist to provide opportunities for our students and to serve society. We are one — we must be one — regardless of our role, race or gender, economic status, religious affiliation, or political persuasion. We are one people: we value respect for the dignity of the individual, we value honesty and integrity, and we value learning and wisdom. *School pride*

An inauguration is a time for reflection and renewal — a time for honest evaluation of weaknesses and strengths — and a time for commitment to our vision for the future. By the circumstance of time and place shaped by social, economic, political, and religious realities, this university has served not only as a refuge for those who teach and learn, those who seek, question, and experiment to push forward the frontiers of knowledge — this university has served as a microcosm of American society. Throughout our history we have vigorously pursued our mission of teaching, research, and service, but we have also functioned as a laboratory for leaders, a proving ground for social change, a pioneer in scientific and cultural exploration, and a catalyst in America's struggle for a free and just society. When the doors of the Lyceum swung open on that brisk November day in 1848, a long, exciting, and sometimes difficult journey was begun.

The challenges we confronted cut across the entire spectrum of human experience and emotion — obstacles and opportunities, tragedy and triumph, shame and honor, darkness and enlightenment. On more than one occasion, our very existence was seriously threatened. We are, however, a resilient people, a people of strength and commitment, and those qualities are reflected in the life of this university.

Through the ceremonial passing of the medallion, the future of the university is entrusted to us. As a community we publicly acknowledge our acceptance of the sacred responsibility that we share. We will surely be judged by what we do. But, as President John Kennedy so eloquently stated, we will also be judged by what we are. In a 1961 speech to the State Legislature, he said: "For of those to whom much is given, much is required. And when at some future date, the high court of history sits in judgment on each of us, recording whether in our brief span of service we fulfilled our responsibilities, our success or failure in whatever office we hold will be measured by the answers to four questions:
Were we truly people of courage?
Were we truly people of judgment?
Were we truly people of integrity?
Were we truly people of dedication?"

We are at the edge of a new age, a new century, a new millennium. It is clear that effective and efficient use of technology will be critical to the success of every university. But we realize that technology is not a goal; it is a tool that will make us more efficient in fulfilling our mission to teach, to serve, and to extend the boundaries of useful knowledge. Building on the foundations laid by such dedicated scholars as nineteenth and twentieth century leaders Frederick A.P. Barnard and Arthur Guyton, we will continue to expand our role in providing relevant research for business, industry, and health care. We will serve the educational, social, and environmental needs of the state and nation, and, indeed, the global village.

In this coming age of great change, challenge, and opportunity, we must be open and innovative; but there must also be continuity. During our long journey, we have discovered some great truths, the "old verities," as Mr. Faulkner said. So while we seek, we must also remember.

Excellent teaching is the oldest tradition of this university, begun in 1848 by four faculty teaching classes to eighty students — and excellent teaching must continue to be an expectation if we are to attract and serve an outstanding and diverse student body. William Alexander Percy has reminded us that teaching involves much more than the transfer of knowledge. Describing a favorite teacher, he wrote:

"As with all great teachers, his curriculum was an insignificant part of what he communicated. From him you didn't learn subject . . . but life. Tolerance and justice . . . fearlessness and pride . . . reverence and pity . . . are learned in a course in mathematics . . . if the teacher has those qualities."

Each of us remembers a teacher, or teachers, who made a difference in our lives. They are the teachers who make major investments of themselves in their students, in the classroom, in the laboratory, in the library, at the computer terminal, and out on the campus.

We must never forget that people are the essence of this university — intrinsic and indispensable to our meaningful existence. Against the backdrop of our unique history, enabled and empowered by inherited assets and strengths, and challenged by the compelling needs of a complex world, we accept President Kennedy's challenge, and we will move forward with courage, sound judgment, integrity, and dedication. An organization committed to excellence must have focus and a sense of direction. In our quest for recognition as a great public university, we will:

(1) Strengthen our library and enhance our electronic information systems;
(2) Reward our productive faculty and staff;
(3) Attract the brightest and best students;
(4) Increase support of our teaching and research activities, and;
(5) Transform the Honors Program into an Honors College.

Regarding the Honors College, I have the privilege of announcing that Jim and Sally McDonnell Barksdale, 1965 graduates of the university, have endowed the Honors College with the largest single private donation in the history of the university. Their gift of $5.4 million will provide opportunities for honors students and faculty unsurpassed in American higher education. Today, we gratefully and proudly announce the creation of the McDonnell-Barksdale Honors College at the University of Mississippi.

Earlier this year, our faculty and foundation board accepted my challenge to pursue a chapter of Phi Beta Kappa. No public university in Mississippi has been recognized by that prestigious organization. We believe this university, with its strong liberal arts tradition, and the state of Mississippi deserve that recognition. Our united efforts to enhance the quality of our academic programs should support the Phi Beta Kappa initiative and will assure that we provide an ideal environment for learning and teaching.

Pursuing these goals and others, we will expand our involvement in relevant, life-enhancing research, renew our commitment to excellent teaching, and reach out to serve with compassion and dedication.

I accept this office not as a stranger, but as one who came to this university as an eighteen-year-old and found a home. Like many of you and thousands of other students, I was welcomed, challenged, nurtured, guided, and loved.

The faculty, staff, and my fellow students introduced me to a world of opportunities — the joy of learning and teaching, the rich resource of knowledge so readily accessible at this university and the true meaning of friendship. One of our challenges is to assure that these opportunities are available to all students.

The halls of this university and the hearts of our people are open and inviting. The resources entrusted to us are available and will be utilized for the noble purpose of enhancing lives.

To serve as chancellor of the University of Mississippi is a privilege and an opportunity far beyond my powers to express. On behalf of all who love and care about this university, I accept the trust symbolized by this beautiful medallion, and I pledge to honor that trust with a fidelity worthy of this great institution. God bless you, and God bless the University of Mississippi.

I closed my notebook and walked back toward my seat. To my surprise, the audience was still applauding when I sat down. I looked over at Gloria Kellum. She raised her eyebrow, leaned over, and whispered in my ear.

"Are you out of your *damn mind?*"

Symbols & Substance

38

On October 13, 1996, I was welcomed to the executive offices of the Phi Beta Kappa Society. My host was Douglas Foard, who served as executive secretary of the society. His offices were on the third floor of an historic building off Dupont Circle in Washington, D.C.

When I first talked to Mr. Foard by telephone several weeks earlier, he had expressed genuine surprise that Ole Miss didn't already shelter a chapter of Phi Beta Kappa. On several occasions over the years, we had filed applications with the society. We were a fine, old liberal arts university with an outstanding faculty and excellent students, but for one reason or another we had never survived the application process. Since the time of our first telephone conversation, Mr. Foard had done his research.

Sitting in a leather chair across from Mr Foard's desk, I said, "Doug, why do you think Ole Miss has been denied membership in the past?" Then, I followed with the *real* question: "And what do we need to do in order to be favorably considered by the congress of Phi Beta Kappa?"

Mr. Foard turned the tables and started to ask me questions — about the university, our faculty, students, scholarships, athletics, and research. As he inquired about our school, Mr. Foard offered to provide the guidance we needed to get the application process underway.

We talked for nearly two hours and identified the challenges Ole Miss faced. In fact, we pinpointed five or six rather daunting barriers standing between us and the opportunity for our students to be awarded the internationally respected Key.

My "to do" list included (1) increasing our library holdings; (2) increasing faculty salaries for liberal arts faculty; (3) creating and maintaining a nationally competitive academic program for very bright stu-

things important to him

dents; (4) being removed from NCAA probation; and, finally — and perhaps most importantly — (5) addressing racial issues, including disassociation of the university from the Confederate flag.

At the end of our meeting, Mr. Foard added, "And the application process must be *faculty* driven."

As I left Mr. Foard's office, I thanked him for his generosity, candor, and time.

Flying back to Oxford, I considered the scope and difficulty of the process. None of the obstacles we faced would be easily conquered. And I expected we might face some resistance in distancing ourselves from Confederate symbols. But I was committed to earning a chapter.

Back in Oxford, I invited all Ole Miss faculty who were members of Phi Beta Kappa to a reception at Memory House. About twenty-five professors came to the gathering. I spoke for a few minutes about my hopes for a Phi Beta Kappa chapter, and I outlined the shortcomings identified at the meeting in Washington, as well as my plans to address each impediment.

Then I added, "This application needs to be faculty driven. If any of you are interested in working on the process, please let us know."

As the meeting adjourned, I talked with some of our top scholars about the challenge. In the back of the room, an English professor named Ron Schroeder approached our Provost Gerald Walton.

"I'd like to be a part of this," he said.

39

After a promising 1995 football season, Tommy Tuberville's team took a step backwards during 1996. We edged out one great victory toward the end of the season over Georgia; however, our only other wins came over Idaho State, Virginia Military Institute, Arkansas State, and Vanderbilt. We were pummelled by Auburn, Tennessee, Arkansas, and LSU. In the season finale, Mississippi State dominated the Rebels in a 17-0 loss.

On the Sunday morning following the Mississippi State game, I walked over to the fieldhouse. As I entered the coaches' meeting, I thought someone might have died. The mood was not just somber, it was morose. Assistant coaches stared at the wall. Others had their heads in their hands. Tommy looked like he'd been kicked in the stomach.

"OK, guys," I said, clapping my hands, "We've got to get back up, start working toward next season."

My encouragement was greeted with silence.

"What's going on?" I asked.

Coach Tuberville did not mince words. "We can't recruit against the Confederate flag."

A couple of weeks later, Warner Alford, Eddie Crawford, and I flew to Florida to play a round of golf with Jerry Hollingsworth. Jerry, one of our more dedicated alumni, came to Ole Miss from the small Southwest Mississippi town of Centreville. His family couldn't afford to pay for his college, so he lived in an upstairs room at a physician's clinic, where he worked as a janitor in exchange for rent. Jerry's second job as a student was in the Ole Miss cafeteria. That covered his dining expenses.

Jerry graduated in three years and then went on to Harvard Medical School. Four years later, he received his medical degree and established a successful practice in the Florida Panhandle. During the Vietnam War, he served as part of Project Hope in a military hospital in Korea, where he was provided an unusual automobile. The tiny car was a Toyota Celica.

Jerry was more than impressed with the quality and efficiency of the car, and when he returned home to Fort Walton Beach, he applied for one of the first Toyota dealerships in America.

As we rode together in the golf cart and played the Sandestin course, I told Jerry about my discussions with Douglas Foard, as well as what Tommy Tuberville had said in the coaches' meeting.

"I'm afraid I'm going to have to deal with the Confederate flag," I mentioned.

"You know," Jerry responded, "you'll need a great public relations firm to help you with that battle."

I agreed that a top firm would be a valuable asset, but I was candid about our financial state. "The university doesn't have that kind of discretionary cash."

We didn't discuss the matter again and continued our round of golf. On the drive back to the airport, we detoured by Jerry's office.

"Wait here a moment, if you don't mind," he said. Within a few minutes, he came back to the car. "This should cover the cost of professional help," he said.

Jerry handed me a check. It was made out to the University Foundation — in the amount of $200,000.

Upon my return from Florida, my first telephone call was to Harold Burson. Harold came to Ole Miss as a sixteen-year-old freshman from Memphis. His parents were immigrants from England. The Bursons were in the hardware business, but their Memphis store did not survive the Depression. To support the family, Burson's mother sold clothes door-to-door. To pay the costs of his undergraduate education, Harold worked as a "stringer" and cub reporter for *The Commercial Appeal*.

Harold served as a public affairs officer in World War II, after which he pursued a career in public relations in New York City. Soon he had a reputation as an extraordinary publicist (his first client was featured in *Time*, *Life*, and *Reader's Digest*), as well as a groundbreaking thinker in integrated marketing. In 1953, Harold joined Bill Marsteller to establish Burson-Marsteller. Since then, the agency had grown to be the largest, most respected public relations firm in the world. Harold's clients included General Motors, Tylenol, and Coca-Cola, and he managed offices across the United States and eighty-one foreign nations. In the 1980s, Burson-Marsteller was the first public relations firm to gross $100 million in a single year.

But what mattered most to me was that Harold Burson loved Ole Miss.

When he picked up the phone, I said, "Harold, I need your help."

When he asked for details, I explained that I wanted to have a better understanding of the university's image. And that I also wanted to change the perception of Ole Miss nationally, as well as internally. Finally, I said, I wanted to secure a chapter of Phi Beta Kappa. "And I'm going to have to deal with some of our symbols," I added.

"Such as?" he asked.

"Primarily," I answered, "the flag."

Harold agreed on the spot to help, and he assigned three of his brightest people to the project. We scheduled an initial meeting for late February.

When the team members from Burson-Marsteller arrived on campus in late February to begin the review of our image, they met with students, faculty, staff, administrators, alumni, and representatives from athletics. Everything seemed to be on the table for discussion — from self-perception to academic programs, street signs to architecture, landscaping to mascots. Nothing, it seemed, would be overlooked.

At dusk on Wednesday evening, I walked across campus to attend a reception at Barnard Observatory, named for the third chancellor of our university, Frederick A.P. Barnard.

Despite a severe hearing impairment, Barnard was a brilliant, progressive scholar. He grew up in Massachusetts and graduated second in his class at Yale. Barnard, appointed chancellor in 1856, was hugely popular with students, but Mississippi politicians, clergy, and press accused him of turning the university into a *citadel of atheism* and *a hotbed of abolitionism.*

During his time at the university, Barnard worked diligently to build an "ideal university" by expanding courses of study, purchasing scientific instruments, and emphasizing original investigation, not simply memorization. Barnard built what would have become the world's most advanced observatory. He commissioned Alvan Clark & Sons to build the greatest refracting telescope ever known. It would hold the world's largest ground lens at eighteen-and-a-half inches. The building was completed in 1859, but the Civil War broke out before the telescope arrived at our campus. Union soldiers intercepted the telescope, put it on a train, and it eventually landed at Northwestern University, where it is still in use today. On occasion I have thought about asking Northwestern to return it.

Barnard eventually went on to be president of Columbia University — and Barnard College was named in his honor. When entering the historic building, I often thought of Chancellor Barnard, a man who embraced excellence and had an unwavering vision for the future of the university.

I stepped inside Barnard Observatory and mingled with students and faculty dressed in business attire. I moved from group to group, hoping to speak to as many people as possible, when I recognized a student who seemed a bit out of place. She wore blue jeans and a sweatshirt, held a reporter's pad, and was walking toward me. I went to greet her, hoping to make her feel more comfortable.

"Chancellor Khayat," she said, holding out her hand. "Do you have a moment? I'd like to ask you a few questions."

"Well, of course, Jenny," I said.

I suggested we move to the end of the hall where it would be quieter. Jenny Dodson, the news editor at the student newspaper, and I walked down the wooden, antebellum hallway toward the east wing of Barnard Observatory. When we reached the end of the hall, I sat down on an old radiator so we could talk at eye level.

Ms. Dodson laughed and said, "I guess I really have you on the hot seat."

I smiled and checked the radiator for heat, even though I knew it hadn't been used in decades. Then Ms. Dodson asked her first question.

"Is it true that a public relations firm is on campus reviewing the university symbols?"

"Yes," I said. "Our plan is to review everything that affects our image."

"Does that include the flag?" she asked.

"Our plan is to look at everything, so I guess that includes the flag."

Ms. Dodson made a note and then asked, "So are Colonel Rebel, the nickname Rebels, and *Dixie* all up for review?"

I paused, weighing my response carefully. I spoke slowly so that Ms. Dodson would get every word right.

"For way too long," I said, "the public perception, and sometimes our internal perception, has been inaccurate and too heavily influenced by negative events of our past." I watched as Ms. Dodson made notes on her pad. When she'd caught up with me, I continued, "We need to get rid of negative perceptions. They impede our mission and our destiny."

Ms. Dodson asked a few more follow-up questions. At the end of our talk, I reiterated that everything was on the table, even items as mundane as new street names that would make the campus more inviting.

"We're entering the process with no preconceived notions," I told her.

The next morning I picked up a copy of *The Daily Mississippian* and took it into my office to read the story. The front-page headline ran across all five columns — *Several university symbols up for image review.*

As I read the piece, I was struck by how accurate Ms. Dodson had been in her reportage. She didn't misquote me, she interviewed a balanced group of students, and she correctly related the history of the Confederate flag's being disassociated from the university in 1983. *Fine journalist*, I thought.

What I failed to realize, and had no way of knowing at the moment, was that this story, published on Thursday, February 27, 1997, in our small, student-run newspaper, would spark a media firestorm. The story would be picked up by every major national media outlet.

And my life would never be the same.

Several university symbols up for image review

JENNY DODSON
News Editor

Almost 14 years since the Confederate flag was officially disassociated with the university, other university images may now face the same fate.

Colonel Reb, the nickname Rebels and the fight song Dixie are all up for review by two independent marketing firms commissioned by Chancellor Robert Khayat to improve the image of the university.

"For way too long the public perception, and sometimes our internal perception has been inaccurate and too heavily influenced by negative events in our past,"

Khayat said. "We need to get rid of negative perceptions. They impede our mission and our destiny."

Representatives from the firms are examining the image of Ole Miss through meetings with students, faculty, administrators, staff and alumni. From those meetings they will make recommendations for any changes to any of the school's existing official symbols or names.

The firms will turn in their proposals and budgets to Khayat within two weeks. The first firm to visit Ole Miss came last week, and another firm will visit next week.

The representatives met with

nine students on Friday and a large group of alumni, faculty, administrators, staff and students on Saturday.

Brandon Powell, a white senior Southern studies major, sat on the student panel last week.

"They (the firm representatives) were trying to gauge student reaction if they tried to down play Colonel Reb and the Rebels on campus." Powell said. "They asked how we would react to seeing some of the symbols of the university changed."

Shekela Joiner, a black graduate student, attended both meetings and said she believes the university symbols will change, but "the students are the key.

"The students have to ultimately be the ones to do it," Joiner said. She said the Confederate flag is still carried by students today because the administration made the decision to ban the flag as a university symbol without student involve-

ment.

"The administration can develop a plan tomorrow, but until they have the students behind them, it's going to be hard," she said.

Please see **Changes**, page 6

Evers-Williams speaks to UM

TONY PLOHETSKI
Senior Staff Writer

Wednesday's threatening skies stopped few people from attending the Myrlie Evers-Williams lecture, as the crowd poured over into Fulton Chapel aisles.

Evers-Williams' note-free

Evers-Williams' second visit to Ole Miss, but she said an ice storm hindered her from seeing much of the campus the first time.

While neither she nor Evers attended Ole Miss, she said her late husband had applied to attend the university's law school during the 1950s but was denied because of

in my life, in Edgar's life, this is my state. There is a degree of anger, but lots of love," she said.

Evers-Williams said several years after her husband's death, she had feelings of hatred, until one of her three children reminded her of one of Evers' messages.

"One of my children heard me

The Daily Mississippian front page from February 27, 1997

40

When Jenny Dodson's story was picked up by the Associated Press, the Lyceum became a flashpoint for radicals on the far right, liberals on the far left, and every point in between.

The story ran in *The Clarion-Ledger*, *The Commercial Appeal*, *The Times-Picayune* and *The Atlanta Journal-Constitution*. Letters to the editor poured in by the hundreds. Most dripped with sarcasm and anger.

A letter from a lawyer in Jackson that ran in *The Clarion-Ledger* suggested we rename the football team "The Guilt." He added that we should change the school colors to "blush red."

Another letter recommended steps that included "eradication of magnolia trees and antebellum architecture" on campus.

From a far different perspective, the president of the Black Student Union told a reporter that Ole Miss still operated on "a plantation mentality." She added, "This is a university. It's not a shrine for the preservation of the relics of the Civil War."

Despite the fact that Ole Miss officially disassociated itself from the Confederate flag in 1983, in the minds of the general public, the symbol and the university seemed synonymous.

In early March, *The New York Times* dispatched its Atlanta bureau reporter Kevin Sack to Oxford. Mr. Sack arrived in my office for the first time on March 5, 1997.

I liked him the moment we met. Kevin was not a large man. He stood five feet ten inches and couldn't have weighed more than 170 pounds. Kevin was personable and warm, and didn't seem to have any preconceived notions about Ole Miss and the South. I assumed that living in Atlanta had given him some opportunities to understand the cultural differences between the Northeast and the Deep South.

I explained to Kevin that this review and study being conducted by the PR firm was initially about our general image. I had asked for professional help because I wanted to know what we could do to improve Ole Miss and, at the same time, change the negative perceptions associated with the university.

Kevin stayed on campus for several days and we talked at great length. We enjoyed several meals together, and I invited him to sit in the chancellor's box for a football game in the fall.

While on campus, he interviewed students, faculty, and alumni, as well as Harold Burson and me.

But Kevin was particularly curious about the emotional reaction to the public discussion about the flag. Especially its association with Ole Miss. I didn't even understand it at the time, but the emotionally complex, often blind devotion to Confederate symbols ran deeper than I had ever imagined.

Interestingly, our attempt to conduct a comprehensive review of our university — how we were perceived by others and why they had positive or negative feelings about us — soon shifted to a single-issue controversy about the flag.

When Kevin's story broke in the *Times* on March 12, 1997, the headline read: *Symbols of the Old South Stir a College Campus.* The two photos accompanying the piece included an image of the Confederate monument in the Circle and a photograph of me.

That's when the real trouble started.

41

The letters, telephone calls, and fax messages started pouring into the Lyceum. They came from all corners of the United States. Some arrived from Europe.

A few supported my efforts in the image review, but the vast majority came in the form of condemnatory allegations. By far, the loudest, meanest, and most prolific came from people from states other than Mississippi. That such a local issue had become national, even international, in scope astonished me.

From the outset, the letters focused on my "treasonous behavior" and attempts to destroy the "heritage" of the South. The writers — from Montana, South Carolina, Maine, and Michigan — somehow claimed an ownership interest in the state of Mississippi, Ole Miss, and the university's athletics spirit program, though they had absolutely no connection with the university.

But some did come from Mississippians. Letters from friends, classmates, former teachers, and coaches pleaded with me to stop erasing symbols that held deep meaning for them and the school they loved.

One letter contained a tape recording from a Mississippi minister's sermon. The preacher, from a nearby church, delivered a rousing message to his congregation about how it was absolutely and simply "un-Christian" to consider any changes in the use of the Confederate flag.

Among the boxes that arrived at the Lyceum was one bearing a return address I recognized. It was from a friend from Starkville (home of our in-state rival Mississippi State). My assistant opened the box and brought it into my office. She handed it to me, and I looked inside. It was a complete set of women's pink underwear. The note inside read: *Try these, Robert. They should fit.*

I dictated a return note thanking him for the thoughtful gift and encouraging note. Then I placed the box of underwear in a corner of my office.

But not all the communications from friends and associates were as lighthearted. At my home on a Saturday morning, I received a telephone call from a former coach — a man I had called a friend for nearly 40 years.

"You are destroying the university," he shouted into the receiver. I listened quietly until he finished yelling.

"I'm sorry you feel that way. I hope we'll get through this process together," I said. He hung up on me.

He wasn't the only friend to call . . . or react. During the first two weeks of the controversy, my office received more than 150 letters. Some of the messages were nothing more than angry diatribes. Most expressed confusion about my motives.

When I fielded telephone calls, my attempts to rationally discuss the subject were complete failures. I faced a complex, emotionally charged issue that evoked feelings I could not combat. The best I could do was listen, be as polite and civil as possible, and empathize with any pain or discomfort they felt during the process.

Those of us who grew up in the white South, and particularly Mississippi, were so accustomed to Old South songs and sights and symbols during sporting events that the origins of the emblems weren't carefully considered. Nor was the pain they caused others.

In my childhood bedroom, two small, vividly colored Confederate flags hung over my bedroom door. I saw them every morning when I awoke and every evening when I climbed into bed. I didn't know anything about the history of the flags, but I loved the red and blue colors. As I grew and started to follow football, I associated the flag with the great Ole Miss football teams of the 1940s and 1950s. And as a teenager, when I heard the term "Johnny Rebel," I assumed the reference was to Johnny Vaught's Ole Miss Rebel football squad.

I think that many dedicated Ole Miss football fans from the 1940s to the 1990s had similarly naïve — if not innocent — attachments to the symbols. For many of us, the fact that the flag was being waved on behalf of extremist political positions didn't matter. Of course,

Governor Ross Barnett had embraced the darker side of the symbols during the integration crisis at Ole Miss, taking center stage at halftime of a football game to link the school's traditions with the importance of maintaining segregation. But for most of us, most of the time, those symbols had been more benign. That may seem naïve in retrospect, but those who embrace symbols don't always think about what they represent to others.

On any given fall Saturday, the Ole Miss stadium was packed with tens of thousands of fans cheering on great athletes. The cheerleaders would throw bundles of colorful flags into the student section of the stadium, the smell of bourbon and cigar smoke wafted through the stands, the air was filled with music from the Ole Miss Band — the Pride of the South — and the crowd chanted the "Hotty Toddy" cheer in unison. And, during Coach Vaught's tenure, the team usually won the game.

Not unlike the spectacle of a religious tent revival, the drama and action and sounds and sights of college football turned otherwise mild-mannered men, women, and children into screaming, joy-filled zealots. Mothers and fathers brought their sons and daughters to the games, as they had for generations, to share — and pass along the traditions of — the revelry.

Those friends and alumni who didn't fully understand our review process believed it was these memories I was trying to take away.

42

The University of Mississippi opened its doors in 1848. As a Deep South university founded before the Civil War, it's no surprise that for the first one hundred and fourteen years we were a racially segregated school.

To say that the Civil War left a lasting mark on the university is a huge understatement. When the war broke out, most of the students joined the Confederate army. In the fall of 1861, only four students showed up and classes were cancelled. Almost all of the students joined a Confederate unit called the University Greys. The Greys saw action in most of the major battles of the Civil War. At Gettysburg every member of the unit was either captured, wounded, or killed. None of the Greys enrolled again after the war.

The Lyceum was used as a hospital to treat Confederate and Union soldiers after the Battle of Shiloh. And after the war, the university was led from 1874 to 1886 by former Confederate general A.P. Stewart.

Despite our deep ties to the Civil War, by Mississippi standards, the university was considered by many to be liberal. We were one of the first universities in the South to admit women when we became coeducational in 1882. And in 1885, we were the very first university in the Southeast to hire a female faculty member.

During the fall of 1962, while the crisis at Ole Miss grabbed national headlines, I was involved in a very different kind of integration. I was in my third year with the Washington Redskins. The Redskins were the last NFL team to integrate. But in 1962, several black players were signed. One of them was Bobby Mitchell. Bobby was an extraordinarily talented receiver and runner, and he was exactly the spark the Redskins needed. Although Bobby played college football at Illinois, he spent his childhood in Arkansas. Bobby and I discovered we had

.nuch in common.

We were both huge fans of Randy's Record Shop on radio station WLAC. The station broadcast early rhythm and blues. Bobby and I both heard, for the first time, Ray Charles, Fats Domino, and Chuck Berry on WLAC. During training camp in Carlisle, Pennsylvania, Bobby and I became close friends. In fact, I had been encouraging him to come visit me in Mississippi after the season ended.

As the tensions grew during the latter part of September 1962, Bobby and I followed the events in the newspaper and on television, and we talked almost every day about the growing controversy. Both of us wondered what would happen the day James Meredith came to the campus for registration. The Cuban missile crisis was heating up at the time, but the Ole Miss-Meredith story took over the front pages of the nation's newspapers. Bobby and I speculated. He feared the worst, while I thought that if Governor Barnett would stay out of it, integration might be noisy and nasty but it wouldn't get out of control. It never occurred to me that we would experience a full-scale riot.

I was wrong. The tragic series of events permanently scarred the university and, to some degree, the state. I can only imagine the emotional toll it took on James Meredith.

Watching the television news reports with Bobby from my apartment in Washington, I found it difficult to believe that my beautiful campus was under siege. As Bobby and I watched the battle taking place in the center of the campus, we kept our conversation as light as possible. I told him that all of the screaming and rock throwing would be over soon, and he could come to see us and "really get to know" Mississippi.

Bobby tilted his head, smiled, and said in a deep Arkansas drawl, "Bob, you must be crazy. I'm never coming to Mississippi."

Given what we were seeing on television, I could not blame him.

Unfortunately, the riot was real. The images of rioters, U.S. Marshals, National Guard troops, and tear gas were permanently etched in the nation's psyche.

It was a sad time for Ole Miss, James Meredith, our students, the people of Mississippi, and the nation. And I felt helpless being so far away from home.

But Ole Miss was finally integrated. The admission of black students finally — albeit far too late — became a reality. The events of 1962 did open the doors, ever so slowly, for more and more qualified Mississippians. However, black students were not initially encouraged to attend Ole Miss, and many were reluctant to do so. Their families had no interest in sending their children to a school where they were not wanted or welcome. There was also concern, I'm sure, about their safety.

The response to breaking the color barrier at the Redskins could not have been more different from what happened at Ole Miss. The players were greeted with enthusiasm. The white players generally welcomed Bobby Mitchell and other black players with open arms. We wanted to win.

Too many people in Mississippi chose a different route. They could have prevented the riots, but they were more concerned about resisting change. In protecting the status quo, the damage they inflicted on the university's reputation was almost insurmountable. The stigma plagued us for more than thirty years.

Harold Burson's team got busy. They conducted a telephone survey of 1,500 randomly selected individuals in the South. The interviews consisted of twenty questions about five colleges and universities — the University of Alabama, the University of Georgia, the University of North Carolina, the University of Mississippi, and Arkansas State University.

At the conclusion of the survey, Burson-Marsteller presented us with a comprehensive report on the image of Ole Miss, including comparisons to other Southern institutions.

The survey produced some fascinating overall results. The college considered "the best" by those surveyed was the University of Alabama. In the follow-up question — "What makes you think Alabama is the best school?" — the number one answer was "Bear Bryant."

The news about our image was depressing. The vast majority of the survey participants knew nothing about Ole Miss. It appeared that we had *no reputation* to speak of. But among those who did have an opinion about Ole Miss, they still perceived it as a "racist" institution. And most of them associated the Confederate flag with the school. Since 1962, the Confederate flag had been adopted by the Ku Klux Klan, skinheads, and Neo-Nazis. Worldwide, the flag had become a symbol of hate, particularly among those groups that held negative feelings about black people. The survey clearly confirmed our earlier unscientific conclusions about how we were perceived. The results were clear. Among our symbols, songs, mascots, and names, the Confederate flag was by far the most damaging to us.

The survey confirmed we had much work to do. But I made a firm commitment to change these perceptions by addressing the most detrimental representation associated with our university — the Confederate flag.

However, we had a challenge. Owning and displaying *any* flag was the right of every U.S. citizen. And that right was protected by the First Amendment to the Constitution of the United States.

43

I thought the flow of letters and phone calls would subside, but the weeks following *The New York Times* story proved to be some of the most volatile.

The Heritage Defense Committee launched a letter-writing campaign that resulted in more than 3,000 letters arriving at the Lyceum accusing me of *lynching Ole Miss*. The pre-addressed envelopes were printed with the plea: *Stop Robert Khayat from destroying our university*.

The form letters from fringe groups were certainly a distraction, but the most hurtful communications came from those closest to me. Longtime friends and associates wrote caustic letters expressing their bitterness toward me. Others ridiculed my actions as "selling out" to liberal interests. Still others mocked my efforts to take an objective look at our public image.

But that wasn't as difficult as the personal encounters. There were friends who shunned or simply ignored me. Walking across campus or around the Oxford Square, I would make eye contact with friends and see their smiles disappear. They would press their lips together tight and look away as they passed me.

I felt an emptiness every time it happened. But what made it worse was knowing that my actions made them feel this way, as if I had been a disloyal friend.

I have always believed in the power of prayer, and never before during my career as a leader was divine intervention more wanted or needed. Whenever I could slip away from meetings and calls, I would say a four-point prayer. First, I would pray for *wisdom*. The wisdom to make sound, fair decisions in the face of such incendiary topics. Next, I would pray for *courage*. Courage to know when to step up to a challenge. Courage to stand up to the onslaught of opinions. Third, I prayed for *energy*. For the physical, mental, and emotional resources to see me through this process. I feared I might crumble under the destructive fatigue, and I often found myself asking, "Is it really worth it?" The final piece of my prayer was for *peace*. I knew I wouldn't survive if I could not find the time for rest and solitude. I needed to be at my best during this time.

The prayers brought me a great deal of comfort, but at times I couldn't remove myself, emotionally, from the controversy.

My sister Kathy sent me a page she had removed from a collection of notes children had written to God. The page Kathy gave me was written by a boy named Frank, and it read: "Dear God, I am doing the best I can. Frank." I kept Frank's note in the top drawer of my desk and pulled it out whenever I needed a smile . . . or some inspiration.

There were also times when none of this kept me out of the fray. I simply couldn't ignore the calls and letters and pleas. That's when I would reach out to Harold Burson.

"They are killing me," I told him. "Let them have their damn flag."

Harold's voice and demeanor were calm. "Robert," he said, "you can't do that." He would remind me of all that was at stake. The future of the university, a capital campaign with $200 million still to be raised, a Phi Beta Kappa chapter . . . not to mention doing what was right. Harold went on. "You are the only person in the world who can do this."

Harold was generally able to talk me back down. His counsel proved invaluable.

As the days turned to weeks and the weeks turned to months, I wavered. At times I was certain we were doing the right thing. At other times, I had great doubts.

During a particularly rough day in June, I had been grilled by television reporters and two new factions — one that supported retaining the song *Dixie*; another that considered it racist and insensitive.

It was never my intent to address any symbol or song except the flag. I suppose it was natural for many people to think I wanted to stop playing *Dixie*, but I have always loved the song and the excitement it evokes at sporting events.

That afternoon, with the sun beginning to set, I wanted to escape. I wanted the chatter to disappear. I wanted the fighting to stop. I wanted all the talk of flags and mascots and songs to go away.

I sat on my porch and daydreamed of a simpler time. A time in my childhood when I spent my days on the Pascagoula River. For eighty miles or so, the river runs through the swampy bottomlands of southeastern Mississippi in a rich network of channels and bayous before it empties into the Gulf of Mexico. The Pascagoula is frequently brackish — a mixture of fresh and salt water — and is home to cypress swamps and pine ridges, the predatory falcon and the spindly-legged egret. Like the land through which it flows, the river is home to a diverse population — alligators, raccoons, otters, turtles, muskrats, snakes, and bald eagles. They seek refuge and food in and along the river and its soggy banks.

Growing up in Moss Point, my friends and I were children of this river. The Pascagoula was our soundtrack as we paddled and drifted, swam and floated in her waters. The croaking of the frogs and the rhythm of the current, the call of the birds, the splash of jumping fish, the rustling of the tall grasses when disturbed by fox … this was the sound of my childhood.

The Pascagoula River is also known as the Singing River. According to Native American legend, the peace-loving Pascagoula Indians were facing attack from the physically superior Biloxi Indians. Rather than accept enslavement or certain death at the hands of the Biloxi tribe, the Pascagoula Indians joined hands and began to chant a song of death as they marched into the river. Led by the women and children, they marched on until the waters extinguished the last voice.

In the late evenings during summer and autumn, the hum of the river is like a swarm of bees in flight. It begins as a soft buzz, then grows louder and nearer until it surrounds me.

After all these years, I still tune into the rhythms of my surroundings. I try to be mindful of the sounds that emanate from soil, foliage, air, and waterways — a result of my days and nights spent on the Pascagoula River.

When I am in unfamiliar territory — geographically or emotion-ally — this earth-song is muted, but when I am centered and on my native soil, music floods my soul. The sound of my childhood river still strikes a chord in my heart, one that unlocks memories of carefree days and brings me a sense of deep peace.

This is my favorite song.

44

"Chancellor," the police officer said as he walked through my office door, "we need to talk."

I stood, took off my glasses, and asked him to have a seat.

The officer handed me a one-page fax. "You need to see this," he said.

I put on my glasses and picked up the handwritten note. It opened, *Dear Traitor, It is clear from your last name that you were not born in the United States of America.*

The writer went into a diatribe of cursing and accusations, not unlike hundreds of other letters we had received. But then, it took a turn.

Try as you may to vilify our heritage and spit on the graves of our ancestors, but I can promise you will never live to see that day. You may think you are safe, but you will never see us coming. Your family will never see us coming.

I handed the letter back to the police officer. "What do we do about this?" I asked.

The officer looked down at the floor. "First, we need to alert the FBI." He paused and looked back up at me. "Then, we need to talk about how to protect you and Margaret. And your children."

When FBI agents arrived at the Lyceum in 1997 in response to the death threats, everything about our routine was scrutinized — from how we opened the mail to how we greeted visitors. They warned us that anthrax attacks were a possibility, as were explosive devices shipped in boxes. The administrative assistants in our offices were, understandably, terrified. I was concerned for the safety of our students, faculty, and staff.

FBI agents asked us to send any threatening mail to their offices for investigation. They insisted that all mail be opened with protective

racism, people did not
want to get rid of the
confederate flag

On May 14, 1997, Mississippi State Senator Mike Gunn spoke in the Circle
at Ole Miss. A gentleman wearing a black hood and sheet (portraying me) symbolically
beheaded Colonel Rebel. Senator Gunn and his associates dramatized the beheading as part
of a four-city tour to persuade the university to retain its Old South symbols.

just because something is a
tradition does not mean it's a
good thing

174 Robert Khayat

masks and gloves, and they placed security guards outside t
cellor's residence around the clock.

Demonstrators continued to converge on campus. At first, they
were simply disruptive. Now we were worried about the safety of our
students. To avoid disruption of normal university life, we were forced
to establish "free speech" zones on campus — and to ban demonstrations in the Grove and the Circle.

The count of letters written by individuals with regard to the university's image review neared 1,000. About 80 percent expressed opposition to retiring any Old South symbols associated with the
university.

Perhaps I should have been fearful for my own safety, but I wasn't.
In fact, I was more determined than ever to do what needed to be
done to move this university toward greatness. The death threats made
me angry. And I planned to use that anger as fuel to fight this battle.

After we received our fourth or fifth death threat, CBS News sent
a crew to interview me and cover the controversy. I was ready for
them. *About the flag, and how he is changing*

"Ole Miss," I said in a prepared statement, "is not the last bastion *old*
of the Confederacy, nor are we the national repository for racial guilt. *tradition*
We are a modern, progressive university with a long and rich history."

Then I told them that we had a university to operate. We had
classes, labs, libraries, academic programs, research, student-life activities, and all the other responsibilities of a modern university.

From that moment on, and in every conversation or public presentation regarding the issue, I acknowledged the errors and tragedies
of the past but fiercely advanced our positive forward movement.

And I reminded them that we had work to do.

The death threats were obviously disconcerting, but things could
have been worse. I needed to remind myself of that.

On August 2, 1990, I was at the White House with President
George H.W. Bush to tape a public service announcement. I was serving as president of the NCAA Foundation, a group dedicated to promoting academic success for NCAA student athletes. President Bush

had played first base during his college years at Yale. He was a strong advocate of higher education, but he also believed that participation in athletics helps young people build character and learn discipline and teamwork. He was also concerned about the low graduation rates of college athletes. He was the perfect person to star in our television commercial.

When I arrived at the White House the morning of the taping, I was escorted to the area where the portico is located. All of the filming equipment was in place, the president's makeup person was there along with the director and the film crew. The morning was perfect — blue sky, slight breeze, lovely flower beds, and a manicured lawn.

The president arrived at exactly nine o'clock, dressed in a blue suit, white shirt, and blue and orange tie. We shook hands and talked for a few minutes. He asked about the purpose of the taping. When he learned I was from Oxford, he started asking about our mutual friend Willie Morris. The president and Willie frequently exchanged handwritten notes.

As the president stood in the designated position for the taping, he motioned for me to come closer.

"Robert," he asked, "do you think my tie is OK?"

I looked down at his tie and paused. What could I say: "Mr. President, you need to go change ties"?

"These are the Illinois colors," he said. "I don't want to offend any school or look like I'm biased."

"Mr. President," I said, "those are also the colors of Florida and Auburn."

He smiled. I told him I thought the tie was great.

As we began taping, an army general appeared and whispered something into the president's ear. President Bush asked us to excuse him. "I'll be right back," he said.

After about five minutes, the president returned, and the taping resumed. A few minutes later, the general reappeared, again whispered in the president's ear, and the president asked us once more to excuse him. This time the president was gone for about thirty minutes.

When he returned, he apologized profusely. He picked up exactly where we left off, delivered his lines with great calm, and successfully completed the spot. We shook hands, and I thanked the president for his time.

"Give my best to Willie," he said. Then he went back into the White House.

Two days later, the U.S. bombed Kuwait. The Iraqi Republican Guard had overrun the small, oil-rich country. Saddam Hussein announced that Kuwait had been annexed and declared the land the nineteenth province of Iraq.

As I followed the news reports about the U.S. offensive, I realized that President Bush had been called away from our taping to make decisions about a military offensive against Saddam's troops.

Each time the president returned from the military strategy sessions, he seemed as pleasant and relaxed as he might have been at a family gathering.

I was thankful that the issues I dealt with daily were not of the same magnitude as President Bush's. He would make decisions that, literally, cost thousands of human lives.

I also learned a valuable lesson about leadership and compartmentalization.

In our personal lives, compartmentalization can be a dangerous exercise. However, for a leader in the midst of a crisis, it's vital for survival. President Bush moved easily from one setting to another, leaving his emotions and concerns about the impending crisis in a compartment that didn't spill over into all the others.

I found myself in a similar, albeit smaller, situation. Almost daily as chancellor, I was required to move from a conversation with an angry individual to an awards ceremony, to a funeral visitation, to a civic club speech, to a meeting about our symbols.

I feared the controversy over the Confederate flag was tainting everything I touched.

I was determined to get back to mental and emotional normalcy, so on the morning of August 27, 1997, I put the flag controversy in a box and picked up a copy of *The Daily Mississippian*. The front page photograph featured a few freshmen sitting in the grass wearing khaki shorts, t-shirts, and flip-flops. The caption under the photo simply read: *Girl Watching*.

I noticed that one of the young men was identified as Jerry Abdalla Jr. When I was a law professor, Jerry Abdalla Sr. was a law student. I had only seen Jerry Sr. once since he graduated, but I knew he lived in McComb. I didn't know if he was practicing law or if he was running a business, but I thought he'd like to see the newspaper clipping.

I cut out the photo and caption, wrote a note to Jerry Sr., telling him how great it was to have another Abdalla at Ole Miss, and invited him to come see us.

Within a few days, I received a call from Jerry Sr.

"We need to talk," he said.

We scheduled a visit for the following week.

When Jerry arrived in Oxford he explained that he had not been practicing law. He had been working with Croft Industries, a company that manufactured vinyl and aluminum windows and patio doors. The company was founded in Jamestown, New York, but moved its operations to McComb in the early 1960s. Jerry told me the company employed about 500 people and was one of the largest aluminum, vinyl window, and storm door suppliers in the country.

Then, Jerry said that a foundation — the Joseph C. Bancroft Charitable and Educational Fund — had been created by the founder.

"I'd like to use some of the profits from our investments to help Ole Miss," he said.

"Great," I said. "What do you have in mind?"

Jerry wasn't exactly sure what he wanted to do with the funds, but he wanted them to make an impact.

It's difficult to talk directly about money, but I didn't have any idea how much money he was considering giving or the scope of a new project.

"Jerry," I asked, "do you have any figures in mind?"

Jerry nodded. "About $60 million."

45

I picked up the telephone and invited Carolyn Ellis Staton to join Jerry and me in my office. I asked Jerry to tell Carolyn all about Croft Industries and the Bancroft Foundation. Within a few minutes Carolyn introduced the concept for an international studies program. Jerry loved the idea.

Carolyn and her colleagues immediately started to produce a detailed outline of the institute, while Jerry, his accountant, Bob Byrd, and our CFO, Rex Deloach, spent the next few weeks hammering out an agreement.

The following day, Lee Paris called my office to talk about a new campus chapel.

As far back as 1956, when I was a freshman at Ole Miss, I had overheard discussions about building a new chapel on campus. There was lots of talk, but little action.

In 1975, when Polly Williams became director of religious life, the topic was revived. She convinced Chancellor Porter Fortune to form a committee to explore options for a new chapel. The committee developed a plan, talked about a site, and accumulated nearly $12,000. One of the most passionate undergraduate students on that committee was Indianola native Lee Paris. Again, although the idea of a chapel had merit, the committee had little power to push the university to take concrete steps.

Twenty-one years later, Lee Paris called to schedule an appointment to discuss the chapel. Lee was now a successful businessman in Jackson. He came to my office with his father, Henry Paris.

Lee and Henry wanted the building to be clearly marked as a house of worship and prayer, but I had bad news for my friends. I explained that a chapel on public property couldn't have a cross or other religious symbols that identify the building. I added that the chapel would also have to be architecturally compatible with other buildings on campus.

Lee and Henry left my office feeling rather dejected. I couldn't blame them. To conceive and build a nonsectarian structure that would meet the needs of all students, as well as withstand the close scrutiny of those who object to the presence of a religious structure on government property, was challenging.

Over the next few months, we made some progress. We asked the University of Mississippi Foundation to build the chapel. The foundation is a private, not-for-profit organization. It is not funded by tax-payer dollars.

Then, without my knowledge, Lee and Henry Paris decided to provide the chapel's lead gift in excess of a half-million dollars. They were also determined to have a symbol that I believed might provoke the ire of groups that defend the First Amendment directives that separate church and state.

Lee and Henry Paris scheduled a meeting at the offices of the Jackson headquarters of the Mississippi chapter of the American Civil Liberties Union.

The state ACLU board had gathered, along with its legal council, to hear the Parises' plan for a stained-glass window to be erected in a yet-to-be-built chapel on the Ole Miss campus.

Henry grew up in the small Mississippi town of Lexington. He was the only son of Jewish parents. When Henry's best friend decided to go to Ole Miss, Henry chose to join him. Friends and relatives had warned him — *Henry, Jewish people don't go to Ole Miss.* They suggested he try another school, perhaps Tulane, but Henry didn't listen. He followed his friend to Oxford.

The first year on the Ole Miss campus wasn't easy for Henry. All the fraternities except one — a small Jewish fraternity — rejected him based on his religious affiliation. But Henry was gregarious and likable and gently tenacious. He was selected to be an Ole Miss cheerleader, and his personality filled a room. Soon, Ole Miss students started to not only accept Henry as part of the Ole Miss family but also enthu-siastically embrace him. By the time he was a senior, the student body elected Henry as Colonel Rebel — the university's equivalent of Mr. Ole Miss. During this period, Henry met fellow student Rose Leonard of Kosciusko. Rose's grandmother was a founding member of the national Delta Gamma sorority in the 1870s.

As Henry addressed the members of the ACLU, he told the story of his courtship of Rose. The two lived in the Mississippi Delta. When they decided to marry, Rose's Presbyterian church refused to bless a union between a Christian and a Jew. Henry's temple in the Delta had a capacity of a few dozen individuals. Henry and Rose's options were limited. They decided to marry at the Delta Gamma sorority house on the Ole Miss campus.

As Henry told the ACLU board about the obstacles he and Rose overcame during the 1950s, in what was then considered a mixed mar-riage, he also talked about the importance of a nondenominational place of worship on the Ole Miss campus.

The Paris family loved Ole Miss, and they wanted to support a place of worship for students of all beliefs and denominations; how-ever, Henry and Lee also wanted the chapel to house a stained-glass window that represented the union of Henry and Rose — and the faiths of Judaism and Christianity.

Henry and Lee had commissioned a design that blended the Star of David together with a cross, clearly marking the building as a house of worship. Lee showed the ACLU board an illustration of the win-dow.

The board president said, "We've never had anyone ask for per-mission in advance."

Lee told the group that the Paris family was not going to invest a sum worthy of a lead gift if they would eventually have to remove the window. He made it clear to the ACLU board that their gift wasn't assured unless the window that featured the union of the Star of David and the cross would be permanent.

The lawyer for the ACLU explained that the U.S. courts had been split on when a religious symbol could stay on a public building and when it had to be removed.

"In one case in Bartlesville, Oklahoma," the lawyer explained, "the symbol was removed because it was strictly a religious icon." Then he continued, "In the second case, at Stephen F. Austin, the religious symbol was determined to be nonreligious because it also served as a family crest." The lawyer paused and then asked, "Is this a family crest or symbol?"

Henry raised an eyebrow and looked over at his son. Lee smiled and nodded.

"Yes," Henry said, as he turned back toward the ACLU board members. "It is."

"And how long has this been a family symbol?" the lawyer asked.

"About thirty seconds," Henry said.

The Parises left the room while the Mississippi chapter of the ACLU board discussed the family's stained-glass window design. When the board members called Lee and Henry back into the room, the board president told them the ACLU would not oppose the window.

Henry was overjoyed, but Lee wasn't finished. A 1982 graduate of the Ole Miss law school, Lee asked, "Could we have something in writing?"

The lawyer explained that a commitment against future litigation would have to come from the executive director at the national headquarters in New York.

"Well," Lee said, "let's get him on the phone."

46

On September 23, 1997, despite the fact that we were knee deep in the chaos surrounding the Confederate flag, our leadership team left the campus for a retreat. We drove to Old Waverly Golf Club, located about ninety miles southeast of Oxford in West Point.

Magnolia trees line the main drive to the beautiful clubhouse. A picturesque lake greets visitors and borders the attractive houses and condominiums that face well-planned, winding streets. The landscaping is pristine. I felt a sense of serenity.

As we arrived on Friday afternoon and settled into the comfortable accommodations, I sensed something important was going to happen.

As we gathered in our meeting room, I stopped to make a mental note of the moment. I knew this weekend would be transformative. Before we began the formal agenda, I asked everybody to quietly look around the room. *giving the school national attention*

"Try to form a lasting mental image," I said. "When this retreat is over and successful, I hope all of us will look back to this day, this first meeting, and remember planting the seeds that will blossom into wonderful opportunities for our students." *landscape*

Perhaps I was overly optimistic, but I thought it was clear we were all tired of mediocrity, poor public perception, and the negative feelings that lingered on our campus. I had spent the last year and a half working closely with everyone in the room. I knew their talents and potential. They were smart, gifted, enthusiastic individuals. With that group focused and united — and with a soaring national economy — I was confident that we were on the cusp of something extraordinary.

Rex Deloach had engaged a seasoned facilitator to lead the retreat. We had worked with him in advance to ensure that the topics for discussion were tailored to the needs of the university, but we also en-

athletic program ←

to earn money ← *football ←*

couraged creative thinking and free discussion.

Every participant was equipped with pens, paper, and markers. We challenged every person to dream, to open up, to inspire each other and to ultimately reach agreement on a list of topics we would call "key strategies."

While at the retreat, I reflected on my days as an undergraduate at Ole Miss. In the years 1956 to 1960, there were no major wars, and the economy was strong.

Enrollment at Ole Miss was about 3,000, and most of our students were from Mississippi. We knew each other well. It wasn't uncommon to go home with a friend for the weekend, and most of us attended local churches when we stayed on campus.

In looking back on those years, most of my college friends and I came to think of our time at Ole Miss as magical. However, too few people had access to our secure little world.

It was certainly naïve on our part, but it was all we knew. As students, we were so accustomed to "separate but equal" that conversations about race, except those led by a handful of faculty, were simply not a part of our lives. The only other time we talked much about racial tension was when it came to sports.

For me, an early personal experience with Mississippi's segregation policy came in 1959 and 1960. I was the catcher for the Ole Miss baseball team. We won the SEC Championship both years. The SEC champions received an automatic bid to the NCAA tournaments that led to the College World Series.

Our coach, Tom Swayze, announced in an understated way that our season would end when the SEC championship was determined. Even if we won the SEC title and were eligible to play in the NCAA playoffs and College World Series, we would not compete. We couldn't comprehend the rationale, but we did not dream of challenging our coach, much less the governor or the legislature. I never really knew who made or enforced the rule, but I do know that most of my teammates wanted to continue to play, regardless of the opponent.

Dan Jordan, an outstanding student and star pitcher, was president of our student government association. At Coach Swayze's request,

Dan wrote a letter to the president of the IHL and the governor requesting a reprieve, but he received no response.

The last game in the SEC tournament against Florida, which we won, was the end of my status as an undergraduate student athlete at Ole Miss. Within a month, I was in Chicago, in a locker room next to Roger Brown, a 300-pound black player who had a long and successful career in the NFL.

It never occurred to me that anything was odd about playing on an integrated team. I had spent my childhood in Moss Point living with black and white kids — playing, swimming, mowing yards, eating, and exploring every kind of mischief we could discover.

My life would have been rather empty without those friends. My childhood and teenage years were much richer because of these friendships.

As a young boy, it seemed a little strange to me that black and white people attended different schools and churches, but one thing that truly made me feel sick was the presence of "White Only" and "Colored Only" signs painted above public restroom doors and water fountains.

My generation should have addressed these issues earlier. But we didn't. The delay left many scars on many people — and on Ole Miss. But now, we needed to focus on progress.

During the course of the retreat, I started to daydream about the possibilities and opportunities for Ole Miss. I enthusiastically and confidently offered my ideas and dreams.

I told the group that I wanted better visibility, and a better reputation, nationally. I wanted higher enrollment, more alumni involvement, and increased revenue. For students I wanted a better educational experience, an enhanced library, and more diversity among students, faculty, and staff. I wanted state-of-the-art technology, more money for research, and higher salaries to recruit top faculty. Oh, and competitive, winning athletics programs that maintained the highest standards of integrity.

"Is there anything you don't want?" someone asked.

During a break, Rex Deloach, who is perhaps the most level-headed, calm man I know, said, "Robert, they think you're crazy."

"I want the best for our students," I told him.

What I didn't say was that I wanted Ole Miss to be a magical experience again for all our students. A newer, better, more diverse Ole Miss. A place of peace and happiness and growth for every student, regardless of race or background.

For me, the retreat at Old Waverly was a spiritual experience. It was more than simply a renewal of the emotional ties I'd had to Ole Miss since 1956. I was overwhelmed by the candor, inventiveness, originality, and resourcefulness of every person in the room. I was exposed to new thoughts and better processes. I had every reason to believe that Ole Miss could become a great American public university.

At the close of the retreat, we had identified twenty-one key strategies. Donna Patton, who served as recording secretary at the event, said she would create a final document and circulate it in early October to all participants.

I get a strange, warm sensation when something good is underway at Ole Miss. Never before had the feeling been stronger.

Draft

GOALS AGREED UPON BY ADMINISTRATIVE TEAM
THE UNIVERSITY OF MISSISSIPPI
FRIDAY, OCTOBER 10, 1997

1. Enhanced Visibility, Perception, and Reputation

2. Re-engineering

3. Leadership Institute

4. SREB Doctoral I -- 100 doctorates

5. Increased Enrollment

6. Faculty and Staff Development

7. Increased Alumni Participation

8. Increased Revenue from All Sources

9. More Cost Efficient

10. Enhanced Total Educational Experience

11. Phi Beta Kappa

12. Enhanced Library

13. Increased Diversity Among Faculty, Staff, and Students

14. Enhanced Quality of Facilities

15. State of the Art Technology

16. Enhanced Student Support Services

17. Enhanced Environment for Research

18. Dynamic Institution-Wide Planning Process

19. Competitive Faculty and Staff Compensation and Career Opportunities

20. Maintain Integrity, Competitiveness, and Equity of Athletic Programs

21. Strengthen relationship with UMMC

The memo, circulated to all participants in the retreat,
that outlined our twenty-one key strategies

47

I believe every inch of the campus at Ole Miss is precious, almost sacred ground. Consequently, any decision to build a structure requires careful planning, serious study, and visionary thinking.

As chancellor, I made it my job to understand the physical history of the school, the significance of each building, the value of green spaces, trees, walkways, streets, and landscaping.

The leaders who came before me at Ole Miss — those who made decisions about how the campus should be arranged and developed — made very few mistakes. In my opinion, some errors were made in the design of buildings, but for the most part the architectural integrity of the campus had been maintained. Where mistakes were made, we had worked to correct the appearance of buildings that were out of harmony with the others.

The early planners of the university — one of whom was Frederick Law Olmsted, who also designed Central Park — identified an east-west centerline that begins off campus on University Avenue and continues to the western boundary of the campus. The central doors of the Lyceum are perfectly situated on that line as are the library entrance and exit, Magnolia Drive, and the entrance to Guyton Hall. All other buildings are situated around that center line, creating symmetry and harmony.

It seemed to me that all the pieces were finally coming together to build a new chapel. However, we could not agree on the ideal spot. I had received dozens of suggestions, including placing it in the center of the Grove, but nothing felt right.

One morning as I walked the campus, I decided to take a different route.

I generally walked from the chancellor's home, down Fraternity Row, through the Grove, and up the hill near Garland and Mayes dormitories. But on this morning, I decided I'd walk through the parking lot surrounded by Bondurant, the library, and the cafeteria. I generally avoided the area because it was so unattractive. Even worse, the garbage disposal area for the cafeteria was always littered with industrial-sized garbage bags. It smelled bad, too.

As I reached the west entrance of the parking lot at sunrise, I felt strange. I stopped walking and stood perfectly still. Suddenly, I felt as if an electric current were running through my body. Not a painful shock, but a tingling sensation. At that moment, a vision came to me. I saw a beautiful red-brick chapel facing west, with a portico facing the library. I saw the parking lot as a well-tended green space with a large fountain in the center.

A moment later, the peculiar feeling went away . . . but the vision was etched in my mind forever. I thought of one of our outstanding faculty members, Ann Fisher-Wirth, a poet and environmentalist, looking out of her office window only to see a trashy parking lot and a cafeteria waste disposal area.

One thing was certain. This parking lot had to be transformed.

Lee and Henry Paris had great success with the ACLU. They had a letter in hand from the executive director at the national headquarters. The letter stated that no ACLU funds or resources would ever be used to remove the Paris family symbol from the chapel at Ole Miss. With that assurance, the Paris family committed $500,000 toward the cost of construction.

Next, I went to Philadelphia, Mississippi, to visit my old friend Bill Yates. Bill and I were in school together — both as undergraduates and in law school. Bill was not only smart, diligent, and popular, but he was also more capable than any of us realized at the time. While earning a degree in engineering, a commission in the U.S. Army, and a law degree, Bill was running a construction company. While I was living the life of a full-time student with a part-time job, Bill was bidding on jobs and managing construction projects.

When Bill joined his father in 1964 at W.G. Yates & Sons Construction, it was clear from the outset that he was a visionary. Yates

Construction grew from a small-town company in the early 1960s to an internationally recognized leader in construction. Yates was ranked among the top twenty-five construction companies in the world.

Bill and his wife, Nancy, along with their children William and Carolyn, had always been great friends to Ole Miss. And because the project was being funded through the University Foundation, we weren't required to go through a typical bid process.

"Bill," I said, "Yates has got to build this chapel."

We talked about the size and scope of the project and Bill agreed on the spot.

"And what are you going to need from me personally?" Bill asked.

"$500,000," I said.

My next stop was at the home of Frank and Marge Peddle. They came to Oxford soon after World War II. The Peddles were active supporters of St. Peter's Episcopal Church, as well as many community organizations and civic initiatives. They gave generously to the university, and Frank served on the faculty for a number of years.

Marge and Frank had distinctive interests — quite different from each other. Frank, an accomplished pianist, was an avid supporter of developing the local airport. Marge's secret love was baseball. When we built our new baseball stadium, Marge wanted us to have the tallest flagpole in the SEC — as well as the largest American flag. She provided funding for both.

Marge and I sat in her living room in their home on Eagle Springs Road. When I asked her if she and Frank would be willing to help with the chapel, she said, "I always knew you were going to ask us to help with the bell tower."

"I hope you will."

"Let me talk to Daddy," she said.

My final stop was to meet with Don Frugé, president of the University of Mississippi Foundation. I asked him to take the lead on the development team. Don assumed responsibility to lead the effort to build and pay for the chapel. He and his wife, Mary Ann, worked together on the project. They developed a plan to raise the $3.8 million necessary to make the dream of a new chapel a reality. The plan included naming opportunities for pews, windows, spaces, and chancel furniture.

With the Paris, Yates, and Peddle families on board, and the foundation team directed by Don and Mary Ann, I felt certain that we could turn my sunrise vision into a reality.

48

Not long after the retreat, *New York Times* reporter Kevin Sack came back to campus to attend a football game. It was a glorious Saturday in October, when the Rebels were scheduled to play at home against the LSU Tigers.

To say that the fans were enthusiastic doesn't do the scene justice. As we walked through the Grove and Circle, excitement filled the air. Chants of "Hotty Toddy" broke out spontaneously, and the Ole Miss band's sounds echoed across campus.

Inside the stadium, Kevin seemed rattled. The stands were filled, from our perspective, with a sea of Confederate flags. Tens of thousands of flags waved to the tempo of the Pride of the South band as they played *I Saw the Light, From Dixie with Love*, the Ole Miss fight song, and, of course, *Dixie*. The crowd roared in response to those songs, and the flags, held high in the air on sticks, never touched the ground. A college football game is truly a colorful spectacle. It's a photographer's dream.

The *New York Times* photographer who accompanied Kevin captured powerful, panoramic photographs of the flag-filled stadium.

Ole Miss won the game 36-21. It was a resounding victory for the school, but we took another step backward in our public perception. The *New York Sunday Times* magazine ran Kevin's story along with the image of a stadium consumed by Confederate flags. We were in the national news again. Other media outlets picked up the story, and the furor intensified.

All I wanted to do was focus on the strategies we'd identified to make Ole Miss a great university. Not only was the flag issue not going away, but we had no means to stop our fans from waving these red and blue pieces of cloth that were so damaging to our image.

In the months that followed *The New York Times* report, I had recurring thoughts of my father.

In 1947, he ran for supervisor in Jackson County and was elected to office. County supervisors in Mississippi were responsible for the operation of county government at the grassroots level. In the 1940s, running for political office meant walking door-to-door throughout the district, getting to know the voters personally, and asking for their votes.

The domain of the supervisors included streets, drainage, bridges, health care, education, local jails, recreation, economic development, and more. People in the district called my father "Mr. Eddie." They asked him for — and expected him to deliver — jobs. They also asked him to help find stray dogs, get a relative transported to the state hospital, repair driveway culverts with oyster shells, pave church parking lots, and clean up after storms.

My father was a gifted public speaker and thrived on the interaction with his audiences. His favorite topic was Mississippi, and the message was positive — his emphasis always on moving forward, onward, and upward. At his own expense, he traveled across the state addressing civic clubs, high school graduates, sports clubs, and churches. He was obsessed with promoting Jackson County and Mississippi. He was well-respected, admired, and loved by many.

Mr. Eddie was chosen to serve as secretary of the Mississippi Association of Supervisors, a job that included lobbying the Mississippi Legislature. In those days, the speaker of the house was the most powerful person in state government (including the governor). During my father's early years as the lobbyist for the association, Walter Sillers served as House speaker. Mr. Sillers was from Cleveland, a town located in the heart of the Mississippi Delta.

Each July, Dad would load his car with coolers full of shrimp, oysters, flounder, speckled trout, and whiskey. Then he would drive to Cleveland to visit with Mr. Sillers. The two of them would sift through the supervisors' legislative proposals for the January term. After Mr. Sillers identified the passable from the unpromising proposals, my father gave him the treasures from the Coast and drove back to Moss Point. After the trip, my father knew exactly which legislation to push and which to discard. Not surprisingly, Mr. Eddie's legislative package always passed.

Within our family, we often wondered why Dad was so driven. As we matured, we came to understand the discrimination and emotional abuse that dominated his early life. He was a first-generation American whose parents had immigrated from Lebanon. After landing at Ellis Island, they found their way to Biloxi. The family home was on the second floor of a brick building that housed the family grocery store on Howard Avenue, Biloxi's main street. My father had four sisters and one brother, all of whom had strong Middle Eastern features including olive-brown skin, dark eyes, prominent noses, and black hair. My father was tagged with the nickname "Crusty" because of his dark skin.

My father and his dark-skinned siblings ran the streets of Biloxi working odd jobs, going to school, and, in my father's case, participating in athletics. At five feet nine inches, he was by far the tallest of the siblings. His academic performance and success in athletics led to a work scholarship to Millsaps College. His first year at the college, he was blackballed by all the fraternities.

The Great Depression was smothering the nation at the time, but my parents found a way to marry. My father completed his degree and, in 1932, accepted a teaching position at Moss Point High School. When my parents first attended the Methodist Church in Moss Point, my father was asked to move from a forward pew to one more near the rear of the sanctuary.

I suspect that these rejections stimulated him to work harder to be successful and respected. Reputation was *always* a family concern.

From our father, my brother and sisters and I learned discipline, personal responsibility, the importance of a strong spiritual life, and generosity. My brother and I also learned something about athletics. My father taught me how to placekick a football and how to play catcher on the baseball team.

"Those two positions are vital," he told me, "and hardly anybody wants to do either!" Then he added, "You'll always get to play."

My father was uncommonly kind to black people at a time when racial prejudice was at its height in Mississippi. He always told us, "Treat every person with respect."

My father worked hard and broke down old barriers to make sure black men and women could vote, as well as serve on juries. He worked tirelessly helping blacks and whites alike to find jobs, to have access to adequate health care and affordable housing.

On the other hand, he was never "out front" supporting integration of schools, churches, or other public places. My guess is he tried to balance his concern for humanity with the realities of politics in Mississippi during those transitional years.

My father made two critical missteps in his public life. The first, made while riding a crest of popularity in the county and state, was deciding to challenge long-term U.S. House of Representatives member William F. Colmer. My father lost to Representative Colmer twice. Soon after the second failed attempt to unseat the incumbent, the Internal Revenue Service began investigating my father.

None of us in our family knew about the investigation until one morning in the spring of 1973. At the time, I was a faculty member at the University of Mississippi law school. Fittingly, I was teaching a course called Local Government Law. Our class met at 10 a.m. At 9:45, I received a telephone call from my father. He called from a pay phone.

"Robert," he said, "I think I'm going to be indicted by a grand jury before the end of the day."

At first I thought he was joking, but soon I realized he was dead serious.

"For what?" I asked, still in shock.

"Income tax fraud and evasion."

I couldn't believe it. The man didn't have any money. We lived modestly. As far as we could tell, he never thought much about wealth for himself — or for us.

Immediately following our telephone conversation, I stood in front of fifty law students and preached about upholding the highest standards and ethics when handling taxpayers' dollars.

My father was correct. He was indicted. The story dominated the headlines and broadcasts statewide. The pretrial activities seemed to go on forever. The Khayat prosecution was a hot news item. I began to dread walking down our driveway to retrieve *The Clarion-Ledger* every morning.

When I went to the law school, I was sure every person there was staring at me. I wondered how my mother would survive. She had hated politics from the very beginning.

Somehow we all lived through the prosecutorial process. Ultimately, my father reached a plea agreement. He pled guilty to a misdemeanor and a fine. The plea caused us all lots of embarrassment and pain, but Dad avoided a jail sentence. As part of the plea deal, he was allowed to continue to serve as supervisor.

Mr. Eddie continued to be reelected by the people of Jackson County for three terms.

My father's second life-changing mistake came in 1982. There was a move to change the organization of county government from the beat system (where supervisors held all purse strings) to a unit system (where a county administrator handled all finances). Despite my encouragement to embrace the new system of accountability, my father refused to recognize the benefits of the new system. He was dedicated to the old way. When someone was in need, my father wanted to receive the call and provide the assistance — whether the task was as small as providing transportation or as large as repaving a driveway.

The summer of 1982 brought with it allegations and prosecution by newly elected Jackson County District Attorney Mike Moore. Moore alleged "misuse of county property and resources for private benefit."

Local law enforcement officers arrived at my parents' home in Moss Point late in the afternoon. They entered the house and handcuffed my father. My mother watched in horror as the officers escorted her husband from the house and placed him in the back seat of a patrol car.

There were eight counts in the indictment. All eight were to be tried individually and separately. My father would be on trial eight times, no matter how small the alleged crime (one count charged him with asking for and receiving thirteen steaks from a grocery store to give to a legislator).

The pretrial publicity was relentless, and the legal expenses were a huge challenge. Following the first trial, which resulted in a hung jury, we all realized that my father could not afford the financial or emotional expense of seven more. We met as a family and decided to enter into negotiated plea discussions. The plea bargain resulted in a guilty plea to one count of the indictment, a misdemeanor, a $2,000 fine, and the resignation from his elected office.

The door on my father's public career was closed. He never fully recovered from the pain and embarrassment. He lived the final four years of his life in quiet lethargy. He continued to be active in church, to hold his head up, to love his family, and to nurture close friendships, but he was a different person from the Mr. Eddie so many people had known and relied on for so many years.

The final years of my father's life provide a great study in cultural change. Attitudes about public officials and tax-funded organizations changed during his career. My father was unable, or unwilling, to adapt to the new morality of politics or protect himself. He was not alone. Ambitious prosecutors sought indictments and convictions of many well-respected, long-term elected officials. During the early 1980s, fifty-five of Mississippi's 410 supervisors were convicted in the undercover initiative Operation Pretense. All were forced out of office. Some went to jail. Thankfully, Dad avoided incarceration.

My father was charged with crimes based on behavior that had been considered acceptable his entire career. He was forced out of office for doing the very things that had kept him *in* office for thirty-seven years.

Times changed and players changed, but my father did not. A well-lived life of service and kindness ended on a very sad note. He made a positive difference in the lives of thousands of people and sacrificed much of his family life to public service. Lasting, tangible results of his work remain, yet he ended his life feeling demoralized. He felt that the family reputation that meant *everything* to him was now beyond repair.

The similarities between the life of the father I loved and the history of the university I loved were not lost on me. I feared that Ole Miss might suffer a similar fate. Our university had so much that was good and strong and positive, but all that was being overshadowed by racism's legacy.

We had to change with the times. The alternative was unthinkable.

49

Ron Schroeder and I met in the Lyceum to discuss the Phi Beta Kappa application. Ron was a scholar and a member of Phi Beta Kappa at Northwestern University. He was also one of our English professors. He was committed to leading the efforts from the faculty side, and I was grateful. Mr. Foard had been clear. The application needed to be faculty driven. I also knew that Ron would need a great deal of assistance from the administration in pulling together everything required of the four-volume application, and I knew the perfect person for the job — Mary Ann Connell.

Mary Ann served as university attorney. She is one of the most kind and loving people I've ever known. Whether working at the Episcopal church or negotiating with contentious attorneys, she maintained a calmness and civility that should be a model for all people — especially lawyers.

The application process was in good hands with Ron Schroeder and Mary Ann Connell. However, the substance of the application — the five realms identified by the Phi Beta Kappa executive director — was still a long way from being resolved.

As the leadership team and I began to tackle the key strategies, we also wanted everyone — faculty, staff, students, and alumni — to take ownership in the initiatives we'd outlined. We met regularly to discuss each of our twenty-one key strategies.

During one of our many meetings, I mentioned my frustration with our students and alumni for continuing to wave the Confederate flag. I wanted to distance us from the flag, but I could not do anything that violated a First Amendment right. Freedom of speech, press, and expression were dear to me. Individuals certainly had the right to express themselves. What our fans didn't realize was that when 30,000 individuals express themselves, that expression represents the institution.

Our leadership team met regularly to think of ways to convince our fans to stop waving the Confederate flag. We tried talking to influential alumni. We tried education. We asked coaches to spread the word to fans. Then, in one of the meetings I was unable to attend due to travel, someone nonchalantly suggested, "Why don't we just ban sticks?"

After the meeting, Leone King called me to report on the meeting.

"They're talking about banning sticks," she said.

I didn't understand. "What did you say?"

"The team is suggesting banning sticks as a way to keep the flag from showing up."

"Leone," I said, "schedule a meeting with Pete Boone and Mary Ann Connell . . . as soon as possible."

The idea seemed like such a simple solution. Surely, I thought, it couldn't be this easy.

With input from Pete and Mary Ann, we developed a policy based on banning sticks. We thought it was a policy we could enforce. First, in the interest of safety, we extended the ban on umbrellas to cover all sticks and pointed objects at Ole Miss sporting events — including umbrellas, flag sticks, and even corndog sticks.

In the interest of fan enjoyment, we included more items in the "banned" category — alcoholic beverages, banners, and flags larger than twelve-by-fourteen inches.

The policies were all about public safety and enjoyment. They had nothing to do with an individual's right to expression. The following week, we issued a public statement about the new policies.

Then we waited. We waited to see if it would work.

Moving Forward

50

Pat Patterson grew up in the small, northeast Mississippi community of Hatley. His family farmed, but their home had no electricity. In 1949, Pat joined the National Guard, primarily, he said, so he could get his first pair of new shoes.

He worked for a few months at a pants factory before he was called to active military duty in 1951.

After serving his tour, Pat enrolled at Ole Miss to study accountancy and turned out to be a financial whiz. He graduated in 1955 and, after stints at Touche Ross & Co. and Lockheed, ended up as the executive vice president and chief financial officer for Donrey Corporation — a media company that owned television stations and billboards in Arkansas and Nevada.

Pat worked with Donrey until 1994. Upon his retirement, he was also vice chairman and trustee for the Reynolds Foundation — a philanthropic nonprofit started by Donald Reynolds, the founder of Donrey.

Rex Deloach suggested that he and I ask Pat to make a gift to Ole Miss, or, at least, help us present a request to the Reynolds Foundation. Rex called Pat and arranged a visit.

We met at Pat's home in Fort Smith, Arkansas. The house was surrounded by a thirty-acre championship golf course. The course had three bent-grass greens, an irrigation system, and eighteen tees situated at varying distances and angles to simulate an eighteen-hole course.

Pat knew why Rex and I were there.

"How much money are you talking about?" he asked.

"Three million," I said, "primarily to support the School of Accountancy."

"If you're going to ask for money," Pat said, "ask for some real money."

Rex and I heeded Pat Patterson's advice. We put together a proposal for the Reynolds Foundation to invest $16.5 million in Ole Miss.

We earmarked $6 million to endow the School of Accountancy, which would be named in honor of Pat. We requested $2.5 million to help re-engineer the technology and business systems at the university, and we asked for $8 million to support the library and increase our holdings to more than one million volumes.

We needed the additional holdings for the Phi Beta Kappa application, but the last part of the request to the Reynolds Foundation was important for other reasons, too. Our library is a sanctuary — a holy place at the heart of the university, located in the center of campus. It has a personality that helps define our community. It's not only a repository of the collective thinking of our civilization, but it also enriches our lives by providing generation after generation with the opportunity for an intimate relationship with those who recorded, observed, challenged, and inspired humanity.

Our library is a constant reminder that our mission is to discover, understand, and disseminate knowledge.

We submitted our request to the Reynolds Foundation board. Two months later, I received a letter from Donald Pray, president of the Reynolds Foundation board. The letter indicated that the foundation would make a one-time gift to fully fund the requests. Mr. Pray also noted that this was the first gift the foundation would award to a group outside Arkansas or Nevada.

I called Mr. Pray to thank him and arrange a date for a ceremony. I also called Governor Kirk Fordice and asked him to join us for the celebration and to help us express appreciation to the Reynolds Foundation.

We hosted the reception and event on a beautiful spring day in the Circle. More than 100 people gathered. After introducing everyone, the governor spoke to the crowd. Then, he introduced Mr. Pray.

Mr. Pray stepped to the microphone. He carried a large briefcase. After a few comments about the dedication and brilliance of Pat Patterson, Mr. Pray opened the briefcase. It was empty except for a single check made out to the University of Mississippi for $16.5 million.

None of us, including the governor, had ever seen a check that large. Mr. Pray presented me with the check.

Then Governor Fordice leaned over and said, "Let me take a look at the check."

I handed it to the governor, who examined it carefully. Then he deftly placed the check in his coat pocket.

"If that ends up in the general fund, Governor," I said, "it will disappear."

Smiling, providing a bit of theatre for the crowd, Governor Fordice returned the check.

51

I thought the 1960 College All-Star Game would be the last time I ever lined up across from the colossal Big Daddy Lipscomb. I was mistaken.

Because I was the placekicker for the Redskins, but the sixth offensive lineman, I played only if one of the other linemen was injured. Even then, I was usually in the game for no more than a few plays.

One of our 1960 preseason games was against the Baltimore Colts. The week before the game, our left guard sprained his ankle. Coach Abe Gibron told me that I would start at left guard. "You'll play the whole game . . . and kick."

On our first set of downs in Baltimore's Memorial Stadium, I ran from the huddle and took my place on the line of scrimmage. I looked up and saw the number 76 staring back at me.

Big Daddy didn't remember me from the All-Star game, and he didn't call me "Sweet Pea." But he did come at me as if I were a seasoned, professional guard. I wasn't. Big Daddy still outweighed me by eighty pounds and he was at least six inches taller. It was no contest. Big Daddy tossed me around like a rag doll.

The Colts dominated us. With a huge lead in the third quarter, Baltimore's coach Weeb Ewbank pulled Big Daddy from the game. It was a great relief. I'm not sure I would have survived the fourth quarter.

The next time I met Big Daddy was on September 25, 1960, in our season opener against the Colts. Again, we played in Memorial Stadium, and, again, an injury to a teammate put me in Big Daddy's sights.

By now I had figured out how to scuffle around and avoid direct contact with him. I spent more time eluding Big Daddy than blocking him, but at least I survived. I was even able to get in his way on occasion and impede his efforts to rush the passer or disrupt play.

Big Daddy was the only player on the Colts squad who played college football, but he was football savvy. If he suspected I was going to pull in either direction to block for a running back or the quarterback, Big Daddy would simply reach out one of his huge hands and grab my jersey. It was, technically, a holding violation, but in the interior of the line, surrounded by guards, tackles, and a center, the hold generally went unnoticed.

By delaying me — and preventing me from making my blocking assignments — the play usually resulted in a loss of yardage. I went back to the huddle only to be greeted by an angry and confused quarterback or running back.

Before the game ended, I figured out that I needed to leave a split second ahead of the snap. It was the only way to elude the grasp of the giant.

We lost the game 20-0.

During the 1960 season, including the All-Star game, I started as a lineman in only three football games. All three times, I faced Big Daddy Lipscomb.

It seemed as if it were my fate to face Big Daddy whether I liked it or not. He simply would not go away.

race would not go away.

In late 1997, Andy Mullins received a call from his former boss William Winter. Andy had served on Governor Winter's staff in the 1980s, and the two remained close friends.

Governor Winter had just been appointed to an advisory board for President Clinton's Initiative on Race. The president believed the program was critical to prepare the country to embrace diversity. The primary directive, initially, was to convene in towns across the country and engage in a dialogue about race. Ultimately, President Clinton hoped the program would lead to healing racial and ethnic divisions wherever they existed.

Governor Winter, a 1943 graduate of Ole Miss, told Andy he thought it would be a great thing to bring an initiative on race, as a town hall meeting, to Ole Miss.

Andy walked to my office, told me about the governor's idea and said, "What do you think?"

I was always interested in open dialogue and communication. Honestly, though, during the last few months, I had been so traumatized, had grown so weary of talking about symbols and race and tradition and flags and songs that I had a difficult time getting excited about the prospect of another forum on race. But I also didn't want to tell Governor Winter — or President Clinton — no.

"If the City of Oxford will partner with us," I said, "we'll host it on campus."

I was beginning to think that fate had selected a new adversary for me. This time it didn't come in the form of a six-foot, eight-inch football player — and it didn't have a sixty-minute time limit.

Oxford's most famous native son, William Faulkner, wrote in *Requiem for a Nun*, "The past is never dead. It's not even past."

He was right. Ole Miss' past, it seemed — especially with regard to race — was going to stare me in the face every day of my chancellorship.

It simply wasn't going to go away.

Oxford Mayor Patricia Lamar agreed to co-host the Initiative on Race event with us. I called William Winter.

"Governor Winter," I said, "we would love to host the town hall meeting." I added that the City of Oxford had agreed to partner with us.

"We'll be coming in March," he said.

Andy organized a committee to plan and prepare for the event. One of the members, Susan Glisson, had been coordinating the graduate program at the Center for the Study of Southern Culture while she finished her dissertation. Susan had been working to bring the eminent African-American historian John Hope Franklin to Ole Miss to participate in a Black History Month celebration. She had run into dead end after dead end in her attempts to reach Dr. Franklin. As it turned out, John Hope Franklin had been appointed by President Clinton to chair the advisory board for the Initiative on Race. He would be coming in March.

Susan organized a grassroots effort to prepare for the town hall meeting. She met weekly with ten different committees made up of more than 160 students, faculty, and staff, as well as residents of Oxford. Each committee focused on race and its role in specific realms, including arts, business, health care, housing, environment, labor, education, and religion. By the time March 17 arrived, the committees had prepared talking points.

At 7:00 p.m. on that Tuesday evening, a thunderstorm descended on Oxford. I was worried it would hurt attendance, but Fulton Chapel was packed. People even stood against the wall. The crowd of 650-plus was a fairly even racial mix.

After my opening remarks, Dr. Franklin approached the podium.

"President Clinton has called for a new dialogue," he said. "A dialogue where our differences will be viewed as an asset, not a liability. A dialogue where we will respect our differences and never use them as a basis for exploitation."

Dr. Franklin went on to tell, with great calm and dignity, his story of growing up as a black man in the segregated South. Then, he called for the dialogue to begin.

"No one can speak for you," he said. "Let a new discussion begin — an unprecedented conversation on race — where acrimony and name-calling are left behind."

What followed was a discussion in which each speaker — whether young or old, male or female, black or white — approached the microphone with the same purpose. To be heard. A steady stream stepped up to the microphones to talk about race in our community and in the world. At times, emotions ran high as members of the audience recounted their personal experiences with racism, yet the evening was marked by respect for the speakers and their often disparate views.

Then, a gentleman from DeSoto County announced, "It's my freedom to fly the Confederate flag." I thought, *Here we go.*

What happened next was, by far, the most moving moment of
evening. Two Ole Miss students — Allison Grisham, a white student, and Jada Love, a black student — walked on stage together. The
two friends held hands as they spoke. The hushed crowd listened as
Allison explained why it was so important for students and alumni to
quit waving the Confederate battle flag at Ole Miss football games.

"I understand that for many of you it is simply a demonstration
of school spirit," she said, "but the need for the university to be wel-
coming to all students far outweighs the perceived tradition of the
flag."

Then Jada told the audience how painful it was for her to be in a
stadium at *her* university and see *her* classmates — and their parents
— wave a flag that represented oppression, brutality, inequality, and
slavery.

As the two young women left the stage, they received the most
enthusiastic ovation of the evening.

When the three-hour program finally closed, I watched as the gentleman from DeSoto County moved across Fulton Chapel to continue
the conversation with Allison and Jada. That was the point of the
meeting. Before he left, he agreed to never wave the flag again.

The meeting could not have gone any better. We witnessed a lively
yet civil dialogue, and I was proud of our town, community, and university.

I congratulated Andy and Susan on their fine work and mentioned
that I felt Ole Miss was poised to be a catalyst for real change.

"We should be having this conversation every day," I told them.
It wasn't lost on me how far I'd come in embracing this gathering.

Prior to the event, I had been asked to serve as a host for John
Hope Franklin. When the event ended at about ten o'clock, I offered
Dr. Franklin a ride to his hotel. We'd both had a full day, and although
tired, I knew sleep wouldn't come any time soon for me. I was still
too roused from the momentous event.

I was eager to discuss the evening with Dr. Franklin, but I didn't
want him to feel obligated. After all, he had to be in his mid-eighties.

talked about the two white and
black friends who came on to the
stage holding hands

"Dr. Franklin," I said, "You've had quite an evening. Are you hungry?"

"Why, yes I am," he said.

I offered an apology that none of Oxford's finer dining establishments were still serving. "Kitchens generally close at ten o'clock around here."

Our options were limited to fast food and convenience store fare, neither of which sounded particularly appealing.

"I usually have a bowl of cereal at this time of night," I said. "It seems to make me sleep better."

"Well, let's do that," he said.

At 10:30 p.m., Dr. Franklin and I sat at the kitchen table in the chancellor's residence and ate cereal.

Dr. Franklin was the nation's leading scholar of African-American history. His books and scholarship changed the way the world thought about slavery and reconstruction. During his life, he worked side-by-side with Dr. Martin Luther King Jr., W.E.B. Du Bois, and Thurgood Marshall. His book *From Slavery to Freedom: A History of African-Americans* sold more than three million copies. It is considered the definitive survey of the American black experience.

Dr. Franklin's father earned a law degree, but the state of Louisiana would not allow him to practice. So his father moved to the all-black town of Rentiesville, Oklahoma. The following year, John Hope was born, and the family relocated to Tulsa. He understood racism. As a boy, he was forced off an all-white train, he was made to sit in a segregated section of the Tulsa Opera, and he witnessed, firsthand, the Tulsa race riots of 1921, when black neighborhoods, including the one that housed his father's law office, were burned to the ground. At the age of eighteen, he was denied admission to the University of Oklahoma because of the color of his skin.

Even as a world-renowned scholar, Dr. Franklin could not escape racism. On the evening before receiving an award at the White House, a woman at a private club in Washington mistook him for an attendant and asked him to fetch her coat.

On this occasion, John Franklin did not speak of all that he had endured. He told me about his wife, Aurelia, and his son, John. He also told me about his lifelong hobby of cultivating orchids (one species of the flower had been named for him).

Dr. Franklin was deeply interested in Ole Miss, especially the controversy over our symbols. I told him about all that we had encountered in the last year, including the strides we'd made, along with a few missteps, and my hopes for the future.

"I'm afraid we'll be fighting our old reputation for a lifetime," I told him.

He looked up from his cereal bowl. "Not if you keep doing what you did tonight."

I wish we could have talked for hours. I was spellbound.

The following week, I wrote letters to each of the advisory board members of President Clinton's Initiative on Race, including Dr. Franklin. But when the letter arrived at Dr. Franklin's Durham home, he wasn't there to open it. He was in Denver, Colorado, for the next scheduled town hall meeting. The topic of discussion for the Colorado meeting was racial stereotypes. When the moderator introduced the chair, John Hope Franklin, dozens of Native Americans yelled out from the audience. They were there to protest the President's Initiative on Race, specifically the lack of Native American representation on the advisory panel.

As John Hope Franklin outlined his hopes for the evening, the yelling continued. He made it through his introduction. Then, actor Edward James Olmos questioned the panel about how the indigenous people of this continent could sit by silently, when 95 percent of the history studied in schools was European American.

The raucous group yelled louder and louder, and the moderators lost control of the program. As the rants and screams continued, John Hope Franklin leaned over to William Winter.

"I wish we were back in Mississippi," he said.

Dr. John Hope Franklin

52

As chancellor, I was learning a lot about human nature. What I had learned during the past year was this: Most people want progress, but very few want change. This is true even if the change is a clear improvement.

The image review backlash caught me off-guard. I would try to move forward avoiding unnecessary controversy. But I knew that our next improvement would be greeted with outrage. We were about to change sorority and fraternity rush.

In the grand scheme of things, this appeared to be pedestrian, if not trivial, certainly compared to the flag. However, those who are emotionally and financially invested in Greek organizations place a high value on every aspect of sorority and fraternity life.

We had good reason for wanting to move rush from August to mid-fall. We believed an eighteen-year-old should not make permanent decisions before he or she became comfortable in a new life at the university and away from home.

By delaying rush, first-year students could establish relationships, get settled in classes, become familiar with their new environment, and have a better feel for the different social organizations.

Most of the resistance to change came from alumni. Some of the women who supported and guided the sororities had particular difficulty accepting the change. They seemed even more more tied to the traditional way than the men. In fact, some of the reaction was as vehement as those who resisted the review of symbols.

The only reasonable counter-position we heard was that the sororities and fraternities needed the income from pledges to offset the loss from graduating seniors. That didn't come close to outweighing the benefits.

There was one exception to the usual dynamic of resistance to change. In the fall of 1998, three students, all in separate incidents but within the same week, were hit by automobiles. In all three mishaps, a student had stepped between cars parked on the perimeter of the Circle. Fortunately, no one was seriously injured. I decided to use the accidents as an impetus for change.

The longstanding tradition of parking cars on the Lyceum Circle had been a burr in my saddle for years. The area is so beautiful, I found it offensive to use a garden spot as a parking lot.

Over the years, I found myself saying, "If I were chancellor, I would not allow parking on the Circle." After the accidents, I thought, *Now I am chancellor.*

I sent a memo to the university traffic committee expressing my concern over the danger of pedestrians walking between parked vehicles into lanes of traffic on the Circle. I gave the committee two recommendations: First, that parking on the Circle be restricted to visitors or handicapped drivers/passengers. Second, I suggested we reduce the campus speed limit to 18 miles per hour.

The committee accepted my recommendations.

When the new speed limit signs went up, I was interviewed by a number of news reporters.

"Why 18 miles per hour?"

"It's Archie Manning's number," I said.

Suddenly, the change became a great idea. The Associated Press picked up the story, and newspapers across the country ran pieces on the tribute to one of Ole Miss' most beloved players.

Our policy on banning sticks — and we hoped Confederate flags — from Vaught-Hemingway Stadium was about to be tested. The first game with the ban in effect was November 6, 1998, against Arkansas.

Our security guards were instructed to block anyone from entering who violated any of the new policies. That included anyone with sticks, an umbrella, alcohol, or a flag larger than twelve by fourteen inches. We provided containers for umbrellas, sticks, bottles, cans, or any other potentially harmful item.

I was nervous. What if 30,000 people showed up at Vaught-Hemingway with flags? What if they refused to discard them? Would we have a nasty incident?

The day of the game, the Ole Miss alumni and students were completely cooperative. Although a few flags had to be placed in the trash receptacles, most fans left them at home.

Of course there were exceptions. Richard Barrett, a lawyer and self-proclaimed white supremacist, and his two clients from New Jersey entered the game while concealing a three-by-five feet Confederate flag. During the game, they displayed the flag against the back wall of the stadium.

A university police officer asked the gentlemen to remove the flag, reminding them of the new policies. The men refused to remove the flag. The officers called UPD Captain Calvin Sellers, who warned the gentlemen that failure to comply would result in their arrest.

They removed the flag . . . but they weren't through testing our resolve. The following week, Richard Barrett, on behalf of his two clients from New Jersey, filed suit against the University of Mississippi in federal court claiming that they were denied their First Amendment freedom of expression rights.

When interviewed by newspapers about the suit, Mr. Barrett said, "The people of Mississippi have just as much right to wave a flag as the hippies had to burn the United States flag." He continued, "If you have the right to burn a flag, you certainly have the right to wave a flag. We'll take this fight all the way to the Supreme Court."

As long as the courts didn't overturn our policy, we seemed to have solved the Confederate flag issue. The flags completely disappeared from our stadium, but the sights and sounds of an Ole Miss football game were still a spectacle like no other.

I thought it might be a good time to invite Kevin Sack, my new friend from *The New York Times*, for another campus visit.

53

Kevin arrived on a gorgeous Friday afternoon in the fall. He spent the afternoon speaking with Susan Glisson and the two students who came to the stage so dramatically during the town hall meeting on race. He interviewed historian David Sansing, as well as Janice Murray, an African-American art faculty member who had come to Ole Miss from Yale.

On Saturday, he joined me in the chancellor's box for a football game against LSU. There was not a Confederate flag in sight.

The next week, a feature story appeared in *The New York Times* with the title "The Final Refrains of *Dixie.*" The article was glowing. Kevin referred to Ole Miss as a "more diverse, more selective, more rigorous school." He compared us to other top SEC schools. He called our turnaround "worthy of Nixon to China" and wrote that we had "recast the school's image by aggressively confronting its shortcomings both real and perceived."

He wrote about President Clinton's Initiative on Race and recounted the story of Allison Grisham and Jada Love's confronting the man who wanted to wave his flag. He mentioned that the national advisory committee agreed that the very best dialogue took place on the Ole Miss campus.

Kevin included my comment, where I acknowledged that our history included the Civil War and the Civil Rights movement, "but this is 1998. We are a fully integrated, open, caring, nurturing, vital community, and I am ready for the rest of the country to understand that is where we are."

He even quoted Phi Beta Kappa Executive Director Douglas Foard, who called Ole Miss a "much improved academic institution" and added, "it's a much more serious place for students to study and for faculty to do research and teach."

The story not only validated our efforts, but it was also a huge step toward changing the national perception of Ole Miss. It also helped with our self-perception.

Back in my office, I glanced over and saw the box I had received from the friend in Starkville nearly nine months earlier, the one containing women's underwear. I clipped a copy of *The New York Times* article and wrote this note: *I can't seem to make these articles of clothing fit. Perhaps you should try them. Warmest regards, Robert.* I placed the note and article on top of the pink underwear, handed the box to Sue Keiser and asked her to ship it back to Starkville.

Rex Deloach came to discuss some financial matters. Upon the early retirement of a university finance director, I was able to convince Rex to work for the university full time. He was whipping us into financial shape. We instituted new policies, based on Rex's analysis of the budget, to eliminate the "use it or lose it" system. We simply empowered department heads to roll forward any unspent balances into the next fiscal year. If they chose to save funds for equipment or travel, they could do so without fear of losing those funds.

Almost immediately, spending habits changed. They became more consistent. Departmental chairs and signatory officers knew that they had authority to manage their budgets, and they rightfully inferred that was an expression of respect for each of them. Suddenly, morale improved. Department heads sensed that they had ownership of our university. More power was vested in people across the campus, not just at the Lyceum.

When Rex arrived in my office, he held the final invoice from Burson-Marsteller. I held my breath. I couldn't imagine the $200,000 Jerry Hollingsworth had given us would cover the time and work the firm had put into our survey and national image campaign.

"How much?" I asked.

Rex handed me the invoice and said, "$198,000."

"Let's get them paid," I said, rather relieved.

Rex took the invoice back. "And one more thing," he said. "Our 23,000 acres of forestland in south Mississippi generates about

$150,000 a year."

I rolled my eyes and nodded. The maintenance and oversight of the land five hours south of campus had been a headache for every chancellor since 1887.

Rex smiled. "How would you like to turn that into $2 million a year?"

• • •

Tommy Tuberville's 1998 Ole Miss Rebels got off to a marvelous start. With overtime victories against SMU and LSU, the team record stood at 6-2 — and that included an overtime loss to Alabama.

Tommy put together a talented team that featured two talented sophomores, quarterback Romaro Miller and running back Deuce McAllister. Deuce, in fact, was on pace to become the first Ole Miss running back to rush for 1,000 yards since Kayo Dottley did it in 1950.

Tommy's reputation was growing. Sportswriters called him "the Riverboat Gambler" because of his willingness to try anything to win games, especially when Ole Miss was the underdog. Tommy would go for it on fourth down, he would fake field goals, he would try onside kicks in the middle of a game. During his tenure, Ole Miss upset a number of favored teams, including LSU and Georgia.

Coach Tuberville's off-field behavior had flair, too. On a Friday night in Nashville prior to the Vanderbilt football game, I sat outside a country club, where a small group of alumni were gathering. A couple of dozen other cars were in the parking lot. I sat in my leased Ford and listened to the Friday Night Opry while I waited for Coach Tuberville to arrive. We were both scheduled to speak to the group.

In his four years as head coach, Tommy had done a fantastic job getting our fans excited about football again. They returned the favor with enthusiastic support, including pats on the back, invitations to dinners, golfing trips, exclusive fishing outings, and other celebrity perks, including investment opportunities.

As I waited for Tommy to arrive, I remembered our conversation prior to the first press conference, when I offered my three pieces of advice on keeping things in perspective.

Suddenly, I heard the loud blast of sirens. Three police motorcycles, two police cars with sirens and lights, and a chauffeured Lincoln Town Car rolled into the parking lot. Coach Tuberville had arrived.

I sat in my car and shook my head as Tommy and his entourage entered the clubhouse.

I suppose it's difficult for coaches to stay grounded when they are showered with praise and adulation. The press certainly makes them seem like stars; they are sought after by television personalities and they are paid like Wall Street bankers. Only the most secure person could maintain balance in the midst of that circus.

As the 1998 season came to a close, the luster of the season started to fade. We were shut out by Arkansas, manhandled by Georgia, and drummed by in-state rival MSU by a score of 28-6.

Despite the three consecutive losses, we were invited to play in the Independence Bowl.

As is so often the case when a coach's reputation soars, rumors circulate about other schools' attempts to lure the winning coach away. After the loss to Mississippi State, a sportswriter asked Tommy if he had entertained other coaching offers. Tommy denied the rumor. Then he added. "They'll have to carry me out of Oxford in a pine box."

Two days later, Tommy Tuberville flew from the Oxford airport to Alabama. At a press conference, he announced he had accepted the job of head football coach at Auburn University.

Part of the fan base was depressed. The Ole Miss program had made so many positive strides under Coach Tuberville. Other Ole Miss fans, however, were enraged. Posters of Tuberville sporting a Pinocchio nose were splattered all over town. One of the local newspapers ran a full-page piece juxtaposing Tommy's photo with a recent image of President Clinton during his testimony at the Monica Lewinsky hearing. The headline read: *Only the Truth*.

Despite the general feelings of dismay, I eventually realized it was an opportunity. A chance, perhaps, for us to hire a man who left a lasting impression on me four years before.

I placed a call to New Orleans to the home of Archie Manning.

"Archie," I said, "Can I ask you a few questions about David Cutcliffe?"

54

In February of 1998, I received a telephone call from Dick Scruggs. Our families had deep ties. Dick's mother attended Millsaps College with my father in the 1930s. We both grew up in Jackson County. In 1962, when I was teaching and coaching at Pascagoula High School, Dick was a sophomore. He was in my homeroom, and he played on the football team I coached. Dick called me "Coach."

"Coach," Dick said, when I picked up the telephone, "Diane and I want to give something back to the university."

"Wonderful," I said, "What did you have in mind?"

"We'd like to give $25 million."

"That's really wonderful," I said, trying not to sound too giddy. "What would you want us to do with the money?"

"What would you like to do with it?" he asked.

It's rare to have a gift of this magnitude that hasn't been earmarked for a particular program or department.

"I'd like to see it go to supplement liberal arts faculty salaries," I said.

I realized my pitch didn't sound particularly alluring, but it was long overdue. Plus, it was a vital component in our quest for a Phi Beta Kappa chapter.

Dick and Diane agreed to contribute the funds for salary enhancement. Later, David Nutt agreed to join them in their effort. The private gift for salary enhancement from the two families would top $30 million.

I have an obsessive personality. I cannot remember a time in my life when I wasn't obsessed. It started with household chores. I wanted to finish my chores first, perform the tasks to perfection, and get the best report from my mother and father. Later, the compulsion moved to sports — perfection in kicking field goals, blocking, batting and catching. After that, my passions expanded to the law, to teaching, to manicuring my lawn. When it came to my lawn, I paid attention to every detail. I carefully edged the drive, made certain no grass was growing up a tree trunk, and trimmed trees and shrubbery exactly as directed by the professional landscapers. I learned how and when to fertilize, water, and use weed killer. I was terribly frustrated if grass grew between the cracks in the concrete. And I raked our guest parking area — made of pea gravel — after anyone had parked there and left tire marks.

Also, I had always been distressed with the poor reputation of my state — at a level of consternation that probably wasn't healthy. When I became chancellor, my preoccupation with making Ole Miss a great university reached a level that I can only describe as manic. I awoke every morning with ideas for improving the school — or improving the perception of the school — racing through my mind. I went to bed at night in the same mindset. Most nights I dreamed about the university or students or some project we had undertaken.

My devotion to Ole Miss had a grip on me that I could not escape. But even I wasn't prepared for the frenzy of activity that ensued in 1999 and 2000. Rarely did a day pass when someone didn't call with an opportunity or a gift or an idea to improve Ole Miss. The outpouring of support and affection was somewhat overwhelming. When we needed $30 million for salary enhancement, it came. If we needed $3.8 million to build a chapel, the people who could make that happen showed up in my office. If it took $20 million to build a performing arts center, a foundation appeared that met the need. And when the school was long overdue for a championship football team, a young man named Manning committed to play football at Ole Miss.

Some might call this synchronicity . . . or luck. To me, it felt like divine intervention.

In the fall of 1999, Jim Barksdale called to schedule a meeting. We met in early November at the chancellor's residence on campus.

After we caught up on our wives and children, Jim said he and

Sally had been discussing what they could do to help our state.

"We want every young child in Mississippi to be reading at the third-grade level within three years," he said.

I wasn't sure this kind of progress was even possible.

"How do you plan to do that?" I asked.

"We're going to start a reading institute that does nothing but focus on early childhood education." Jim added that it was the single greatest obstacle Mississippi faced.

Jim said he and Sally wanted to make the gift to the state of Mississippi. They wanted all the universities to share in the work to be done, as well as the $100 million they planned to put into the program.

"What can we do to help?" I asked.

"Tell me what you can do."

My first thought was that we could help with the announcement, to fashion the story in a way that might repair some of the damage to the state's reputation. And I knew just the person to call to help with that project.

Then, I thought of something else.

"Let us take care of the money," I suggested. "We can invest the funds in the university's foundation."

55

Archie Manning could not have been more enthusiastic about David Cutcliffe — as a coach, a friend, and a human being. David started his coaching career as a student assistant under Alabama's legendary Bear Bryant. Later, at Tennessee, David moved up the coaching ranks. In 1990, he was appointed quarterbacks coach. Three years later he moved to offensive coordinator.

Archie's son Peyton had played quarterback for the Volunteers under Coach Cutcliffe. Peyton, during his four years playing at Tennessee, shattered every school quarterback record, broke most SEC passing marks, was selected an All-American, and won nearly every major national award except the Heisman Trophy.

With Archie's endorsement, we invited David Cutcliffe to visit the campus, and I immediately knew we would make him an offer. On December 2, 1998, just a few days after Tommy Tuberville left for Auburn, we hired David as head football coach for the Ole Miss Rebels. And he had to hit the ground running. Ole Miss was scheduled to play Texas Tech in the Independence Bowl on New Year's Eve. David had thirty days to learn players' names, implement some of his own game plan, and teach the team a new system . . . or learn the one left behind by Tommy Tuberville.

The new coaching staff had time for fewer than a dozen pre-bowl workouts, so they decided to learn the old system. If that weren't enough pressure, a few days before the bowl game, David suffered from an inflamed pancreas. But he never quit. He won the hearts of all Ole Miss fans during the days before the bowl game. It didn't hurt that we beat Texas Tech 35-18. Deuce McAllister scored three touchdowns — one on a swing pass, one on a running play, and one returning an onside kick forty-three yards for a score.

After the game, Coach Cutcliffe set about building a program at

Ole Miss that was all his own. He also had some recruiting business in New Orleans. Archie's youngest son, Eli, was a high school senior. He also happened to be one of the most promising and highly sought-after college prospects in the country.

I wanted the $100 million gift from Jim and Sally Barksdale to get the national press it deserved. I also thought it would be another important story that might change the perception of Mississippi. So I called my friend and Ole Miss alumnus Campbell McCool. Campbell owned and operated one of the most innovative advertising and public relations firms in Atlanta. McCool Communications represented Delta Airlines, CNN, Bridgestone, and dozens of other large companies.

Campbell had also co-chaired the Rowan Oak Society with the Barksdales' daughter Susan. The society's mission was to raise money for the renovation of William Faulkner's home, as well as create an endowment that would fund its maintenance. I knew Campbell loved Ole Miss. I also knew he could help us get the media attention the gift merited.

Campbell accepted my invitation to meet in Oxford with Jim and Sally, Gloria Kellum, Andy Mullins, and a handful of other trusted staff members. I wanted to keep the gathering as small as possible because we didn't want the news to leak before we could hold a press conference.

As I had done at the faculty retreat a year earlier, I asked everyone in attendance to look to his or her right and left.

"Remember this moment," I said. "What we're about to do will change the state of Mississippi."

Then I asked Jim and Sally to tell the group about their plan to invest $100 million in early education and reading for the children of Mississippi.

Campbell asked, "When are you planning to announce this?"

"Sixty days," I said.

"You'll never keep it a secret that long," Campbell told us.

56

I had known about Trent Lott since childhood. He grew up in Pascagoula, a town that shared a border with Moss Point. His future wife, Tricia Thompson, was a dear childhood friend of my sister Kathy. The two girls spent many of their days together and Tricia was often at our home.

I'm several years older than Trent, so we really didn't become good friends until our days at Ole Miss. I was a law student and Trent was an undergraduate.

Trent was popular and well-known on campus. In fact, he was a cheerleader. He even worked part-time as a student recruiter for Ole Miss. Then he entered law school.

In 1967, after Trent earned his law degree, he moved with Tricia from Oxford to Pascagoula. At the same time, Margaret and I moved to Moss Point. The four of us filled a U-Haul truck with our meager household possessions and made the move together.

Trent joined a fine law firm in Pascagoula but was soon lured to Washington to serve as the chief of staff for Congressman William Colmer, a longtime member of the House of Representatives (and the man who defeated my father twice). When Mr. Colmer reached the age of retirement, Trent — declaring himself to be a Republican — ran for the Fifth District seat being vacated by Congressman Colmer. Trent won handily against a popular Gulfport Democrat, Ben Stone, in large part due to Richard Nixon. In the 1972 election, President Nixon won 87 percent of the Fifth District vote. It was the most pro-Nixon, pro-Republican district in the nation.

Trent served four terms as a young member of the House. Then he was elected Minority Whip. Though none of us could have guessed how politically astute Trent would become, he proved to be an able congressman with an unusual ability to build consensus and reach middle ground on divisive issues. Over the years, Trent developed a strong base of support in the Fifth Congressional District of Mississippi. He was also gaining respect and popularity in the U.S. House and in other districts of Mississippi.

Then, in 1987, John Stennis announced his retirement after serving forty-two years in the U.S. Senate. Trent ran for the seat and won.

Trent worked tirelessly for the people of Mississippi and used his extraordinary people and political skills to develop working relationships with Democratic members of the Senate. And he held steadfast to a lesson that had served him well — "compromise is the key to survival."

Ole Miss has always produced great leaders and Trent Lott was no exception. I can remember, as a teenager, reading about people in government or business or sports whom I admired. Generally, at the end of the news article or feature story, the writer would mention that the person had graduated from the University of Mississippi. Early in my chancellorship, it occurred to me that there should be some kind of formalized leadership training at Ole Miss. I believed there was a place for the creation of a special program or institute for our aspiring student leaders.

I approached Senator Lott with the idea, but initially he was reluctant to commit to the venture. When he became majority leader, I strongly urged him to agree to the creation of the Trent Lott Leadership Institute, an academic program that would combine public policy and political science to provide opportunities for students interested in becoming leaders whether in government, business, ministry, education, or other professions. Finally, Trent agreed.

However, we still had to fund the initiative. In one of our conversations about raising money to support the institute, we stumbled upon an idea. Trent and I both loved music. We brainstormed and ultimately conceived "Ole Miss at the Kennedy Center"— a gala honoring Senate Majority Leader Trent Lott.

We agreed that all performers would be Mississippians, and all would agree to donate their time and talent. We also agreed on a ticket price: $1,000.

57

We planned to announce the Barksdales' $100 million gift on the steps of the old Central High School in Jackson on January 19, 2000. Two days before the announcement — just before McCool Communications' media blitz — *The Daily Mississippian* broke the story. Jim, Campbell, and I were none too happy about it, but we knew it was a tall order to keep a $100 million story quiet. Nonetheless, the official announcement was greeted with the excitement and fanfare for which we had hoped, and the major media outlets in the country covered the gift.

The following morning, *The New York Times* ran a front-page story. It read, "The gift is thought by authorities on philanthropy to be by far the largest ever made in the field of literacy. And because the donation will establish an institute at the University of Mississippi, it is also one of the five largest donations by a private individual or foundation to a public university, according to rankings maintained by *The Chronicle of Higher Education*."

The *Times* didn't just publish the feature story. The following day, the editorial board published an opinion column. In it the editors wrote, "The gift represents a transfer of wealth from people on the cutting edge of society to people who are struggling just to get started. It also sets an inspiring example for Mr. Barksdale's fellow high-tech millionaires, many of whom are still in full wealth-accumulation mode."

During the weeklong media frenzy, Jim and Sally appeared on television and radio shows around the country. It could not have been more positive, and people were talking about Mississippi leading the way in privately funded literacy.

When Jim and I appeared on the *Today Show*, Katie Couric questioned Jim about the enormity of the gift. Jim told her, "When we die, if there's a dollar left, it's because I've miscalculated."

58

When Larry and Susan Martindale came to visit Oxford, the first thing we did was take a walk through campus. I explained that one of my goals was to enhance the natural beauty of the campus.

"Deferred maintenance," I commented, as we walked by buildings in need of repair, weed-infested flowerbeds, and patches of dirt. The deterioration was patently obvious. "It impacts the perception of the campus — negatively — internally and externally."

I wasn't telling Larry anything he didn't already know. As owner of several Ritz-Carlton hotels, he understood the importance of a first impression. At his hotels, nothing but the best would do, and that included landscaping.

I explained that academic programs, student-life programming, salaries, library acquisitions, technology, and a variety of other university needs were always going to be funded, at least with state-appropriated money, before maintenance and beautification of the grounds.

At the end of our walk, Larry and Susan told me they wanted to help improve the beauty of the campus and agreed to a significant multiyear gift . . . if we moved campus beauty up the priority list and invested some additional funds in the effort.

"You can count on it," I said.

Then, the Martindales really surprised me. In addition to funding the beautification effort, the Martindales wanted to be hands-on partners in transforming the Ole Miss campus.

The first thing they did was introduce me to a young man from Atlanta who consulted with us to get the efforts underway. He and I selected a visible part of the inner campus as a pilot project. The improvement — in both function and beauty — was a bit overwhelming. That area, located between the library and the old gymnasium, quickly became a favorite route for pedestrians. I was convinced we had to expand the effort.

I knew we needed someone permanent to lead this effort. The consultant suggested I visit Dr. Harry Ponder, a professor of horticulture at Auburn University. I told Dr. Ponder about our dreams for our campus. I asked him for names of graduates of his program who might be able to help.

"I want it to be the most beautiful in the nation," I said.

"You're the first university president who has ever called," Dr. Ponder replied.

Then, he gave me the names of two young graduates of his program, and I arranged interviews.

One of the recent graduates was Jeff McManus. When he arrived on campus, we walked the grounds and talked. I was taken with him immediately. He was personable and clearly knowledgeable. He was leading the landscape program at the Turnberry Hotel — a five-star property known for the beauty of its grounds and golf courses.

"Jeff," I said, "I'd like for you to join us and make Ole Miss a five-star campus."

"There would be two conditions," he told me.

"What are they?"

"First," Jeff said. "I want to report directly to you."

"Done," I told him without hesitation. I had already planned to be involved in the process. What Jeff didn't realize was that landscaping was one of my great loves. "And the second?" I asked.

"I'll need a pickup truck."

My fantasy is to perform as a musician or produce musical events. I loved promoting an event at the Kennedy Center. In May of 1999, the very best musicians and entertainers from Mississippi, including Marty Stuart, Mary Ann Mobley, Gary Collins, Guy Hovis, Sam and Mary Haskell, Laurie Gayle Stevenson, and Morgan Freeman performed at the center, but the primary draw was Trent Lott. The main hall was sold-out. In addition, several large corporations made substantial donations to support the formation of the leadership institute.

At the gala, I was seated next to Secretary of Health and Human Services Donna Shalala. We spent part of the evening talking, and she loved the sound of the Mississippi musicians. We had a common Lebanese heritage and had met when she was chancellor at the University of Wisconsin-Madison from 1988 to 1993. By the evening's end, I felt like we would be lifelong friends. I invited her to come visit the Ole Miss campus, and Donna assured me she would make the trip.

At the end of a magnificent evening that showcased Mississippi's finest musicians, I felt certain we had a good start funding the Trent Lott Leadership Institute.

I was back in Oxford when I heard the final tally. The event had produced $13 million.

59

On February 28, 1878, the Mississippi Legislature created the Agricultural and Mechanical College of the State of Mississippi near Starkville. It became one of the national land-grant colleges established after the U.S. Congress had passed the Morrill Act of 1862.

Attempting to be balanced, Congress gave the University of Mississippi 23,000 acres of timberland in Stone, George, and Harrison counties. For more than 100 years, we had "managed" the forestlands with very little benefit to the university and with plenty of headaches for university administrators.

We generated a small annual income from harvesting the timber. In recent years, every time we harvested, a local television crew arrived to film the rough-and-tumble cutting and clearing of timber and ran a story about keeping America green. Then, predictably, I would receive critical mail and phone calls.

When Rex Deloach asked me if I'd like to turn $150,000 per year into $2 million a year, I had no idea what he meant. I don't think anyone had ever thought of ways to expand the benefit of the forestlands to the university.

"I think we can sell the land for $40 million," Rex said. "In the endowment," he added, "the funds could generate $2 million a year, maybe more."

I had some reservations. First, a university selling land — land that could never be recovered — would have some political implications. Second, I wasn't sure who would pay $40 million for land in the middle of nowhere.

I had been batting ideas around about Rex's concept of selling the timberland when it occurred to me that the 23,000 acres were adjacent to the DeSoto National Forest.

During one of our meetings, I asked Andy Mullins, "Do you think the federal government would buy it back?"

He just smiled and shrugged.

I called our senator and friend Thad Cochran. Senator Cochran immediately saw the value in the plan. He agreed to introduce legislation appropriating up to $43 million to enable the U.S. Forest Service to purchase the land.

Andy outlined the political and governmental hurdles the sale would pose, but the income potential was so great, we decided to take it on. We divided responsibilities among the three of us. Rex would produce the financial plan. Andy would lead the state government initiative. I would pursue the federal government angle, as well as speak with Governor Kirk Fordice, Secretary of State Eric Clark, and members of the IHL board.

It didn't take long for news to leak that Ole Miss was selling forestland. An opposition group formed in South Mississippi. They called themselves the "Save Our Forest Lands" group. The group leader was an LSU graduate who created an uproar, including individuals calling me to say, "Don't sell. They aren't making any more land!"

As Andy worked with the state legislature, I worked with the governor, the secretary of state, and the IHL board. Though all parties had questions, they bought into the idea at just about the same time Senator Cochran gained authorization for the appropriation.

Rex had obtained three appraisals of the land, which ranged from $39 million to $42 million. We agreed that the fair price was $40 million.

Andy worked a deal with the Legislature to restrict the funds to the university endowment with earnings to be used strictly for repair and renovation of buildings and support systems on the Oxford campus.

Andy and I met with a representative from the U.S. Forest Service in Jackson at Eric Clark's office for final execution of the documents. We delivered the deed to the land. Then the forest service representative handed us a check.

Immediately following that meeting, Andy and I went to see Governor Fordice. We reported the consummation of the sale.

Governor Fordice said, "You are telling me that the United States government has just paid you $40 million to purchase land they gave to you in the 1870s?"

Andy and I nodded.

"Sounds like a pretty good deal to me," he said. Then Governor Fordice, who was no supporter of liberal spending by Congress, sat in the chair behind his desk, shook his head in disgust, and added, "No wonder our damn government is broke."

Since Larry and Susan Martindale were spending so much time working with us to beautify the campus, they decided to purchase a home in Oxford. I couldn't have been happier. Susan and Margaret had become friends, and the four of us spent many hours together. In addition, the Martindales' funding and support were beginning to yield results.

Pete Boone suggested, as a show of gratitude for Larry and Susan's work, that we name the newly renovated student services building — a building formerly known as the Old Gymnasium — Martindale Hall.

"It makes sense," Pete said. "Larry played every home game in the old gym when he was an undergraduate on the basketball team."

The Martindales had, in short order, changed the way people felt when they arrived on campus. The first impression was vastly different from two years earlier. Naming the old gym in their honor was a fitting tribute.

Jeff McManus and his team were setting a standard for everyone on campus. He was not only a great landscaper, he was also an amazing leader. In one of his first acts, he asked me if he could reduce the size of his staff from thirty to twenty-one.

"But I'd need to keep the same budget," he said.

Most of Jeff's employees were making minimum wage. The attrition rate was high. He wanted to weed out those who weren't going to work for excellence, keep those who would, and pay the remaining employees a better wage.

Next, Jeff started training his staff, including touring universities in the Southeast to see how they did things. Jeff implemented efficiencies and made certain his staff acted and performed consistently with our vision and mission. I quickly grew to trust Jeff completely.

One day he came to my office and said, "We need to raise the canopy of the trees in the Grove."

I knew that meant cutting off the lower limbs of trees. And I knew that any cutting of trees was sensitive business.

"If we raise the canopy, the grass will grow better," he said. "Most people won't notice," he added.

"How high do you want to raise it?"

"Twenty feet," he said.

I've always believed that I should employ people who are better at their job than I would be, and I also believe in giving them the authority to make decisions. But I was nervous about cutting all the limbs off trees in the Grove from the ground up to twenty feet.

"Why don't we start with twelve feet?" I suggested. "And can you do the work at night?"

Jeff laughed. He knew I was kidding, but he also knew I wanted to avoid a controversy.

"If there is no uproar over twelve feet," I said, "let's come back and go to twenty."

Jeff and his team trimmed the trees to twelve feet. No one said a word and the impact was stunning. Jeff had been right all along.

Philadelphia

My family on vacation in 1951. Left to right: William "Fishbait" Miller (doorkeeper to the House of Representatives), Congressman William M. Colmer, Edna Khayat, Edward A. Khayat, Eva P. Khayat, Robert Khayat, Eddie Khayat, and Kathy Khayat

60

On the morning of October 19, 2000, John Hope Franklin boarded a train in his hometown of Durham to travel to Philadelphia, Pennsylvania. At about the same time, Gloria Kellum, Jeff Alford, Ron Schroeder, and I boarded a plane at the Oxford/University airport. Our destination was the Triennial Council of Phi Beta Kappa.

The council, made up of 300 delegates from 230 colleges and universities, convened at the Sheraton Society Hill Hotel. On day two of the convention, the delegates would vote on whether Ole Miss was worthy to shelter a chapter of Phi Beta Kappa.

We had worked for three years to get to this point. In early 1997, Ron and I had delivered a 107-page preliminary application to Phi Beta Kappa headquarters in Washington. It was the third time Ole Miss had submitted an application since the 1970s. In February of 1999, a small group of Phi Beta Kappa members — the Committee on Qualifications — visited our campus. It was a successful trip, and I sensed they liked what they saw at Ole Miss.

Three months later, we discovered, the visiting committee recommended our application to the Phi Beta Kappa senate. After a seven-month review, the senate recommended us to the full council.

Ole Miss had never made it this far in the process. Though I believed we were more than deserving of the honor, I worried about the perceptions the delegates might have about our university.

To say that I was nervous would be a tremendous understatement. I'd become somewhat obsessed with sheltering a chapter at Ole Miss. We were not only *the* University of Mississippi, but we were also one of only four flagship universities that did not have this distinction. The others were the universities of Alaska, Montana, and Nevada.

Ole Miss was being considered along with seven other universities, including Auburn, Truman State and St. Joseph's.

At 9:00 a.m. on Saturday, October 21, Phi Beta Kappa President Frederick Crosson called the second plenary session of the Triennial Council to order. The first item of business was to vote on new chapters.

Each of the eight prospective universities was discussed separately. Of course the discussion was conducted in alphabetical order, which put us last. A member of the Committee on Qualifications first gave a report on the school. Then, the delegates asked questions. The banter was lively and the questions ranged from graduation rates, number of nonwestern subjects offered, diversity, the presence of faculty unions, and student/faculty ratios. Four hours passed before the report on Ole Miss.

The Phi Beta Kappa representative who offered the report on Ole Miss was positive and upbeat about the strides we had made at the university. She mentioned the library holdings and the honors college and the endowment for faculty salaries.

At the conclusion of the report, one gentleman asked, "What are the graduation rates?"

The same question had been asked of Auburn University. Their answer was 64 percent.

"The percentage is in the low 50s," she said.

Another member of the committee came to our defense. "Remember, there are more first-generation college students at Ole Miss. And many also work part-time, skewing the percentages based on a five-year graduation rate."

There were other questions about minority enrollment and diversity among the faculty.

Then, John Hope Franklin stood and walked to the front of the hall. When President Crosson saw Dr. Franklin, he said, "The chair recognizes former Phi Beta Kappa President John Hope Franklin."

The gentleman who sat at my kitchen table two years earlier stood in front of 300 delegates. He wore a dark suit with the Presidential Medal of Honor on the lapel.

He stood, silently, for a moment. The room was quiet. Then John Hope Franklin spoke.

"Distinguished colleagues, I am here today to speak on behalf of Ole Miss. I think you all know that I understand discrimination. I urge you today to cast your vote for the University of Mississippi based on its merits, not on an outdated, inaccurate reputation. I have been to the Ole Miss campus. I have participated in discussions with their students and faculty, and I can say, without hesitation, that they are doing as good a job addressing the issue of race as any university in America. I thank you for your consideration."

President Crosson closed the question-and-answer session, thanked the committee for its hard work, and called for a vote. He reminded the delegates that the voting on chapters was by delegation and secret ballot. All non-delegates were asked to retire from the hall.

When Dr. Franklin and I ate cereal and talked in 1998 at the chancellor's home, I did not know he had served as president of Phi Beta Kappa, and our application was never mentioned.

He came to the convention without being asked. He helped us at his own expense.

Leaving the conference hall, I saw an African-American delegate sitting at the very end of the back table. As I passed him, I glanced down. His ballot was on the corner of the table. He had already cast his votes. Next to the University of Mississippi, he had checked the box that read "No."

I found a seat in the hotel lobby outside the convention hall. And I waited.

I'd visited Philadelphia as a child. In 1951, we took our one and only family vacation. The six members of the Khayat family piled into an unairconditioned Chevrolet Bel Air and headed up the East Coast. We stopped in Atlanta for our first night. In Washington, we visited the Capitol and the Library of Congress. In Philadelphia, we saw the Liberty Bell and Ben Franklin's print shop. We swam in the ocean at Atlantic City. In New York, we toured the Metropolitan Museum of Art, Grand Central Station, and Central Park. The six of us stayed in a single room with a kitchenette at the Hotel Astor. Our mother cooked our meals in two pots she'd purchased along the way and we ate in the hotel room.

One of our last stops was a trip to Yankee Stadium, home to Babe Ruth, Yogi Berra, Mickey Mantle, as well as dozens of football greats. As a thirteen-year-old boy, standing next to my brother, Eddie, leaning over the stadium rails, I'd never been so thrilled. We sat in the stadium seats and talked about all that had happened here before.

My father looked over at his two sons. Eddie's face was broken out with a terrible case of acne, and he was mad at the world. I was a skinny, clueless kid with a crew cut.

"Someday," my father said, "I'll come watch you boys play at Yankee Stadium."

Nine years later, on October 16, 1960, I stood in the cool shadows of a stadium tunnel. This was the place I had dreamed about for a decade. My fellow Redskins and I began to move along the tunnel. When we passed through the dugout and into the light of day, I stepped onto that hallowed ground. Before stretching and calisthenics, my teammate Billy Brewer and I ran out to the center field wall to touch the plaques honoring Babe Ruth and Lou Gehrig. We were about to play a professional football game, but we might as well have been tourists. I saw former Ole Miss great and New York Giants quarterback Charlie Conerly. I shook his hand and said hello.

As I ran back across the turf at Yankee Stadium, I thought of the history embedded in the soil and in every blade of grass. I felt as if I needed to shout or cry or maybe turn a cartwheel. As I moved through the scent of hot dogs, beer, and cigar smoke and listened to the distinctive public address announcer, I wished that my high school friends could have been running alongside me.

The Giants were a much better team. In the previous season, their defense, under the direction of Tom Landry, led the league in rush defense and pass defense. Their offense, directed by Vince Lombardi, had scored 284 points. They finished the regular season 10-2 and played against the Baltimore Colts in the NFL championship game. The Giants' roster included Frank Gifford and Charlie Conerly, Sam Huff and Jimmy Patton, Rosey Grier and Pat Summerall.

The previous year for the Redskins was a bit of a different story. My new team had been last in scoring, as well as last in points scored against. We opened the 1960 season being whipped by the defending champions, the Baltimore Colts, 20-0. Our only win came against a newly formed expansion team — the Dallas Cowboys.

The Giants took a quick lead. Pat Summerall kicked a long field goal, followed by a Frank Gifford touchdown. In the second quarter, with the Giants leading 10-0, they stopped us on their forty-three-yard line. Our coach called for the field goal unit.

We huddled, broke, and the team fell into formation. I stood on the Giants' forty-seven-yard line. Our center, Jim Schrader, wrapped his hands around the ball. Our holder, Dick James, dropped to one knee, held his fingers on the dirt where he would place the ball, and extended his right arm toward the line of scrimmage. The Giants players were yelling, *Hook it! Miss it!*, along with some obscenities, to distract me. The crowd of 60,000 was on its feet screaming.

Then, all the noise disappeared. I focused, just as my father had taught me, just as I had practiced a thousand times before. Shoulders squared. Eyes on the spot where the ball would be placed.

I heard the snap and the sound of the ball hitting Dick's hands. The placement was perfect. I kept my head down, my eye on the ball, and kicked through until my shoe was a full foot above my head. I couldn't see anything behind the huge linemen, but the ball went through the uprights.

I had been calm before the kick, but after the ball cleared the crossbar my teammates swarmed around me.

I didn't realize it at the moment, but I later discovered I'd made the longest field goal in Redskins history. It was just shy of the NFL record, and it was, by far, the longest field goal of my career.

The convention hall doors burst open. The votes had been counted. Douglas Foard walked toward me.

"Chancellor," he said, "we chose four universities to shelter chapters of Phi Beta Kappa." Then, he put his hand on my shoulder, "And the University of Mississippi is one of them. Congratulations."

The fifty-yard field goal on October 16, 1960, at Yankee Stadium

As I celebrated with Ron, Jeff, and Gloria, John Hope Franklin boarded the train for his return trip to Durham. The eighty-five-year-old was a rare combination of scholar and moral figure. His books transformed the way we understood our own history. His witness to — and leadership in — our efforts to reconcile differences were conducted with kindness and civility. He was a generous, dignified, compassionate gentleman. A man who spent his life fighting for fairness and equality.

On this day, John Hope Franklin fought for Ole Miss. And we were graced by his generosity.

The New Millennium

61

During the 2000 Oxford Conference for the Book, two former journalists for *The Boston Globe* — Curtis Wilkie and Tom Oliphant — were having late-night drinks at the home of Campbell McCool.

Tom mentioned how beautiful the campus looked and how impressed he was with the students, faculty, and — from what he could tell — the academic programs.

Campbell, whose business was to understand media and public relations said, "Yeah, but every time Ole Miss is mentioned in the national media, the next words the greater world hears are *riot* and *race* and *two deaths* and *James Meredith*."

"You know," Tom said, "something that would go a long way toward repairing that reputation would be to host a presidential debate here." He added that the vice presidential debate at Centre College changed the way the world viewed that institution.

The three men went back to their drinks and nothing more was said.

Two weeks later, Tom Oliphant — who has no formal connection with Ole Miss — called Janet Brown, executive director of the Commission on Presidential Debates. He proposed having one of the debates at Ole Miss.

As it turned out, Janet Brown's father grew up on a farm outside Como, just a few miles north of campus. Janet loved the idea.

That afternoon, Campbell called my office.

"Robert," he said, "I want you to think out of the box for a moment . . . and put on your really big idea hat."

When Campbell told me about Tom's idea — especially the part about 2,000 journalists from around the world descending on Oxford and Ole Miss for four days — I was completely on board. Campbell said there was more work to be done. Although having Janet Brown's support was a plus, the chairs of both the Democratic and Republican parties would have to sign off on the location.

"Tom Oliphant is calling them as we speak," Campbell said.

As soon as I put the phone in its cradle, I walked across the hallway to Andy Mullins' office.

"Andy," I said, "what do you know about presidential debates?"

Tom Oliphant took it upon himself to reach out to representatives of the Democratic and Republican national parties. Both parties not only were willing to come to Oxford, but they seemed genuinely excited about the prospect.

At the same time, Andy started researching the logistics of hosting a debate. Janet Brown told him about the process and procedures of getting approval. She told Andy we would need $4 million. Then she mentioned that during a debate, when a sitting president participates — and George W. Bush was surely planning to participate — no automobiles would be allowed within a one-mile radius of the venue.

Andy also called the debate coordinator at Wake Forest, who painted a dismal picture of the amount of time, money, and energy the debate consumed. "Life at the university came to a grinding halt," the Wake Forest representative said.

Andy, Gloria, and I scheduled a conference call with Campbell about the logistical problems of hosting a debate at Ole Miss when a sitting president participated. We explained that we all felt the event, at least the 2004 debate, was too big for us to tackle — in terms of money and logistics. Campbell was clearly unhappy.

"This is the one event that will get people talking about something other than race," he said over the speakerphone. "We need this. And Ole Miss will never have a more significant platform to tell our story."

"We'd have to close down the Oxford square for four days," Andy said. "The one-mile radius is just too much. Where would cars park?"

"Guys," Campbell said, "we have greased the rails for this to happen — to showcase Ole Miss on an international stage. All the powers that be have signed off on it . . . and you're talking about parking?"

We told Campbell how much we appreciated his efforts, as well as Curtis' and Tom's, but that we all agreed it was too much for us at this point.

"Maybe in four years, when there's not an incumbent," Andy said.

"I can't believe you are passing on this chance," Campbell said. "This is why we can't get out of last place." Campbell paused and the room was quiet. I didn't know how to respond. Campbell concluded the call with, "Personally, I think you're all making a huge mistake."

62

One of our university's most distinguished graduates, Arthur Guyton, was born in Oxford in 1919. He graduated at the top of his class at University High School in 1936. After finishing his undergraduate degree at Ole Miss in three years — again, at the top of his class — he attended Harvard Medical School. His residency training was interrupted by World War II, but after serving his country, he returned to Massachusetts to complete his training.

Within a year of beginning his medical practice, Dr. Guyton was stricken with polio. Dr. Guyton's right leg and shoulder were paralyzed. He spent nine months in rehabilitation in Warm Springs, Georgia.

While there, Dr. Guyton designed a special leg brace, created a hoist for moving patients from bed to chair to bathtub, and invented a motorized wheelchair controlled by an electric "joystick." For these inventions, he would later receive a presidential citation. Dr. Guyton had planned to be a surgeon, but the paralysis made that impossible, so he and his wife, Ruth, moved back to Oxford, where he accepted a position on the medical faculty at the University of Mississippi Medical School.

In 1956, based on his classroom notes, he published *Guyton's Textbook of Medical Physiology*. It became one of the most widely read medical textbooks in the world. Dr. Guyton's research and writings, including more than 600 papers and forty books, were legendary. He was considered one of the greatest figures in the history of cardiovascular physiology.

The Guytons had ten children. All of them went to medical school, and all attended Harvard — two as undergraduates, eight as medical students.

In early 2000, I suffered a severe attack of pancreatitis. I went to the emergency room at Baptist Memorial Hospital in Oxford. As I waited for a physician to arrive, my thoughts went back thirty-eight years.

I was twenty-two years old and the picture of good health. I'd just finished my rookie season with the Washington Redskins. That year, I led the NFL in kicking and played in the Pro Bowl. I'd met the girl I would marry, and I felt as if I had my entire life ahead of me.

Although I was having some success in the NFL, I wanted to be a high school history teacher. To complete my degree, I was required to practice teach. My assignment was in Vicksburg. I lived in the YMCA.

On the morning of April 15, 1961, without warning, I woke up with a burning pain in my abdomen. I stumbled down the stairs of the YMCA. Ernest Hovious, brother of my college coach Junie Hovious, took me to Mercy Hospital. The doctor who examined me that day wasn't certain about his diagnosis. He thought that the pain could be stemming from a ruptured appendix. He called my parents to get permission to do surgery. They told the doctor to do what he thought was best. He made a ten-inch incision in the center of my abdomen. When he saw my inflamed pancreas, he was alarmed. Surgery is not recommended to treat pancreatitis.

I didn't regain full consciousness for weeks, and I was heavily sedated at all times. The nurses fed me through an IV. I didn't eat a bite of food.

I remained at Mercy Hospital in Vicksburg for eighty-two days — from April 15 until early July. My mother spent every night with me in room 315. She slept in a lounge chair next to me when I had drains placed in my abdominal cavity, tubes down my throat, IVs in my arms. She also watched and waited as I went through blood transfusions and three separate surgeries.

Midway through my hospitalization, a priest was called to my bedside. The doctors and medical staff at Mercy Hospital did not believe I had a chance to survive. They told my mother and father to prepare.

I was dying. My parents stood at my bedside. The priest administered last rites.

The night I reached my lowest point, on the brink of death, my brother and sisters were called to Vicksburg. The doctors had given up. As my family circled around me, I was suddenly pain free, and felt cool. I saw translucent figures in a mist that was blue and gray with hints of green.

Though I didn't know it at the time, a black preacher in Moss Point, 170 miles away, a man I didn't know, got out of bed at midnight. He knelt next to his bed and prayed for me throughout the night.

By dawn, my condition had improved. From that day forward, my health improved each day. I couldn't explain what happened. Neither could my doctors.

I had lost so much weight, my grayish skin hung from my bones and I hadn't eaten solid food in months. Toward the end of my stay, my friend Bo Ball — after a night out on the town in Vicksburg — came to visit. When he entered the room, I cocked open one eye and said, "My God, you look like hell."

The day I suffered the attack of pancreatitis, I weighed 245 pounds. When I was finally discharged, I was down to 160.

In 2000, the physicians at Baptist Memorial Hospital seemed as perplexed about how to treat me as the doctors at Mercy Hospital in 1961. Pancreatitis is apparently rare, and the recommended treatments sometimes seem counter-intuitive to a doctor.

Thankfully, on the night in 2000 when I suffered my attack, the sixth child of Dr. Guyton — Dr. Jean Gispen — was on call. Jean is a patient, caring physician. She also had the Guyton curiosity and intellect. She found a medical text that covered pancreatitis, studied it, and returned to my hospital room with an understanding of how to treat me.

That night, Jean Gispen saved my life.

63

By the time I was five years old, before I started going to school, I had the run of our Moss Point neighborhood. Everything was within walking distance — the church, the school, the lake, the woods, the cemetery, and the store. I spent my days playing cowboys and Indians and hide and seek in the cemetery. I grew wise in the ways of avoiding the older boys who would harass, if not bully, the kids my age. Some days, I had chores or piano lessons, but on most days, I made my way through the neighborhood to see my friends.

One of my regular stops was to see Walter. A small man, no more than five feet five inches, he could not have weighed 125 pounds. He lived alone in a small shotgun house. It was in the backyard of the old man and woman for whom Walter worked.

Walter spent his days doing chores the old woman told him to perform. He cut the grass with the push reel mower, loaded sacks of feed onto a wagon, weeded the small garden, gathered pecans, harvested figs, ran errands, and milked the Jersey cow that stayed in a narrow stall in the barn.

No matter what Walter was doing, he would let me give him a hand. If I arrived during mealtime, I would join Walter while he ate. In the summers, he took his meals on the back porch of the big house. In the winters, he ate in the kitchen.

If I happened to come around at the end of the day, Walter would let me come inside his home. Eight brick pillars supported the small, one-room house, lifting it nearly three feet off the ground. The cool, dark space underneath was a haven for small animals escaping the heat. Unfinished wooden steps — stained gray by exposure — led to a small porch. The house had no electricity or gas or running water, and it was sparsely furnished. A pot-bellied stove sat in one corner of the house, its exhaust pipe running up the wall and out through

Me fishing in 1943, Moss Point

the tar-paper roof. There was an iron double bed and a short, weath-ered chest with two drawers. On top of the chest, Walter had a porce-lain pitcher, a bowl, and a coal oil lamp. A small mirror hung above the chest. It hung from a single nail. Next to the bed were a ladder-back rocking chair and a small table, where Walter kept his Bible and pipe.

Walter's meager wardrobe, surely given to him by the old man, hung on nails on the inside of the front door. He owned a couple of dark trousers, three blue chambray shirts, and a mismatched navy suit.

When Walter was outside, doing chores, he was quiet. But at the end of the day, he talked constantly. He talked about the old man and woman, his accomplishments from his day's labor, as well as what was to be done tomorrow.

As I listened, Walter performed his end-of-the-day ritual: a shave. He removed his damp work shirt and hung it on a nail. He lit the coal oil lamp that illuminated the small room, and I could see the stark contrast between his undershirt and his dark skin. Then Walter poured water from the pitcher into the bowl, soaped his face with a shaving brush, and dragged the straight razor across his face. I was fascinated watching him methodically, masterfully scrape away the shaving cream with the shiny blade. With each stroke, he dipped the razor in the water to clean the blade.

When he was finished, Walter carried the bowl to the porch and emptied it in the yard. Then he went back inside and sat in his rocking chair. He filled his pipe with tobacco, lit it with a match, and started to rock. Without saying a word, we both knew that it was time for me to go home.

In the winter of 2001, the Ole Miss basketball team, under the direction of Coach Rod Barnes, won the SEC tournament with a vic-tory over Kentucky. With a record of 25-7, the Rebels were ranked No. 15 in the country.

The excitement of March Madness was in full swing, when our team was invited to play in the NCAA Midwest Regional Tournament in Kansas City. The Sunday before play began, the tournament directors announced the draw. Ole Miss was to play Iona College, a 22-10 team that had won the Metro Atlantic Athletic Conference.

On Tuesday — three days before the opening game — Sue Keiser handed me a copy of *The New York Daily News*. It told the story of a January 2, 1957, basketball game between Ole Miss and Iona College.

On that day, Ole Miss had traveled to Owensboro, Kentucky, to play in Kentucky Wesleyan's All-American Holiday Tournament. Ole Miss was on the court warming up, when Iona College ran in from the locker room. Ole Miss Coach Country Graham gathered his players together. Iona had one black player on its team, a sophomore from Brooklyn named Stanley Hill. Coach Graham had been instructed by Mississippi Governor J.P. Coleman to refuse to play against any integrated team. As Stanley stood on the court, practicing layups, the Ole Miss coach and players walked back into the locker room. Stanley Hill stood perfectly still in the middle of the court.

Tip-off time passed, and the announcer said over the loudspeaker, *Iona College wins by forfeit*. All eyes in the coliseum were on twenty-year-old Stanley Hill.

Later that night, back in the hotel, several of the Ole Miss players went to Stanley's room to apologize for the hurt and indignation the governor's stance caused. Stanley accepted the apology but didn't understand why someone would refuse to play a game because of race.

The next morning at breakfast, Country Graham apologized to Iona's coach Jim McDermott. "But I can't disobey the governor's order," Coach Graham told him.

When I finished reading the story, I was outraged. I called our sports information director and asked him to look up the game. A few minutes later, he told me there was no record of a 2-0 loss (the score statisticians use to record a forfeit) to Iona. He added that there wasn't even a record of Ole Miss participating in the tournament. The school record book had been washed clean.

I was suddenly thrown back to my senior year at Ole Miss, when we won the 1960 SEC baseball tournament but weren't allowed to play in the NCAA tournament because other teams were integrated. I simply accepted it. I asked no questions. Coach Swayze asked Dan

Jordan to write a letter requesting a reprieve, but other than that, no one on the team protested. We simply obeyed our orders.

I also thought of Walter. He was a kind man, and I like to imagine that he enjoyed my company and attention. But there was so much I didn't know about him. I knew nothing about his family or how he came to work for the old man and woman. I didn't know if he'd ever been married or had children of his own. I didn't know where he was born or if he ever went to school.

Perhaps most telling is that I was never curious about Walter's surname. It wasn't until many years after his death that I discovered his full name was Walter Oliver.

No one in the community seemed to know it, and certainly no one called him Mr. Oliver. Not even the children. He was just Walter. He lived behind the old man and woman voluntarily, but the way they treated him — and the way Walter reacted to them — was a remnant of a long-ago era.

I wish I could see Walter again. If I had the chance, I would thank him for being so kind to a young boy who was fascinated by the way he shaved and milked a cow. I'd apologize for not asking about his family or childhood, and I'd confess that I was so very sorry for not knowing him as Mr. Walter Oliver.

But it was too late to say all those things to Walter. And it was too late to go back to 1960 and ask the questions I probably should have asked. But it wasn't too late to reach out to Stanley Hill.

I asked Jeff Alford, our public relations director, to locate Stanley. Within an hour, Jeff had found him. Stanley lived in a neighborhood called Jamaica in Queens, New York, with his wife of forty-three years, Ruby. Jeff also had his phone number.

"Stanley," I said, when he answered the phone, "you don't know me, but my name is Robert Khayat. I'm the chancellor at Ole Miss."

I told Stanley that I had just this morning heard about the 1957 incident. I apologized on behalf of the university, told him about my frustrations with the egregious rule, and assured him that things had changed at Ole Miss.

Stanley said the experience had been hard. "I felt hurt and humiliated at the time," he said. Stanley had grown up on the streets of Brooklyn, where everyone played basketball together. He'd never experienced prejudice. And it wasn't just the Ole Miss team leaving the court. When he and his teammates tried to enter a Kentucky pool hall, the owner blocked the doorway and insisted that no blacks would ever enter his establishment.

Stanley said he didn't let the hurt turn him bitter. He used the experience to fight for working people through the unions. He was at peace with what transpired forty-four years before.

"Ruby and I were watching television when they announced the pairings," he said, "and we both screamed with laughter."

"Stanley," I said, "would you and Ruby consider being our guests in Kansas City?" I told him the invitation covered airfare, hotel, food, and tickets to Crosby Arena.

When he agreed to take us up on the gesture, he added, "I'll sit with you, but I'll be cheering for Iona."

On Thursday night before the game, Ole Miss Coach Rod Barnes asked if Stanley would come speak to his players.

"I want our kids to understand about our history," he said. "I want them to know what people went through so they could play basketball anywhere against anyone."

Stanley spoke to Coach Barnes and the team and told them of the events the last time Ole Miss and Iona played. At the end of the talk, he was presented with a game ball that had been signed by all the players and coaches.

Reaching out to Stanley was the right thing to do, but I also knew it was a perfect stage from which to show the world a new Ole Miss.

The night of the game, I sat next to Stanley and Ruby. Mississippi Governor Ronnie Musgrove sat on one side of us; Iona College President Brother James Liguori sat on the other. CBS broadcast the game, and it seemed like its cameras were on us as much as the players on the court. During breaks, the broadcasters interviewed Mr. and Mrs. Hill and asked Governor Musgrove and me about Mississippi and Ole

Miss. The game was close, but Ole Miss won 72-70.

At the game's end, I shook Stanley's hand and hugged Ruby. We all promised to stay in touch.

In the days that followed, feature stories about us reaching out to Stanley Hill were published in the *Denver Post*, the *Atlanta Journal-Constitution*, and the *Los Angeles Times*. The *Times* headline read, "A Sporting Gesture Puts New Ending on a Game that Racism Won in '57."

The press did wonders for how sports fans across the country perceived Ole Miss, and I felt that I had new friends in Stanley and Ruby. But most importantly, I felt we had made an effort to begin the healing of a forty-four-year-old wound.

64

In April of 2001, we set aside an entire weekend to celebrate. The Commitment to Excellence fundraising campaign had come to a close. The university had received $525.9 million. In addition, two buildings were ready to be presented to the public — a fully renovated Lyceum and Paris-Yates Chapel.

For 154 years, the Lyceum, the symbolic soul of the university, bore witness to peace and prosperity, as well as hardship and war. Seven generations of students had passed through its halls. But the centerpiece of our campus was weary — tired, worn, and in dire need of a facelift. With funds appropriated by the Legislature, and with the support of Governor Ronnie Musgrove, we were able to fund the $11 million renovation.

Jim Eley was the lead architect on the project, Roy Anderson Construction was the general contractor, and one of our most distinguished graduates, Lynda Mead Shea, was responsible for the interior design. The ultimate goals were to maintain the physical integrity of the building, assure executive office space that facilitated the intensive flow of business, and to capture its distinguished history. We also wanted every space to be beautiful with period decor reflecting the structure's long life.

During the two years of construction, Jim, Roy, and Lynda worked together to create a stunning renovation. As an added bonus, the Lyceum's original cornerstone, laid in 1846, was unearthed during construction. University records indicated that it contained several newspapers, legislative documents, a Bible, some silver coins, and a gold piece.

Several weeks prior to the grand opening of the Paris-Yates Chapel and Peddle Bell Tower, Frank Peddle came to test the carillon.

Frank, one of our former faculty members, was an accomplished pianist. He was also a meticulous scholar. Two years earlier, Frank had done an extensive survey of bell towers and manufacturers. Ultimately, he determined that we needed thirty-six bells. And they needed to be built by a company in Holland. With three octaves, the carillon would have great versatility. Late in the afternoon, as the sun sank behind the trees, Frank played the first song. He chose a slow, haunting version of *Dixie*.

Marge Peddle was also on hand when the final stone was placed at the base of the bell tower. Before the contractor placed the stone, Marge put a note, wrapped in a handkerchief, underneath it.

At the dedication, Lee Paris and his co-chair, Jean Jordan, Don and Mary Ann Frugé, and I spoke. Doug Dale, the architect for the project, was also at the ceremony. He understood the significance and sensitivity of the initiative. Doug is a very private man. His wife was battling cancer. I believe her illness — and its effect on Doug — heightened the spiritual elements of the chapel he designed.

The highlight of the dedication came as Mary Ann spoke. She explained that every religious organization on campus was represented at the ceremony. She then instructed each of them to stand and articulate in one word — yes, only one word — what the chapel would mean to his or her organization.

Then Mary Ann said, "One by one, each representative will proceed to the bell tower. When the last person speaks, we will all join hands as a symbol of the unity of purpose as reflected in one's faith and, concurrently, as a symbol of the beauty of diversity."

As the students from all walks of life uttered their one, carefully selected word and joined around the bell tower hand in hand, the University of Mississippi Concert Singers performed a moving rendition of *What a Wonderful World*.

65

Football taught me lots of lessons. Sometimes, it also opened doors, including the one evening I spent with Elvis.

In January 1961, several of us Ole Miss football players received a call from a classmate who lived next door to Graceland. She was a friend of Elvis. She told us he would like to meet some Ole Miss football players and wondered if we would like to visit him and spend some time with him.

We'd heard that Elvis slept during the daylight hours to avoid fans swarming him every time he was spotted. He didn't go out until after midnight. The call to us came on a cold, rainy Tuesday night at about 10:00 p.m. Of course we jumped at the invitation, and four of us drove to Memphis on a two-lane highway.

I remember, in 1956, when I fell in love with Elvis' music, listening to his songs while surrounded by beautiful girls in the Ole Miss cafeteria. He had the nation in turmoil.

Elvis was scheduled to perform in Memphis on the Fourth of July, 1956, at Russwood Park, a Memphis baseball stadium.

Ken Kirk, somehow, had managed to get three tickets to the concert — one for himself, one for Carl Comer, and one for me. The concert was scheduled for 7:00 p.m.

We left early in the morning for Memphis; we each had five dollars in our pockets. About twenty-five miles north of Oxford, Ken's Ford started to sputter. It stalled and started again and then finally came to rest on the side of the road south of Holly Springs. We abandoned Ken's car and hitchhiked to Memphis.

I had never been to Memphis, but Ken and Carl presented themselves as experienced travelers. We caught a ride with a nice older couple and rolled into Memphis in style.

The woman asked us where we were staying.

"The Gayoso Hotel," Ken said, without hesitation.

The Gayoso was a well-known, older hotel in downtown Memphis. The nice couple dropped us at the front door.

Ken went to the front desk while Carl and I waited on the sidewalk. Ken rented a single room for $7.50, and the three of us moved in. We didn't stay at the Gayoso long. We were anxious to get to the stadium.

We walked about a mile in the blistering heat to Russwood Park. We presented our tickets at the gate and claimed our seats in the stadium.

Elvis walked on stage. He wore all black except for a pink tie and pink socks. As Elvis moved toward the microphone, pandemonium broke out. Fans jumped from their seats, sprinted across the field, and swept onto the stage. Elvis asked them politely to return to their seats.

"You know," Elvis said to the crowd, "those people in New York aren't gonna change me none. I'm going to show you what the real Elvis is like tonight."

Then, Elvis Presley, Scotty Moore (guitar), Bill Black (bass), and D.J. Fontana (drums) launched into *Heartbreak Hotel*. The band rocked, rolled, crooned, and shook that stage for nearly two hours. The songs included *Blue Suede Shoes*, *Long Tall Sally*, *Hound Dog*, and *Don't Be Cruel*.

As Elvis completed the last song, the stadium lights were extinguished, and he was whisked away through the center field gate as hundreds of screaming girls chased his car.

Ken, Carl, and I stood perfectly still, stunned by what we had just witnessed.

We arrived at Graceland at about 11:30 p.m. Elvis had just finished dressing and was ready for a night of fun. He wore white trousers, a white open-collar shirt with an ascot, a blue double-breasted blazer, deck shoes, and a boat captain's hat. The quintessential movie star.

He was also a little awestruck by the four thick-necked, oversized football players. He started asking us about playing SEC football. We regaled Elvis with our best, funniest stories, and at about 12:30 a.m., he said, "Dy'all wanna go to the show?"

"Sure," I said.

"Follow me."

We jumped into separate cars and drove down the Graceland driveway.

Elvis drove three of his friends, and we followed his car to the Memphian Theater in Midtown Memphis. Although the neighborhood was closed for the night, the Memphian was open for Elvis — ushers, popcorn, and Cokes. The projector was ready to run when Elvis went in and sat down. There were eight of us in the theater. The hall went dark, and the film began. The film was *Never on Sunday*, an award-winning black-and-white film, which told the story of Ilya, a self-employed, free-spirited prostitute, and Homer, an American tourist enamored with all things Greek.

Elvis didn't like the movie. The moment it ended, he stood, the lights came on, and we walked up the aisle to the lobby. He said he needed to go to the bathroom and I followed.

As we stood at the urinals discussing the movie, I thought, *What in the world am I doing in a bathroom in Memphis, at a theater at three in the morning with Elvis Presley?* As we walked back into the lobby, he and his pals announced they were going to the skating rink and invited us to join them. We thanked him but declined. We told him we had eight o'clock classes. They left to go skating in the wee hours of the morning, and we drove back to Oxford wondering if we had dreamed the entire night. In fact, we all agreed we wouldn't tell our classmates.

They wouldn't believe it anyway.

66

I was constantly surprised by the loyalty and dedication of Ole Miss supporters but never more than in October of 2002. I received the most unusual, unexpected phone call of all my years as chancellor. It came on a Thursday before a Saturday home football game. The gentleman was from Texas.

After introducing himself, he said, "My father recently passed away."

I offered my condolences. Then the man told me that his father was an avid Ole Miss supporter who loved nothing more than Ole Miss football.

"One of my father's last requests," the man said, "was to have his ashes strewn in the end zone of your football stadium." He added that he was flying to Oxford on Saturday, urn in tow, to do just that.

I was speechless for a moment. When I finally gathered my wits, I freely confessed that I was puzzled and had no idea if there were any laws or regulations that prevented us from granting his request.

"I need to check with the university attorney," I said. "I'll call you later in the day to tell you what she says."

"Oh," he said, "one more thing. Dad asked that his ashes be spread in the exact spot that Bud Slay caught the winning touchdown pass to beat Maryland in 1952."

Mary Ann Connell, who always provided great legal advice, was as stunned as I had been when I asked for her opinion. This was a first, and neither of us knew of a reference to provide guidance.

We talked about any potential risks. We wondered if we would open the floodgates and be inundated with requests from others if we authorized the spreading of the ashes. Also, we didn't know if the church would go along (the deceased man was a Presbyterian).

Mary Ann and I both concluded that there was no legal impediment, and we didn't think it posed a health risk. Then I called Reverend Alan Cochet. He saw no good reason to deny the request.

I called the man from Texas with the news, and we agreed that eight o'clock on Saturday morning would be a good time for the service. We also decided there would be no announcements or invitations. The family of the deceased, the minister, and I would be the only people attending the service.

October Saturdays in Oxford are beautiful, especially on a football weekend. The town and the campus are lovely. The maple and bodock trees are a vivid yellow. The perennial plants and large, old oak and pecan trees haven't yet lost their leaves. Temperatures are generally forty-five to fifty degrees in the morning and mid-sixties in the afternoons. The skies are a deep blue and there is often a gentle breeze.

Game day electrifies the atmosphere not only of the campus and the town but for miles around as happy people roll down the highway with banners waving, their trunks filled with some of the best picnic food on the planet.

We all gathered together and walked through the Grove. At the stadium, we formed a circle in the northeast part of the north end zone. Reverend Cochet read from the burial liturgy and said a prayer. Then, members of the family each removed ashes from the urn and scattered them about as their father and grandfather had expressly requested. The ashes settled onto the turf in the exact spot Bud Slay caught the winning touchdown pass when Ole Miss beat the No. 1 team in the nation.

The day before I left the office for the holiday, I was packing some paperwork to take home, when I noticed a Christmas card. The return address was Jamaica Queens, New York. It was from Stanley and Ruby Hill. Stanley included a handwritten postscript: *Robert, I'm having a good time wearing my Ole Miss cap around the neighborhood.*

Just before I left the office, I heard from Pete Boone. He wanted to schedule a meeting early in the new year. He said, "We need to talk about Colonel Rebel."

67

During September of 2002, we celebrated the fortieth anniversary of integration at Ole Miss. We called the celebration "Open Doors: Forty Years of Opportunity."

We developed a self-guided walking tour of the campus spots that were significant in the 1962 events. We screened documentary films such as "Eyes on the Prize" and "Race & Sports: The Struggle for Equality On & Off the Field." We taped oral histories from eyewitnesses. James Meredith's chief legal counsel, U.S. District Judge Constance Baker Motley spoke to law students. An evening prayer service took place at St. Peter's Episcopal Church honoring Bishop Duncan Gray Jr. for his role in calming the masses.

On October 1, the anniversary celebration began. James Meredith arrived on campus. The U.S. Marshals service presented me with original poster artwork, Meredith's bodyguard spoke to students, William Doyle signed copies of *An American Insurrection*, and the 1962 editor of *The Daily Mississippian* spoke to journalism students.

Just before 7:30 p.m., we gathered for a symbolic walk and the formal address.

As I was waiting with James Meredith, a seasoned reporter from CBS quietly asked if he could interview Mr. Meredith while we waited.

"Fine with me," I said. "But be prepared: he's full of surprises." The reporter raised an eyebrow and said nothing would surprise him.

He approached Mr. Meredith with the microphone.

"Mr. Meredith," the reporter asked, "How does it feel to be the first African-American to attend Ole Miss?"

James turned toward him and exclaimed, "African-American?! I was born in Kosciusko, Mississippi!"

After that, the reporter left Mr. Meredith alone.

At 7:30, the hundreds who had gathered for the fortieth anniversary of James Meredith's arrival took a symbolic walk through the center hallway of the Lyceum to the ellipse between the J.D. Williams Library and the Lyceum to commemorate Mr. Meredith's entrance into Ole Miss.

The evening culminated in a candlelight ceremony on the west lawn of the Lyceum. Myrlie Evers-Williams, the widow of Medgar Evers, spoke. The evening represented one of those rare spiritually stimulating experiences that deeply affected me. It was in many ways symbolic, but it was also substantive. Our current generation of students, who knew little or nothing of the price paid by thousands of people to assure that race would not preclude access, were given the opportunity to see and hear the people who had performed so valiantly in 1962.

The event also provided graphic examples of the deeply held attitudes and feelings that had to be changed to avoid tragedies similar to that of 1962.

68

On March 28, 2003, I stood in the wings of a stage. In a few moments, I would walk onstage to welcome the audience to an inaugural gala celebrating the opening of the Gertrude C. Ford Center for the Performing Arts.

As I waited, I had thoughts of that hot June day, when I stood at the front door of Ms. Ford's house in Jackson. I smiled as I thought of her gruff voice, her propensity for using four-letter words, and the lesson she gave to me about the "plagiarist" William Shakespeare.

I imagined what she would have said if she could witness the opening of the $25 million state-of-the-art theater that bore her name. It was a beautiful building. The 88,000-square-foot facility had seating for an audience of 1,150.

Sam Haskell and his wife, Mary Donnelly Haskell, helped us plan the gala. Sam served as executive producer for the event. He was a member of the board of directors at the William Morris Agency. He also served as executive vice president and worldwide head of television for the agency. Sam was instrumental in the launch of the television shows *The Fresh Prince of Bel Air*, *Everybody Loves Raymond*, *The Cosby Show*, and *Mad About You*. Mary, a former Miss Mississippi, was a noted actress in film and television, as well as on the stage.

Sam and Mary appeared on stage along with Morgan Freeman, Gary Collins, Guy Hovis, John Maxwell, Gerald McRaney, Mary Ann Mobley, Connie Smith, and Marty Stuart.

The hall was completely sold out. The musical performances were stirring, and our state's finest actors performed scenes from Tennessee Williams' plays and Maxwell's one-man play *Oh Mr. Faulkner, Do You Write?*

The evening went as planned until Governor Ronnie Musgrove started his congratulatory speech. Backstage, as one of the female performers was preparing for her entrance, her exuberant use of hair-spray activated the building's fire alarm.

The sirens blared through the acoustically perfect hall for more than three minutes. When the alarm stopped, the governor laughed, put everyone at ease, and the program continued.

The dedication of the building was the realization of more than fifty years of dreams of Ole Miss people who loved the performing arts. Fulton Chapel, built in 1927 with 900 seats and a small stage, had served as our theater for seventy-six years. Leon Lewis, Tom Papa, and Cheryl Sims were the trustees of the Ford Foundation. They were generous and creative and thought outside the box. Their twenty-year commitment of $1 million per year would help Ole Miss retire the bonds we sold to finance the project. Those same trustees also helped us develop the area near the Ford Center, as well as the ballroom at The Inn at Ole Miss.

The gift of the Gertrude C. Ford Foundation is evidence of the margin of excellence made possible through private gifts. It gave Ole Miss a truly great university performance center.

And it all started with a woman calling me "Mr. Canoe."

When I met with Pete Boone, he told me that just about every coach — from football's David Cutcliffe to men's basketball coach Rod Barnes to track coach Joe Walker to women's basketball coach Carol Ross — had come to him to complain about our mascot, Colonel Rebel.

To me, the mascot seemed harmless — a Disneyesque cartoon character to entertain the kids in the Grove and between plays.

But to the coaches, it was devastating.

College recruiting can be a dirty business. Top athletes are sought after, but with the threat of NCAA sanctions, schools have to be careful in how they approach prospects. About all coaches can do is make friendships, tell the students about the great opportunities at their schools, and tell stories. And recruiters from other schools were telling prospects that Ole Miss was a racist school.

Carol Ross had somehow found a file other recruiters used. The folder held photographs of the 1962 riots, pictures of angry mobs throwing bricks, historical photos of southern plantation owners, and photos of our mascot, which recruiters claimed was modeled on a slave owner. We'd even heard that recruiters from other schools were showing the mothers and fathers and grandparents of recruits film clips of the 1962 riot.

"Do you really want to send your son or daughter to a place like that?" they would say.

Too many black players were running for the hills.

I asked Pete what he wanted to do.

He suggested forming a committee of students, faculty, staff, and alumni. "Let's make this a formal process," he said, "and get as many people as possible involved."

In 1964, I was in the Mississippi Delta. Gerald Morgan, a teammate of mine at Ole Miss, had asked me to speak at his team's annual football awards banquet. I actually was asked to do a lot of those sorts of things. I was playing for the Redskins, and it never crossed my mind to request a fee.

Gerald introduced me to some of his players. Then he said, "Robert, I'd like you to meet a young man who will probably be the best quarterback in Mississippi someday." Then he added, "If he ever begins to grow."

I'd heard similar statements every time I spoke at one of these banquets.

The skinny, freckle-faced, strawberry blond kid extended his hand.

"Nice to meet you, sir," he said. "I'm Archie Manning."

I didn't know it at the moment, but the young man, his future wife, and his children would impact Ole Miss — and the world — in ways I could never have dreamed. And what Archie's coach failed to mention was just how fine a person Archie was.

We often look for role models for young people. Archie is the model for role models.

Archie's Ole Miss story is mythical. In addition to shattering school records in football, he was also a fine baseball player, a very good student, and a friend to just about everyone. His courtship of Olivia Williams and ultimate marriage demonstrated that Archie's wonderful mother, Sis, taught him the qualities of a truly great woman.

In the late 1960s, the Ole Miss baseball team played against Alabama. With the score tied late in the game, Archie hit a triple, driving in the winning runs. As he slid into third base, Professor George Howell, Archie's political science teacher, leaned over and whispered in his faculty colleague Don Vaughan's ear: "That ole boy is going to mess around and make an A in political science."

Ole Miss' relationship with Archie and Olivia was, in my view, unbreakable. What they brought to our university's community, and to our state, is beyond measure. Time and again, Archie has been recognized as the most popular person in our state. If one of the reasons we live is to make life better for others, the Mannings deserve even more attention than they already receive.

Their oldest son, Cooper, signed to play football at Ole Miss. Perhaps the most athletic of the three Manning boys, Cooper was an all-state wide receiver at Isidore Newman High School in New Orleans. In fact, his senior year, Cooper caught passes from his younger brother, a sophomore named Peyton.

Before he ever played a game at Ole Miss, Cooper discovered he had a degenerative spinal condition. Doctors told him he was one hit away from being paralyzed. Cooper never complained. He told his younger brother and best friend, "I would like to live my dream of playing football through you."

Had Cooper been able to play at Ole Miss, Peyton would have followed him to Ole Miss. "It was assumed," Cooper said.

But things didn't work out that way. When it was time for Peyton to select a college, Ole Miss was headed toward probation.

Peyton's choice to play football at Tennessee created quite a stir, but that reaction was short-lived. Anybody who knew the facts understood his decision. Peyton was committed to perfection, and our program was far from it. We wouldn't play on television. We would not play in bowl games. Additionally, Peyton looked forward to playing under Tennessee Offensive Coordinator David Cutcliffe. The Mannings and Coach Cutcliffe developed a deep friendship during Peyton's four years in Tennessee.

Shortly after we hired David to be head coach at Ole Miss, Cooper and Peyton's younger brother, Eli, decided to play for the Rebels.

Eli was redshirted, so we had him on campus for five years. I saw him from time to time walking across campus. In khaki shorts, t-shirt, and loafers with no socks, carrying a backpack across campus, Eli lived his life off field as quietly as possible. The only time I saw him excited off the field was when he was running through the Circle to make class on time.

While a quarterback at Ole Miss, Eli broke forty-five passing records. He threw eighty-one touchdown passes in his college career, and his total career passing surpassed 10,000 yards. He received just about every honor available to a college quarterback, and in his senior year he led the Rebels to a 10-3 record and a 31-28 Cotton Bowl victory over Oklahoma State.

Everyone agreed that Eli had a remarkable impact on Ole Miss, Oxford, and Mississippi. The one thing no one seemed to agree on was our mascot. The committee Pete put together to examine options had evaluated dozens of potential new mascots for Ole Miss. Apparently, no one on the committee could agree on any alternatives.

During Eli's senior year, the committee finally came together. The group voted unanimously to pull Colonel Rebel from the field.

69

The success of the 1998 town hall meeting that was part of President Clinton's effort to have a national discussion of race in America prompted us to look at other ways to continue the dialogue. We knew that any time Ole Miss and race appeared in the same news story, it would be covered by the national media. Given our history and the difficulties we had experienced in the profound cultural shift that occurred between 1956 and 1998, our leadership team concluded that there could be no better place than Ole Miss to talk about race — and how to improve race relations.

We also believed that our experience in recent years in addressing racial issues openly, honestly, and head-on had produced nothing but positive results.

Former Mississippi Governor William Winter had the same response I had at the end of the town hall meeting: *We need to do this all the time.*

The talented director of our Center for the Study of Southern Culture, Charles Wilson, chaired a committee to look into a program or institute that might handle this continuing conversation. The university agreed to contribute funds, and soon an institute on racial reconciliation was formed.

Three years later, the institute was named in honor of Governor Winter. Soon, Governor Winter convinced his friend Susan Glisson, the same young woman who had spearheaded the grassroots efforts for the town hall meeting, to become director of the William Winter Institute for Racial Reconciliation.

The timing couldn't have been better. As the institute grew, a potentially incendiary retrial of a defendant from the murders that took place in Philadelphia, Mississippi, in the 1960s was scheduled. Racial tensions threatened to ignite once again.

Governor Winter had staked out a clear position on racial issues during those turbulent years and had become Mississippi's most visible, respected advocate for equality, respect, and openness as our state and nation struggled through the Civil Rights movement.

The pending trial in Philadelphia could have easily deteriorated into angry confrontations or even violence. It presented the ideal opportunity for our institute to reach out to a sharply divided community. We knew the trial would attract the national press, and we didn't want to stand by and watch Mississippi get nailed again by mishandling racially charged issues.

Dr. Glisson and her team initiated contact with black and white leaders in Philadelphia and suggested a series of community conversations about the upcoming trial. Members of our institute team hosted several events in Philadelphia, encouraged open meetings, candid discussions, and thoughtful considerations of the facts and issues surrounding the trial.

Local leaders in Philadelphia also stepped up to the challenge. Meaningful, heartfelt discussions between white and black members of the community had a significant impact on community behavior before, during, and after the trial.

The experience confirmed what we knew — that thoughtful people at universities can provide invaluable public service by calmly reaching out, promoting civil discussion of highly divisive issues, and opening doors, and hearts, to the essential value of respect.

I believe the William Winter Institute for Racial Reconciliation is one of our most meaningful, high-impact programs. It was vital for the world to know that we were sensitive to matters of race. I wanted the university and the institute to be a model for effectively acknowledging and addressing this difficult component of American life. I was proud of the work the institute was doing.

But we were about to have trouble on another front. As usual, if it wasn't race generating headlines at Ole Miss, it was football.

When Eli was drafted after the successful 2003 football season and moved on to play for the Giants, the Ole Miss football program had a difficult year. We went 4-7, including losses to Memphis and Wyoming.

David Cutcliffe had everything I looked for in a head football coach. He was smart and personable and he represented the university well. He knew the game and he worked hard. And he knew how to assemble a team of assistant coaches. He had five great seasons at Ole Miss, but something shifted in the sixth season. David didn't seem to be up to performing the rigorous responsibilities of head coach. We lost assistant coaches, the recruiting classes were increasingly mediocre, and we were losing to teams we normally beat with ease.

Based on the poor performance of our team in 2004 and the sub-par recruiting classes, Pete Boone asked David to give him a plan for getting us back on track. David either could not or would not respond to the request. After meeting with the two of them for an hour or so, I concluded they were at an impasse, and they would have to resolve the dispute.

It may have been the most difficult personnel decision I faced as chancellor.

Pete prevailed, but there was no winner.

Then the search for a new head coach began. Of course, what we didn't know — and what David didn't realize — was that the arteries in his heart were almost completely blocked. The problem was discovered six months later, and David underwent quadruple bypass surgery.

Pete and I interviewed several potential head coaches. Then we flew to the Dallas airport to meet with Ed Orgeron. Ed was the defensive line coach and recruiting coordinator for the University of Southern California. He also happened to be the highest paid assistant coach in the nation, earning an unheard of sum of $650,000 per year. Ed had also just been named the 2004 National Recruiter of the Year.

When Ed walked in the door, I understood his success. His energy and enthusiasm were almost overwhelming. He was excited about the prospects of leading the Rebels. He talked about how he would convince the nation's top prospects to come to Ole Miss. He even mentioned national championships.

Pete and I had not been overly impressed with the other candidates. We offered Ed the job on the spot, and he accepted. I flew back to Oxford. Pete accompanied Ed to USC. Ed wanted to tell his players in person about his decision, before they heard it on the news.

Ed arrived on the Ole Miss campus to great fanfare. But soon rumors started circulating about his temper and his use of profanity. I received calls and letters asking me to speak to Ed about his cursing and his unorthodox methods of motivating players. Rumor had it he had even torn a set of cabinets off a wall in the coaches' office to express his displeasure with practice.

The culture of football has always included vulgarity and abusive behavior by coaches and players. With few exceptions, my experience was no different. The Ole Miss assistant coaches treated us like dogs. They denied us water. They put us through grueling wind sprints. And they didn't tolerate softness.

At a September practice my sophomore year, one of our running backs received a monstrous hit from a defensive lineman. As the running back rolled on the ground in agony, he took off his helmet. Blood ran down his forehead and nose. He rolled over on his stomach and held his face in his hands.

An assistant coach walked over and stood as the injured player moaned. The coach wedged his foot under the player's chest and rolled him over.

"Lemme see," he said.

The player moved his hands away from his face, and the coach looked down at him.

"Get up, son!" the coach said. "My hemorrhoids bleed more than that every morning!"

In spite of the coaches' disparaging remarks, they knew how to prepare us for games. A typical practice would involve thirty minutes of individual position drills — passing for quarterbacks, blocking and tackling for linemen, route-running for receivers. Then Coach Vaught would blow his whistle, and we'd move into full scrimmage mode. A complete offense would practice against a fully assembled defense. Then practice would end with the most agonizing drill. Everyone hated it. It was called *twenty 50s*.

A football field is just over fifty yards wide. Every single practice ended with us sprinting twenty times across the field. Back and forth. The assistant coaches watched every one of us carefully — and yelled, sometimes vulgarities, at us to increase our pace. If a player "dogged it," the coaches made him repeat the sprint.

We never played a team better conditioned than we were.

Not all the coaches yelled and cursed. Coach Vaught was a quiet, albeit powerful, man. I remember the first time I met him.

Coach Vaught loved golf, and he slipped away to hit shag balls whenever he had time. He built a tee just across the street from his office so he could hit practice balls into the band field.

I nervously approached him. He was wearing his signature khaki pants, white t-shirt, black football shoes, and an Ole Miss cap.

I extended my hand and said, "Coach Vaught, I'm one of your new freshmen . . . Robert Khayat."

He returned a firm handshake, welcomed me to Ole Miss, and asked if I was settled in. After a few more questions — to which I answered "yes, sir" — he turned his attention back to his golf game.

As I walked away, he said, "I look forward to you being a Rebel, Eddie."

The next time I was in the presence of Coach Vaught was nine months later, when spring practice started. I wasn't on Coach Vaught's radar. He spent most of his time with the quarterbacks, not freshmen linemen. But then he said something that put me back in his line of sight.

"Who here can placekick?" he said.

Five of us stepped forward.

We moved to the twenty-yard line with the centers and holders, and we started kicking field goals. After a few kicks, two of the players went back to join the other teammates. That left Bobby Franklin, our quarterback and best all-around athlete; Allen Green, who could punt and placekick; and me. The three of us were the first to arrive each day and the last to leave. We practiced field goals before and after each practice.

One of Coach Vaught's greatest traits was attention to detail. He wanted to take advantage of every football asset. Field goals were rather rare in 1956. But Coach Vaught knew that having a good field-goal squad in your arsenal could provide a huge advantage and frequently win games.

Ultimately, Coach Vaught chose me to perform the kicking duties for the Rebels. Whenever I came off the field after scoring and ran past Coach Vaught, he would clap his hands together and say, "Good job, Eddie."

The New Ole Miss

70

During the past decade, Ole Miss had made tremendous strides. One of our students, Calvin Thigpen, became the university's twenty-fourth Rhodes Scholar. We were touted in several publications as a "Best Buy" in higher education. *The Chronicle of Higher Education* placed us on its list of top thirty universities with the largest endowment per student. Our library surpassed the one million-volume mark. We created a Women's Council for Philanthropy. We opened a Center for Justice and Rule of Law to provide training in fighting cybercrime. Under the leadership of Alice Clark, our research funding had surpassed the $100 million mark for each of the past eight years. The Freedom Forum opened the Overby Center for Southern Journalism and Politics. Our honors college, under the direction of Douglass Sullivan-Gonzàlez, was recognized as one of the top three in the nation. The National Library of the Accounting Profession moved to Ole Miss. We expanded Vaught-Hemingway Stadium to hold more than 60,000 fans. Our landscape services won two national awards. We were named one of four Truman Foundation Honor Institutions. We started the first student-run, converged newsroom for print and broadcast journalism majors. We'd spent more than $500 million renovating and upgrading our buildings. Rex Deloach revolutionized our business systems, and Johnny Williams and Larry Sparks improved those systems. Universities in other parts of the country called wanting to follow our model. And, of course, we started an international studies program, a leadership institute, an institute on racial reconciliation . . . and were awarded a Phi Beta Kappa chapter.

Though some in the field of higher education recognized the progress we'd made, the world still had an outdated view of our university.

In 2005, I asked Andy Mullins to place a call to Janet Brown at the Commission on Presidential Debates. We were all a bit nervous. We hoped the commission didn't view our passing on the 2004 debates as a lack of interest.

Andy told Janet we were interested in hosting a 2008 presidential debate.

"Would you like us to send a site team?" she asked.

Apparently a site team and a technical team had to approve a debate host site before a university could submit an application.

"Sure," Andy said. "That'd be great."

When the site team arrived, Marty Slutsky was in charge. As executive producer for the presidential debates, Marty would make the ultimate decision about whether Ole Miss was capable of handling the debate. Marty is also the lead guitarist for the band McKendree Spring.

Andy and Marty hit it off immediately. When Marty saw the Gertrude Ford Center for the Performing Arts, he told Andy, "I think you have a shot."

During one of the meetings with the site team, Andy asked Marty how much money we'd need to raise.

"A minimum of $3 million," he said. "Probably closer to four." Then he added, "And you'll need a million up front."

"Why is it so expensive?" Andy asked.

"You host 3,000 journalists for four days, and it gets expensive."

"Is it worth it?" Andy asked.

"It's up to you to decide whether it's worth it," Marty told him.

I walked into the meeting to greet the team.

Marty asked about the commitment of the university to host a debate.

I told him with no reservation that we were totally committed.

"Anything it takes," I told him.

I knew the entire world would be watching. It was the perfect opportunity to change the way people viewed Ole Miss. It was a chance to show that we were a great university and to present modern Mississippi to the world.

71

Early in my chancellorship, one of our graduate students at the Center for the Study of Southern Culture, John T. Edge, came to see me. Based on classroom discussions, he proposed the construction of a civil rights monument.

John T. was full of energy and one of the most warm and likable young men I'd ever encountered — and he presented a persuasive case. John T. didn't know that the leadership team and I were already working on a plan to add outdoor art to the campus. At that time, our only outdoor art was a monument dedicated to the University Greys, many of whom lost their lives in the Civil War. Though important and worthy, it was always a flashpoint for visiting journalists.

When I told John T. that I agreed, he seemed a bit surprised. I think he assumed I would resist the idea.

I knew that any talk of building a civil rights monument would stimulate discussion and produce many ideas. I also understood that it would provoke anger and, among some, be divisive.

I thought it prudent to create a diverse committee charged with the responsibility of recommending an artist and a site for the monument.

Creating the committee was a good idea, but allowing a contentious discussion of the appearance and location of the monument would, it turned out, go on far too long. It was my mistake.

I requested recommendations. Some members of the committee inferred that my request meant that their recommendations were binding. But, to the committee members' credit, they spent nearly six years going through a juried process, consulting with experts, and considering the opinions of dozens, if not hundreds, of individuals with some connection to the integration of Ole Miss and the Civil Rights movement.

When they presented me with the winning entry, my heart sank. I had no problem with the artist's work, strictly from an artistic perspective. But I had a huge problem with the way his artwork would alter the campus.

The winning entry, as described by the artist, would "dominate the center of the plaza ellipse between the Lyceum and the library." He proposed two nineteen-foot high concrete structures — one at the west entrance of the Lyceum, one at the east entrance of the library. Atop each was an enormous arch. Between the columns of the archway were two functional, hurricane-proof, etched glass doors. The text etched in the doorways included the phrases "Teach in fear no more," "Learn in fear no more," and "Unite in fear no more."

Although the design did call for more positive, forward-looking verbiage with the text, "Henceforth and Forevermore" and "Freedom and Justice," those words were at the top of the nineteen-foot structures — where no one would see them. I simply couldn't imagine every student, visitor, staff member, or faculty member walking in and out of the Lyceum or library facing the negative, shocking language.

Actually, I didn't think the design was compatible with the university's architecture. The cost was going to be high. The 600-pound functional doors were dangerous. The glass doorways were going to be an open invitation for vandalism and graffiti — especially from those who held on to Old South traditions (which would hurt the university even more), and the size of the doorways overwhelmed the ellipse. On a personal level, I wanted to move forward in a positive manner. I have never denied our past, but a monument should, in my opinion, inspire hope for the future. The discussion about Ole Miss in the national media, and by those who didn't know the new Ole Miss, was already — and always — about fear.

What I didn't realize was that the artist who designed the monument was Terry Adkins, an African-American.

When I rejected the proposed rendering of the monument, one committee person said I "was bound by the process." It was not surprising that, since the artist the committee had selected was black, my decision was considered racist. I didn't even know the color of his skin until then.

People in leadership positions are often scrutinized. Not just by the public but by colleagues too. None of us can withstand close inspection without the revelation of faults and flaws, mistakes and failures.

I have come to believe that many external forces shape and mold us. I am no exception. Conflicts, natural tragedies, economic conditions, and many other factors impact our lives. Frequently, there is no way to prepare for a particular challenge or situation, and you have to go with what you have and who you are. And who you are is often shaped by your family.

My oldest sister, Edna, had a huge influence on the person I became. The oldest of four children, she often had responsibility for looking after the younger ones — my brother, younger sister, and me. Of course, she had her own life to live, but until the day she left for college, she served as a sort of assistant mother at our house.

Edna was sensitive, and her concern for the less fortunate dominated her adult life.

She and her husband had two daughters and settled in to teaching and coaching careers, respectively. Then something happened that dramatically changed the direction of their lives.

Tom decided to pursue a life in Christian service and entered Perkins Seminary in Dallas. Edna's interest in social causes was also increasing. The sensitive spirit that had been with her since childhood began to dominate her. In total contrast with the rest of her family members, she became a political activist. She participated in civil rights marches, anti-Vietnam War demonstrations, and other anti-establishment activities.

Edna changed from a traditional Southern child to a sophisticated, expansive adult who devoted her life to helping the less fortunate. Most of my family leaned slightly right of center. Edna leaned pretty far left. I quickly learned that family conversations shouldn't include politics. Whenever a discussion seemed to be headed there, I tried to move it in a different direction. I wanted to find balance among the conflicting beliefs of the members of my family.

I tried to remember this during my chancellorship.

We tried to work with the artist to adjust his design to meet the needs of the university. It simply didn't work. But I was committed to getting a monument up as soon as possible.

On October 4, 2005, I wrote a letter to John T. explaining that we were committed to placing a civil rights memorial on our campus on the ellipse between the Lyceum and the library and that James Meredith's enrollment — an event that brought equal access to higher education in Mississippi — deserved a memorial.

I outlined the challenges of moving forward with the committee's selection: cost, safety of the operational doors, location within the ellipse, scale, and architectural compatibility.

I thanked John T. and Susan Glisson for their efforts to resolve the issues and for their efforts during the five-year process.

Ultimately, it was my responsibility as chancellor to make a decision. I met with a committee of students, male and female, black and white. Within an hour they agreed that a statue of James Meredith should be a part of the memorial. The black students thought it would be educational. "Nobody our age knows who he is," one told me.

I contacted an architect to give us preliminary designs and reached out to local sculptor Rod Moorhead.

Rod, who had artwork on the campus already, said, "My lifetime dream has been to create a rendering of James Meredith."

He started working immediately. Rod produced a life-sized replica of Mr. Meredith that creates the illusion of him walking through the entrance to the university.

Jim Eley, the architect who designed our performing arts center and led the restoration of the Lyceum, was a truly gifted artist. He understood that we needed to move fast. I could not allow the disagreement about the monument to fester. Jim moved the monument to item one on his list of priorities and created a structure that reflected our architectural personality. He recommended placing it on the green between the Lyceum and the library with the statue of Mr. Meredith placed so that he was entering and walking through the monument. The capstone of the monument displayed the words *Opportunity, Courage, Perseverance,* and *Knowledge.*

On October 1, 2006, a panel of dignitaries gathered to dedicate our new civil rights monument. Those on stage included Morgan Freeman, James Meredith, Governor William Winter, Dr. Joseph Meredith (son of James Meredith and Ph.D. graduate from Ole Miss), and our keynote speaker, the Honorable John Lewis, House of Representatives leader from the Fifth Congressional District of Georgia.

A crowd of more than 1,500 people assembled on the ellipse between the Lyceum and the library. As members of the platform party made their way to the podium to speak, I thought about the long and often difficult relationship between Ole Miss and race.

Through the eleven years I'd been chancellor, I had tried to acknowledge our history while at the same time pushing forward in every aspect of university life.

I was tired of race being a part of almost every conversation. Regardless of our progress, regardless of our efforts to open our doors, regardless of our work to instill in the culture and personality of the university respect for the dignity of each individual, we seemed destined to continue to address and re-address the same difficult and emotional events of our past.

At times I prayed that society — and the media — would let us talk about the promise of our future without rehashing our widely known history. I hoped the creation of the civil rights monument might put a bookend on the events of the past.

But I knew that was unrealistic.

Morgan Freeman ended his speech with these words, "Mississippi is a better state today because of James Meredith, and this is a much better university. Thank you, Mr. Meredith."

Then our keynote speaker, Representative Lewis, spoke.

"This is a day to rejoice," he said. "With the unveiling of this monument, we free ourselves from the chains of a difficult past. Today we can celebrate a new day, a new beginning, the birth of a new South, and a new America that is more free, more fair, and more just than ever before."

Then Representative Lewis brought the crowd to its feet when he talked about his childhood, his role in the Civil Rights movement, including being beaten by a mob in Alabama in 1961, and his role in the historic March on Washington in 1963.

In conclusion, Representative Lewis praised James Meredith and the leaders at Ole Miss for fostering acceptance and equal access.

At the end of the ceremony, the Meredith family pulled the dark cloth from the life-sized monument. The crowd erupted in applause.

As I stood on stage and clapped, I hoped that Representative Lewis was right. I hoped this was a new day, a new beginning, and the birth of a new South. And I hoped we could start a new conversation about building a better society. Together, for everyone.

The Civil Rights Monument and James Meredith statue

72

Through the years I had learned the importance of offices being service-driven, open, and friendly. Sandra Lowery, Shirley Stuart, and Sue Keiser exemplified those traits.

Sandra and Shirley were my schedulers. A strong scheduler can keep your life in balance. A weak one can ruin your days. Shirley and Sandra both helped me do my job efficiently.

They developed a card for each day. It fit perfectly into my inside lapel pocket. Every card had the date, times, places, addresses, and telephone numbers for each appointment.

While Sandra and Shirley prepared the cards, Sue Keiser, my extraordinarily capable and loyal executive assistant, prepared the notebooks. For each event, Sue assembled a blue notebook with all the materials I would need for each meeting, including scripts, speeches, and, most importantly, a list of names of individuals I needed to recognize — and background information when necessary.

Some days we would use as many as six notebooks. In the years Sue worked with me, she never once made a mistake in the notebook.

Although we had been friends before I hired her, Sue always addressed me as "Chancellor." She managed the chancellor's office, served as a sounding board for me, protected me from unnecessary intrusions, and always offered good advice.

By the time 2007 arrived, Sandra and Shirley had prepared more than 3,600 cards, and Sue had prepared more than 10,000 notebooks.

I started thinking about retirement. I was still as passionate about Ole Miss as I'd ever been, but fatigue had set in. During my tenure as chancellor, I'd had two knee surgeries, a right knee replaced, and a right hip replaced. I'd also had rotator cuff surgery and three bouts of pancreatitis. In addition, the stress of the past thirteen years had taken its toll.

In early 2007, the Commission on Presidential Debates' site team approved Ole Miss. Andy worked to put the application together.

When we learned the cost of hosting a presidential debate would approach $5 million, we knew we needed a lead gift. Our first presentation was to the Robert M. Hearin Foundation board. In the past, the board had provided extraordinary support to Ole Miss, as well as to other educational organizations in Mississippi. The members of the board listened carefully, evaluated the opportunity for the state and Ole Miss, and agreed to provide up to $1.5 million as a challenge to other donors. With their support, we were able to attract an additional $3 million from other corporations and foundations.

After we submitted our application, we discovered that Ole Miss was one of nineteen institutions applying to host the 2008 debates. Only four would be selected.

Ed Orgeron continued to recruit great football players, but we couldn't seem to win games. After three dismal seasons, including 2007, when we only won three games — against Memphis, Louisiana Tech, and Northwestern State — Pete Boone and I asked Ed to resign.

Ed's attitude was ideal. He treated us both with respect. Ed shook our hands, thanked us for the opportunity to coach at Ole Miss, and left.

When news spread, Arkansas Athletics Director Frank Broyles called Pete.

"Houston Nutt wants to come to Ole Miss," he said. Frank explained that Coach Nutt was having conflicts with some of the Arkansas alumni and was about to resign. "You should give him a call," Frank suggested.

Pete respected Houston. He had put together tough teams that had always performed well against Ole Miss. They'd also recently upset top-ranked LSU.

"I'm not going to call him," Pete said. "If Houston's interested, he needs to call me."

Within an hour, Pete had heard from Houston. The following day, Pete flew to Arkansas and visited with Houston and his wife. Then he negotiated with Houston's agent.

Pete called to give me all the details. Then he recommended we hire Coach Nutt.

"Great," I said, "he'll be my last head coach."

The next morning, we hired him.

73

In November, Paul Kirk, a member of the Commission on Presidential Debates called.

"Chancellor Khayat," he said, "Congratulations. Ole Miss has been selected to host a debate." He paused for a moment. "And you're hosting the first one."

I thanked Paul and assured him the commission had made a good decision.

Then, we had to get to work.

We decided to make the benefits of the debate worth the investment, and everyone pulled together. The faculty joined in the planning. Political Science Chair Rich Forgette said it best: "The debate presents a teachable moment."

We established sixteen academic courses with a debate tie-in. They were added to the curriculum for the fall, along with fifty-three lectures, movies, panel discussions, quiz bowls, art exhibits, and other special events.

I always knew it was important that as many people as possible get involved. When I discovered that Ole Miss would only receive one hundred tickets to the debate, it became doubly important. I also decided that all one hundred would go to students. We also agreed to put big-screen televisions across campus — with the biggest in the Grove.

The physical appearance of the campus was transformed by the approaching debate. Security measures included a fence that surrounded the perimeter of the Ford Center. Barricades blocked traffic from the edge of the Grove down University Avenue a quarter-mile. A media tent — 10,000 square feet of space — was erected in a grassy field next to the venue. We brought in seven state-of-the-art generators to provide redundant power in case of a failure. We worked, too, to make the campus as beautiful as possible.

Life on campus, and in Oxford, was a little inconvenient, but we were certain it would be worth the effort.

On Tuesday, September 23, journalists started arriving from all over the world.

Our team met every morning at 10:00 a.m. Andy Mullins, who was the leader in planning and executing the debate, generally led the discussion. The Wednesday morning before the debate, as Andy was walking from the Ford Center to the Lyceum, a reporter called him on his cell. Andy stopped just under the Confederate monument at the Circle.

"Mr. Mullins," the reporter said, "Senator McCain just held a press conference and announced he was suspending his campaign until the fiscal crisis in Washington was settled. When asked if he would attend the debate, he said 'No.' What will be the impact on Ole Miss?"

Andy was in shock. "Devastating," he answered. "Just devastating."

By the time Andy reached the Lyceum, his quote had hit the national news.

Our marketing and public relations consultant, Liza Cirlot, joined us.

"Andy," she said, "next time consider a word like 'disappointing.'"

After the consultant left the room, I looked at Andy and said, "I'm sure as hell glad they didn't ask me."

We were all in shock at Senator McCain's unprecedented withdrawal, but we weren't the only ones.

When Senator Barack Obama heard the news, his response was, "He did what?!"

Senator McCain's press conference was played and replayed on the news networks. He said he was withdrawing due to "a historic crisis in our financial system."

In a hastily arranged press conference in Florida, Senator Obama said that the economic crisis made the Friday debate in Oxford "more important than ever." He went on, "It's my belief that this is exactly the time that the American people need to hear from the person who in approximately forty days will be responsible for dealing with this mess. It's going to be part of the president's job to deal with more than one thing at once."

We had no idea what would happen but told ourselves *surely Senator McCain will participate*. We all started looking at options. We proposed a town hall meeting with Senator Obama and were told the Commission on President Debates' stage — which was already assembled on the Ford Center stage — could only be used for a presidential debate.

We suggested pulling the curtains to cover the stage and letting Senator Obama speak to the audience from there.

No, we were told, the sound system belonged to the Commission on Presidential Debates, and the same rule applied.

We noticed that Senator McCain's on-location staff seemed to relax. They were almost lethargic. That made me very nervous. But the veteran journalists, including Tom Brokaw and Curtis Wilkie, assured us that no politician would leave the seat empty when forty million voters were watching.

Tom Brokaw's exact words were, "It'll happen."

Gloria Kellum and I put together a quick statement:

"The University of Mississippi is going forward with the preparation for the debate. We are ready to host the debate, and we expect the debate to occur as planned.

"At present, the University has received no notification of any change in the timing or venue of the debate.

"We have been notified by the Commission on Presidential Debates that we are proceeding as scheduled."

Senator Obama was on the same page as Ole Miss. He told reporters, "We've both got these jets. Let's just fly down to Mississippi. In fact, this is the perfect time. The people of the United States deserve to know how the next president will handle this situation."

Ole Miss actually had friends in high places. We asked Senators Thad Cochran and Trent Lott and Mississippi Governor Haley Barbour — all Ole Miss alums — to reach out to Senator McCain.

Governor Barbour said, "McCain's a maverick. He doesn't do what we ask."

The next day and a half seemed to drag on forever. We were operating as if nothing had changed, but we were all afraid that everything had changed.

Early Friday morning, Andy received a text message — "Obama in the air."

"At least one of them will be here," I said.

At about the same time, a small contractor was working in Morton, a small town just outside of Jackson. His crew was using a Ditch Witch machine while installing an irrigation system.

Mississippi has one high-speed, fiber-optic cable that runs the length of the state. The construction crew in Morton heard a terrible noise, and the machine they used to cut small trenches in the ground started smoking.

A few seconds later, every Internet connection in Oxford, including the university's and the media tent's, went dead.

74

Within a few minutes the redundant backup systems our IT staff had created kicked in. The media had Internet access, but they didn't have the bandwidth they needed for the debate.

Half an hour later, every AT&T repair truck from Jackson and central Mississippi converged on Morton. The contractor sent his men home. The activity caught the attention of a newspaper reporter who asked the contractor about the incident.

"We cut a cable," he said, "but I've never seen anything like this." He looked around at dozens of trucks and repairmen. Then he whispered to the reporter, "Must be some kind of CIA operation."

It took a couple of hours, but the high-speed cable was repaired, and we were ready to go. Except, of course, that John McCain was still not in the air.

The press leading up to the debate was better than we could have hoped. *The Boston Globe* ran a front-page piece with the title: "The Ole Miss Debate Marks Racial Progress." The piece began:

Now, Ole Miss is a diverse university where racial conflict is a topic for history classes, not a fact of everyday life, and it is hosting the first presidential debate featuring a black nominee for a major party.

"I think what we have here is really a confluence of two lines of history, where you have a new Ole Miss, a post-racial Ole Miss, and you have a post-racial black candidate running for president," said David Sansing, professor emeritus of history at the university. "Nowhere in America could these two forces reinforce each other as they do here at Ole Miss."

Barack Obama was a 14-month-old toddler in Hawaii when James Meredith, a 29-year-old Air Force veteran, broke the color barrier at the University of Mis-

sissippi in the fall of 1962.

Ole Miss Chancellor Robert Khayat welcomes the Sept. 26 debate between Obama and John McCain as a chance to show the world an up-to-date image of the school.

The *Los Angeles Times* wrote: "If the debate goes off as planned, it will provide the 160-year-old school with the opportunity to show, once and for all, that it has moved beyond its old, infamous and self-destructive reputation."

And I revealed my hopes to *The Commercial Appeal*: "The media are going to come here and see the James Meredith statue and see our diverse and friendly student body changing classes and they're going to want to tell that story."

Late in the day, a few hours before the debate was scheduled, we received word. Senator McCain was in the air. He was headed our way.

The debate went off without a glitch. And it wasn't lost on the 3,000 journalists that we were hosting the first African-American presidential candidate just a few hundred feet from where the Meredith crisis took place.

When the debate was over, our consultants from the Cirlot Agency estimated that the media exposure Ole Miss received during the four-day event would have cost $25 million in air time, if we'd had to pay for it.

Most importantly, I felt as if the world now had a better picture of the Ole Miss that I knew and loved.

It was time to retire.

Dedication

Chancellor Dan Jones and author John Grisham joined me on stage at the law school dedication ceremony.

75

I waited backstage with bestselling author John Grisham; Chancellor Dan Jones, who succeeded me; U.S. Senators Thad Cochran and Roger Wicker; Mississippi Governor Phil Bryant; Ole Miss law school Dean Richard Gershon; BancorpSouth CEO Aubrey Patterson; Provost Morris Stocks; the Reverend Curt Presley; and Mississippi Supreme Court Chief Justice Bill Waller. We had gathered for a dedication. The university's new $50 million law center was going to bear my name.

The Gertrude C. Ford Center for the Performing Arts was packed with friends, colleagues, and family. I had envisioned that we might congregate outside on a beautiful, sunny day, on the lawn of the new law center, but severe thunderstorms and tornado sightings forced the organizers to move the event inside.

I was, of course, deeply honored that the new building would be known as the Robert C. Khayat Law Center, but the irony wasn't lost on me. It probably wasn't lost on anyone else either.

Even from backstage, I could hear the soft roar of the crowd as old friends greeted each other. As we all walked onto the enormous stage, the audience greeted us with rousing applause. A podium and microphone had been placed in the center of the stage. Eleven chairs were lined up to the right and left of the podium. I sat between Chancellor Jones and John Grisham.

The Ford Center stage was beautiful. It was decorated with fresh-cut flowers from the university garden. The stage was also brightly illuminated, but the lights were in perfect balance. I could see friends and family sitting in the bright red seats.

As I looked out over the audience, I suddenly had a new appreciation for how unpredictable and inexplicable my path to this stage had been. Memories — snapshots really — of the remarkable people who defined my life flooded my mind.

I thought of Sara Davidson's kindness to a homesick kid and John Hope Franklin's kind words about our university. I recalled the talk with Jack Dunbar next to his fireplace and Harold Burson's counsel when I was ready to give up.

I remembered all the mentors who gently passed along lessons: Mr. Mallette and the birdhouse, Cyanide Jones and the gift of a D-minus, my mother's attention to detail, and the day my father pushed two nails into the ground and taught me how to kick.

Then there were the unexpected encounters: The first time Gertrude Ford called me "Mr. Canoe" and the night I first lined up against Big Daddy Lipscomb; Jenny Dodson's interview on symbols and our management team's stroke of genius — banning sticks; and a golf game with Jerry Hollingsworth.

My thoughts moved to my hometown of Moss Point, where everything I needed was within a walk. I longed to see Mama's oak, the store, the old cemetery, the neighborhood kids, Beardslee Lake, the Singing River, and Walter Oliver.

I felt an overwhelming sense of thankfulness for those who had made gifts that transformed Ole Miss: the Martindales for their gift of beauty; the Barksdales for giving our students an honors college; Jerry Abdalla for opening a wider world of study to Ole Miss students. And the Paris, Yates and Peddle families, along with Don and Mary Ann Frugé, who made sure all Ole Miss students had a sacred space to worship or pray.

At this moment, even the lighter episodes in my life seemed important: Eddie's advice to stay off the road to Memphis; a late night with Elvis; a basketball game with Stanley Hill; sprinkling ashes in the north end zone; and Coach Vaught calling me by my brother's name.

As the memories flashed before me, I recognized so many friends in the audience. My freshman roommate, Warner Alford, and his wife, Kay; my colleague Bob Weems and his wife, Janis; and my classmate Bill Yates (whose company built the law center) and his wife, Nancy; and the remarkable Sue Keiser.

Every single person I noticed had a special relationship with Ole

Miss, or me.

I knew that I could never understand the mystery of my relationship with God — or his hand in guiding me. But in remembering the extraordinary people with whom I've crossed paths, my belief in a master plan was affirmed. I felt, without any doubt, that my successes and failures, wins and losses, loves and heartaches, adulation and humiliation, good health and bad, led me to this place. I am a person of faith, and even when I strayed or behaved in ways that I regret, I never doubted God's quiet, careful presence along the way.

I looked to my left and saw my family. They were sitting together on the third row — my wife, Margaret; my daughter, Margaret, and her husband, David; my son, Robert, and his wife, Susannah, and their three children, Molly, Ben, and Betsey. They brought great joy into my life.

My mother and father were gone, but not a day went by when I did not think of them and all they gave to me. They built a foundation upon which I could live. That foundation was built around respect — respect for the dignity of each person.

When John Grisham finished his speech, Chancellor Jones introduced me. I stood at the podium, looked out at the friends who had gathered, and opened the notebook that held my speech. I knew it would never do justice to what I was thinking and feeling. But I would try, once again, to convey to the 800 men and women gathered in the hall how much respect I held for each of them. I wanted them to understand that this respect flowed from love and a faith in God. I hoped they would understand that their friendships mattered in ways that I could never fully explain. They were all family. The Ole Miss family.

And among them, it felt like being home.

Thank you for sharing this personal journey with me. I have tried to be as accurate as memory permits. My hope for this book is to offer thanksgiving to those who enriched my life and to communicate to you intensely personal accounts of a few relationships that comprise my seventy-five years on this earth. I was certainly fortunate. More fortunate than I deserved, but I guess that's one of the definitions of grace.

Through the years, I have felt a deep frustration with my inability to express to God, family, and friends my gratitude for this wonderful life. Perhaps by reducing the story to writing, that need to say *thank you, thank you* will finally be satisfied.

When I look back on my life — the sacred places I've been, the fascinating people I've encountered, and the challenges God assembled for me — I am humbled and profoundly grateful.

It has been the education of a lifetime.

Epilogue

Sara Davidson still lives in Oxford — three blocks away from Robert and Margaret Khayat.

C.N. "Cyanide" Jones received the Elsie M. Hood Outstanding Teacher Award at Ole Miss in 1976.

Ken Kirk and Robert remained lifelong friends. Ken died on November 16, 2009.

Jack Dunbar lives and practices law in Oxford, Mississippi.

On May 9, 1963, **Eugene "Big Daddy" Lipscomb** spent the night out in Baltimore, Maryland. The following morning he was discovered in a friend's house. He was dead from a heroin overdose.

In 1999, Netscape was purchased by AOL. Eventually, AOL merged with TimeWarner, where **Jim Barksdale** served on the board of directors. On December 9, 2003, Sally Barksdale passed away. At Jim's request, the honors college was renamed the Sally McDonnell Barksdale Honors College. The Barksdale family continues to support the college, the university, and the state of Mississippi.

Larry and Susan Martindale live in Shepherdstown, West Virginia. Together they have made extraordinary gifts to the university. The scholarships Larry's mother wanted him to repay totaled $3,500.

Jeff McManus is the director of Landscape Services, Ole Miss Golf Course and Airport Operations.

Gertrude C. "Gayle" Ford died in September of 1996. She is buried in Cuthbert, a small town in southwest Georgia. The Gertrude C. Ford Foundation continues to support the 80,000-square-foot performing arts center at Ole Miss that bears her name. Each year, dozens of Broadway shows, musicals, concerts, and plays are performed at the center — including the annual Shakespeare Festival.

Jenny Dodson (Robertson), the *Daily Mississippian* news editor who broke the story on the review of university symbols, is the manager of global media for FedEx.

Harold Burson is still active in the world of public relations and lives in New York.

Jerry Hollingsworth continues to support Ole Miss. He lives in Crestview, Florida.

Jerry Abdalla is chairman and CEO of Croft Industries in McComb, Mississippi.

In 2006, **John Hope Franklin** received the John W. Kluge Prize for lifetime achievement in the study of humanities. Dr. Franklin died in Durham, North Carolina, on March 25, 2009, at the age of ninety-four.

Lee Paris is CEO of Meadowbrook Capital in Jackson. He and his family divide their time between Jackson and Oxford. **Henry Paris** is retired. He lives in Indianola.

Bill Yates is chairman of The Yates Companies, one of the top general contractors in the world. He and his wife, Nancy, live in Philadelphia, Mississippi.

Frank Peddle died on October 15, 2005. **Marge Peddle** still lives in Oxford.

Pat Patterson died October 2, 2004, after a battle with cancer.

John Grisham lives in Charlottesville, Virginia. His books continue to sell millions of copies every year. He is involved in many charitable causes, including the Ole Miss law school's Innocence Project.

Dick and Diane Scruggs live in Oxford, Mississippi.

From 1985 to 2007, **Dan Jordan** served as executive director of Monticello, as well as president of the Thomas Jefferson Foundation. He and his wife, Lou, an artist, live in Charlottesville.

James Meredith earned a law degree from Columbia University and spent his career as an entrepreneur, speaker, and political activist. His book *A Mission from God: A Memoir and Challenge for America* was published in 2012. He is currently a tree farmer in Jackson.

Stanley and Ruby Hill still live in Jamaica, Queens, New York.

In 2002, **Dr. Jean Gispen** was hired by the university to be the full-time primary care physician exclusively for Ole Miss faculty and staff.

Richard Barrett sued the university in federal court over the ban on sticks. In November 1999, U.S. District Court Judge Neal Biggers ruled that the university was legally justified in banning sticks and limiting banners. In 2000, the Fifth Circuit Court of Appeals upheld that decision.

Tommy Tuberville went on to coach at Auburn and Texas Tech. He is now head coach at the University of Cincinnati.

David Cutcliffe is the head football coach at Duke University. He revived Duke's football program and ended one of the longest bowl droughts in major college football history.

Eli Manning is the quarterback of the New York Giants. He is a two-time recipient of the Super Bowl's Most Valuable Player award. Eli and his wife, Abby, donated $1 million to the university for a need-based scholarship program. In the off-season, they live in Oxford.

Ed Orgeron serves as the defensive line coach/recruiting coordinator for the University of Southern California Trojans.

Houston Nutt works for CBS as a college football studio analyst.

In 2012, SEC schools were paying approximately $25 million to football coaches who were no longer coaching at the university that compensated them.

Carolyn Ellis Staton retired in 2009. She and her husband, Bill, operate a small used bookstore out of a booth in an Oxford antique mall.

Gloria Kellum retired in 2009. She spends her time in Oxford and New Orleans, where her grandchildren live.

Andy Mullins served as chief of staff for Chancellor Dan Jones until 2013. He recently retired after forty-two years in education.

Gerald Walton retired in 1999. He continues to be an active part of the Oxford/Ole Miss community.

Rex Deloach retired in 2001. He and his wife, Ruth Ann Ray, live in Oxford.

• Between 1995 and 2009, enrollment at Ole Miss increased 43.6 percent; minority enrollment grew 78.5 percent.

• Research and development grants at Ole Miss topped $100 million during each of the last eight years of Robert Khayat's chancellorship.

• Under Robert Khayat's leadership, the university's endowment grew from $114.3 million to $472.4 million, a 313.3 percent increase. During the same period, the university's operating budget grew from less than $500 million to nearly $1.5 billion, and its payroll increased from $260.8 million to $667 million.

• Since Phi Beta Kappa, the nation's most prestigious liberal arts honor society, awarded a chapter to the University of Mississippi, 813 Ole Miss students have been inducted.

During the Khayat administration, the Sally McDonnell Barksdale Honors College, Croft Institute for International Studies, Lott Leadership Institute, and William Winter Institute for Racial Reconciliation were created. During the same period, the number of National Merit Finalists in the freshman class more than doubled.

In addition to producing the university's twenty-fourth and twenty-fifth Rhodes scholars, during Chancellor Khayat's tenure, Ole Miss produced five Truman, eight Goldwater, and six Fulbright scholars, plus one Marshall and one Udall scholar.

Ole Miss received the Grand Award for the country's best maintained campus from the National Landscaping Society.

During the Khayat administration, more than $535 million was invested in physical facilities on the Oxford and Jackson campuses. Upon Chancellor Khayat's retirement, an additional $210 million in construction projects were underway on the Oxford campus.

• • •

The Civil Rights Monument and James Meredith statue are among the most photographed locations on the Ole Miss campus.

• • •

Andrew Hacker and Claudia Dreifus spent five years researching colleges and universities across America. Their 2009 book *Higher Education? How Colleges Are Wasting Our Money and Failing Our Kids — and What We Can Do About It* ranked Ole Miss (along with Notre Dame and MIT) as one of the top three values in higher education.

• • •

Robert's brother, **Eddie**, and his wife, Deborah, live in Nashville, Tennessee. His sister, **Kathy,** is a retired teacher from the Moss Point public schools. **Edna** and Tom live in Fountainebleau, Mississippi.

Margaret Khayat Bratt lives in Grand Rapids, Michigan, with her husband, David. She is a lawyer and clerks for the Hon. Robert J. Jonker, U.S. District Court judge.

Robert Khayat Jr. practices law in Atlanta with the firm of King and Spalding. He and his wife, Susannah, have three children, Molly, Ben, and Betsey.

Margaret and Robert Khayat live in Oxford, Mississippi.

The Ole Miss Creed

The University of Mississippi is a community of learning dedicated to nurturing excellence in intellectual inquiry and personal character in an open and diverse environment.

As a voluntary member of this community:

I believe in respect for the dignity of each person.

I believe in fairness and civility.

I believe in personal and professional integrity.

I believe in academic honesty.

I believe in academic freedom.

I believe in good stewardship of our resources.

I pledge to uphold these values and encourage others to follow my example.

Photo Credits

Acknowledgements

This book could not have been written without the enlightened, generous leadership of Neil White. He is a gifted writer and editor who contributed in ways that cannot be measured.

So many people worked to make *The Education of a Lifetime* possible. I thank Richard Howorth for the title, as well as insights from booksellers Lyn Roberts, John Evans, and Joe Hickman. I also thank my great readers Maggie White, Genie Leslie, Deborah Hodges Bell, David Bratt, Margaret Khayat Bratt, Benita Whitehorn, Dan Jordan, Margaret Seicshnaydre, Gerald Walton, Emily Gatlin, Priscilla Grantham, Jamie White, Carroll Chiles Moore, Rheta Grimsley Johnson, Jamie Christian, Margaret Khayat, and Curtis Wilkie.

Assistance from Barbara Lago, Shirley Stuart, Gloria Kellum, Andy Mullins, Carolyn Ellis Staton, Don and Mary Ann Frugé, Sandra Guest, Donna Falkner, and Donna Patton was invaluable.

My hat is off to the talented Le'Herman Payton for the attractive and informative cover design and to Robert Jordan for the cover photography. Also to Connor Covert for the back-cover illustration.

Thanks to my publicist, Stella Connell, of the Connell Agency.

My family, and many friends, encouraged me to pursue this project and I am deeply grateful to Margaret, Robert and Susannah Khayat, Margaret and David Bratt, Kathy Khayat Murray, Barbara Collier, Sue Keiser, and Shirley Stuart.

There are many others to whom I am thankful. My hope is they will know through our friendship the gratitude and affection I feel for them.

ABOUT
ROBERT KHAYAT

Robert Khayat is a former college football All-Star, All-Pro kicker for the Washington Redskins, law professor, and president of the NCAA Foundation.

He holds degrees from Ole Miss and Yale, and was an Academic All-American football and baseball player while at Ole Miss. He has received the NFL Lifetime Achievement Award, as well as the National Football Foundation Distinguished American Award.

Dr. Khayat served as the fifteenth chancellor of the University of Mississippi from 1995 until 2009. He and his wife, Margaret, live in Oxford. They have two children and three grandchildren.

WHAT IS THE
COMMON READING EXPERIENCE?

The Common Reading Experience is a shared intellectual enterprise for new members of the UM community. Through reading and considering a common book, new students engage with each other and with UM faculty in exploring issues relevant to today's global community. Students begin to understand the expectations of college-level academic work, the nature of scholarly inquiry, and the values of an academic community. Chosen by a committee of UM Faculty and students, the Common Reading Text is used in all EDHE classes, all Writing 100/101 classes, and several other classes on campus. This year's selection was chosen after careful consideration of dozens of potential options. *The Education of a Lifetime* gives UM students a unique opportunity to see the development of the university through the eyes of a student, an athlete, a Professor of Law, and a Chancellor. Robert Khayat's experiences also offer a lens through which new students may consider how their experiences at the University of Mississippi will shape their lives and careers. As you read the book, use the following questions to prepare for the first essay in Writing 100/101 and the projects you will compose for EDHE.

THE EDUCATION OF A LIFETIME
QUESTIONS FOR INCOMING STUDENTS

1. Khayat placed a lot of importance on the University of Mississippi gaining a chapter of Phi Beta Kappa, America's oldest honor society and Greek-letter fraternity. Khayat thought hosting a Phi Beta Kappa chapter meant more academic prestige for the school. How important is your school's academic reputation to you? Why? Do societies such as Phi Beta Kappa matter to you as an incoming UM student? Why or why not?

2. On multiple occasions in his book, Khayat mentions how "the world" viewed the University of Mississippi. He thought that for UM to be the type of institution he wanted it to be, "the world" must look favorably upon it. How do you think "the world" views UM in 2015? What does your response to this question mean to you as a new UM student?

3. In 1994, Khayat was behind an initiative to purchase "900 new desktop computers, one for every faculty member and staff" (132-3). This despite the fact that many faculty and staff were not familiar with how to operate a computer. How important is it to you that UM keeps pace with advances in technology? Why? How important is technology to your success as a student? Explain.

4. Why do you suppose Khayat chose to write a book about his life and his experiences at the University of Mississippi? What benefits are there in writing about your life? What are the drawbacks and limitations?

5. Football helped pave the way for Khayat's collegiate education. Later, as Chancellor, successful athletic programs were important to him. What role has athletics played in thinking about where you would attend college? Why? What role do you think athletics will play in the collegiate experience for you? Why?

6. Khayat made no secret of attempting to grow the University of Mississippi's enrollment, and grow it has. In fact, enrollment has increased for twenty straight years at UM, coinciding with Khayat's appointment as Chancellor. As a new student, what impact do you think enrollment has on your education and life in college? Why?

7. Khayat writes, "For most of my life, I have been a member of a team" (43). How was this philosophy important to Khayat's work as Chancellor? Does this quotation speak to you in any meaningful ways, especially as you enter college?

8. Khayat's book is a memoir. As a reader, what do you consider the strong points and the weak points of memoir? Why are these important? How do they help you understand your own reading and writing better?

9. Khayat seemed to agonize over decisions about eliminating (or at least making less visible) symbols that might cause negative perception of the University of Mississippi. He battled between alienating longtime friends/relations and moving UM in what he saw as a positive direction. Over time, he did what he thought was right. How do you balance doing what you think is right and pleasing those who matter to you? How do you think your choices will impact you long term? Why?

10. Khayat's academic career began with a whimper rather than a bang as he struggled to earn a D- in chemistry. Later in his teaching career, he was found unacceptable for the position of Dean of the Law School. Despite those setbacks, Khayat was successful as a student and as a professional. What characteristics did Khayat have that enabled him to move past disappointments? What characteristics will help you to persist in your academic career despite difficulties?

11. Khayat gained a deep appreciation for nature from his mother, an appreciation that became central to the campus improvements he oversaw as Chancellor. In what ways did the natural beauty of the UM campus influence you as you made your college decision? How do you imagine the grounds will influence your experience as a UM student?

Continued

12. Khayat describes a field trip, early in his undergraduate career, to see La Boheme at the invitation of Latin teacher Dr. Doris Raymond. He writes, "She [Dr. Raymond] understood the importance of cultural enrichment; I'd never heard the term. But that night in Memphis was one I would always remember" (32). What cultural enrichment will you seek out as an undergraduate? How will you push yourself out of your comfort zone into unfamiliar intellectual or artistic territory?